Dr Harish Dhillon was the author of sixteen books, including *The Sikh Gurus*, *First Raj of the Sikhs: The Life and Times of Banda Singh Bahadur* and *Love Stories from Punjab*. He had also written numerous articles and short stories. Starting his career at Lucknow University, Dr Dhillon moved to Lawrence School in Sanawar (Himachal Pradesh) as its principal and then on to the two Yadavindra Public Schools at Patiala and Mohali (both in Punjab). He taught English for forty-seven years. After his retirement, he was editorial consultant to *The Tribune* and also acted as the advisor to the Board of Governors at the two Yadavindra Public Schools. He received an award from Punjabi University in Patiala in 2015 for his contribution to Punjabi culture and literature.

THE
SIKH GURUS

Harish Dhillon

HAY HOUSE INDIA
New Delhi • London • Sydney
Carlsbad, California • New York City

Hay House Publishers (India) Pvt Ltd
Muskaan Complex, Plot No. 3, B-2, Vasant Kunj, New Delhi – 110070, India

Hay House LLC, P.O. Box 5100, Carlsbad, CA 92018-5100, USA
Hay House UK Ltd, The Sixth Floor, Watson House, 54 Baker Street, London W1U 7BU, UK
Hay House Australia Publishing Pty Ltd, 18/36 Ralph St., Alexandria NSW 2015, Australia

Email: contact@hayhouse.co.in
Website: www.hayhouse.co.in

Copyright © Harish Dhillon

The views and opinions expressed in this book are the author's own and the facts are as reported by him. They have been verified to the extent possible, and the publishers are not in any way liable for the same.

All rights reserved. No part of this publication may be reproduced, by any mechanical, photographic, or electronic process, or in the form of a phonographic recording, nor may it be stored in a retrieval system, transmitted, or otherwise be copied for public or private use – other than for "fair use" as brief quotations embodied in articles and reviews – without prior written permission of the publisher.

Interior images: Painting of Guru Nanak, Guru Amar Das, Guru Har Gobind, Guru Tegh Bahadur and Guru Gobind Singh
Courtesy: Sobha Singh Art Gallery, Andretta, Himachal Pradesh
Front cover: A rare Tanjore style painting from the late nineteenth century depicting the ten Sikh Gurus with Bhai Bala and Bhai Mardana at the bottom.
Back cover: A granthi reading the Guru Granth Sahib at Amritsar, Punjab. A watercolor by William Simpson (1860).
Japji – The Morning Prayer of the Sikhs by Guru Nanak, translated into English by Khushwant Singh.

Revised Edition published by Hay House India, 2015
First paperback edition, 2018

ISBN 978-93-86832-42-9
ISBN 978-93-84544-45-4 (e-book)

To my children:

Jason, Priya, Naina, Jai, and
of course Tegh

Contents

Acknowledgements ... 9
Introduction ... 11

Part I
GURU NANAK (1469-1539)

Chapter 1
Birth and Childhood ... 18

Chapter 2
Search for an Occupation ... 26

Chapter 3
Travels ... 38

Chapter 4
Teachings ... 65

Chapter 5
The Janamsakhis ... 71

Part II
GURU ANGAD DEV TO GURU TEGH BAHADUR
(1504–1675)

Chapter 6
Guru Angad Dev (1504–1552) ... 86

Chapter 7
Guru Amar Das (1479–1574) ... 99

Chapter 8
Guru Ram Das (1534–1581) ... 111

Chapter 9
Guru Arjan Dev (1563–1606) ... 119

Chapter 10
Guru Hargobind (1595–1644) — 140

Chapter 11
Guru Har Rai (1630–1661) — 162

Chapter 12
Guru Har Krishan (1656–1664) — 171

Chapter 13
Guru Tegh Bahadur (1621–1675) — 177

Part III
GURU GOBIND SINGH (1666–1708)

Chapter 14
The Early Years — 202

Chapter 15
Paonta Sahib: A Centre for Literary and Cultural Activities — 209

Chapter 16
The Battles of Bhangani and Nadaun — 216

Chapter 17
The Birth of the Khalsa — 224

Chapter 18
Sparrows Meet Hawks — 235

Chapter 19
Vichora – The Separation — 245

Chapter 20
The Final Years — 265

Chapter 21
Conclusion — 281

Bibliography — 293

Acknowledgements

This book began its journey in 1995. It was commissioned by Shailender Choudhry of Student Book Store, but by the time it was completed, he had developed cold feet about the project. After a hiatus of two years, Ashok Chopra, (then the publishing director at UBSPD, New Delhi) stepped in and decided to publish it. The rest, as far as I am concerned, is history. Over a period of thirteen years, it has had twelve reprints, the last reprint being as recently as 2012. Then Ashok decided to step in again and bring out an upgraded edition of the book, the thirteenth reprint. So my acknowledgements must begin with a strong expression of gratitude to my friend and mentor, Ashok Chopra, for his unswerving faith in my writing ability.

I am greatly beholden to Dr Wazir Singh for editing the text meticulously and also for suggesting improvements.

I would like to express my grateful thanks to Dr S.S. Dhillon, for obtaining all the source-material for me, to Sohan Singh, who was my PA at Yadavindra Public School when I was the principal there for deciphering my terrible handwriting and typing out the various drafts way back in 1995, and to the late Neeta Sibia, one of my former colleagues, for patiently reading through each draft and giving me her quiet but very valuable advice. My grateful thanks are also due to K.S. Bhalla, for having gone through the text very carefully, word by word, and suggesting important and meaningful corrections and modifications. And finally, a very big 'thank you' to all at Hay House for having given me a beautiful book.

INTRODUCTION

During the time of the founder of the Sikh religion, Guru Nanak (1469-1539), the Punjab we know now was a much bigger geographical unit. In the north, this area was marked by the high Himalayas, the Hindu Kush mountain range, and the mountains of Afghanistan. In the west the river Indus flowed. The south was marked by the desert of Rajasthan. The eastern boundary was not very clearly defined. But, broadly speaking, Punjab was a region of large plains, watered by the rivers Jhelum, Chenab, Ravi, Sutlej, and Beas – the five main tributaries of the Indus (Punjab means 'the land of five waters').

This is the area where the Indus Valley Civilization, one of the oldest civilizations in the world, was born. Stone implements dating back to almost 5,00,000 years have been found here. Copper and bronze implements dating back to 25,000 years have also been unearthed along the banks of the Indus. The ruins of the Harappan culture, found at Ropar, proved the existence of a flourishing urban culture, dating as far back as 2500 BC. 'It was also in Punjab that the Aryans evolved the Vedic religion and composed the great works of Vedic and Sanskrit literatures.'*

The Aryans were followed by wave after wave of conquerors: the Greeks, the Bactrians, the Scythian tribes, and the Huns. After them, at the beginning of the eleventh century came tribes who differed greatly from one another but had one common factor: their religion, Islam. The Ghaznavis, the

---

*Excerpt taken from Khushwant Singh's book *The History of the Sikhs*. (See bibliography for publication details.)

Ghoris, the Tughlaqs, the Suris, the Lodhis, and the Mughals – all invaded North India and ruled it.

The Muslim tribes, when they had settled down in Punjab, directed much of their energies towards destroying non-believers. For over three hundred years, Islam and Hinduism existed side by side in Punjab, in a state of constant conflict. Hinduism had a pantheon of gods and goddesses who were worshipped in the form of idols, and a society that was based on the caste system, while Islam, which was rooted firmly in monotheism, abhorred idolatry and believed in the equality of all human beings.

Some attempts were made to bridge this divide. The Bhakti Movement preached that there was only one God and He was without any form or feature. They advocated that all men were equal and preached against the caste system. The Sufis, too, tried to bridge this divide. For the first time, music was introduced into Muslim religious practice. The Sufis welcomed non-believers both in their homes and in their mosques; and believed that all human beings had a right to observe their own form of worship.

But both these attempts were tentative in nature and any popular acceptance they may have found was destroyed by the Turko-Mongolic conqueror, Timur's invasion in 1398. The Muslim ruling class turned, once again, to killing and robbing the Hindu masses and to destroying their temples. The average Muslim believed that he could gain merit in the eyes of God by converting non-believers to Islam, even if it was at the point of the sword. Religious practices, in both Hinduism and Islam had degenerated into the performance of empty rites and rituals. The followers of Islam believed that circumcision, abstinence from pork, and, fasting during Ramzan were the attributes of a good Muslim. The Hindus meanwhile re-affirmed their belief in the merit of idol worship. They had an even more determined belief in the caste system; in the rituals of washing away their sins in holy rivers, eating vegetarian food, and wearing a holy thread (the *janeu*), all of which they felt would make them pure.

In 1499, Nanak embarked on an attempt to define the common thread running between the two religions, and to free religious practices from all the rituals and the hypocrisy that had come to surround them. His teachings were soon accepted by thousands of followers and the faith (known as Sikhism) became the youngest of the great religions of the world. By the time Guru Nanak died in 1539, he had a sizeable following, mainly in Punjab but also in little pockets along the routes he had taken on his Udasis.

Despite their increasing numbers, the Sikhs were not regarded as a threat by the Mughals, and were treated at best with a degree of cordiality or at the worst with a patronizing tolerance. Babur (1483-1530, the founder of the Mughal Empire in India) had known Guru Nanak personally and had found him to be a true man of God. This is why, not only had he ordered his release from imprisonment after the sacking of Saidpur (in Amritsar), but also deferred to Nanak's wish that all the other citizens be also released. His grandson, emperor Akbar had made a visit to Guru Amar Das, the third Guru's *dera* at Goindwal (in Punjab) and was so impressed by the Sikh way of life that he wanted to make a gift to the Guru. The Guru politely but firmly declined this offer on the plea that his needs were more than taken care of by God. The emperor, not wishing to be thwarted in his generous impulse, made a gift to the Guru's daughter Bibi Bhani, in the form of a *jagir*. It was on this piece of land that Bibi Bhani's husband, the fourth Guru, Guru Ram Das, founded Amritsar. Interestingly, it was also on a part of this piece of land that the fifth Guru, Guru Arjan Dev, built the Harmandir Sahib also known as Golden Temple.

When the fifth Guru began the work of compiling the Adi Granth, rumours were spread that the new *granth* contained passages that were inimical and hostile to Islam. These rumours were strong enough for Akbar to take note of and to have the draft of the granth examined by his scholars to see if there was any truth to the rumours. The scholars found that not only were there no truth in the rumours, but the granth even contained extracts from the works of Muslim saints and scholars. The main reason for this cordiality and tolerance of the newly emerging faith – as time was to prove – was that the Sikhs had not yet defined themselves in any definite terms and were generally regarded as another fringe reformist movement of Hinduism.

This lack of a definite identity was rectified with the completion of the compilation of the Adi Granth by Guru Arjan Dev in 1604 and the building of the Harmandir Sahib, another task undertaken by Guru Arjan Dev in 1588 and completed in 1604. The Adi Granth was installed in the new temple of the Sikhs in 1604. Thus the Sikhs now not only had a religious book of their own, but also a spiritual headquarters of their faith. Their identity had now been clearly and definitely established and there would never again be any doubt that Sikhism was a faith in its own right.

At last, the Mughal rulers woke up to the fact that the new faith was attracting a strong following, and that it might well be a threat to the pre-eminence of Islam in the days to come. The days of the religious liberalism of Akbar were over and done with, and though his immediate successors put on a facade of religious tolerance, they showed enough signs to indicate the extreme religious intolerance that would be the hallmark of the Mughal rule in the times to come. If any proof of this was needed, it came in the form of the sadistic and totally uncalled for martyrdom of the fifth Guru, Guru Arjan Dev in Lahore in 1606. This tragic event marked the end of the easy, comfortable relationship that had existed between the Sikhs and the Mughal rulers till then. From here on there would be only hostility and bad blood between the two and even Guru Gobind Singh's support to Prince Muazzim,(later

Bahadur Shah I), whom he considered to be the rightful heir, in the war of succession after Aurangzeb's death, did nothing to improve the situation.

Under Guru Hargobind, the sixth guru, the process of the transformation of the Sikhs from a non-violent and pacifist community to a people who could stand up and protect their beliefs and ideals, had begun.

Guru Hargobind carried two swords, one symbolizing his temporal (*miri*) powers and the other his spiritual (*piri*) powers. He understood clearly that times had changed and that if the Sikhs were to protect themselves, it could only be through the use of arms. He trained his followers, not only to be physically strong, but also to be skilled in martial arts. He built up an army, consisting both of the infantry and cavalry. He welcomed gifts of horses and weapons. With the new impetus that he provided to the Sikhs, more and more people flocked to his call. They saw in this call, the first real challenge to the cruel and exploitative power of the Mughals, and hence, their first real chance for liberation. Threatened by this growing following, Jahangir, the Mughal emperor, arrested the Guru and imprisoned him in the fort of Gwalior. There had already been anger and hatred caused by the martyrdom of Guru Arjan Dev, and the wise men at the court feared that this arrest would cause this cumulative anger to turn into a violent backlash, which the Mughals would find hard to contain. They advised the emperor to release the Guru, an advice he was sensible enough to act upon.

During Shah Jahan's reign, relations once again reached breaking point between the Sikhs and the Mughal rulers. Guru Hargobind fought as many as four battles with the imperial forces and held his own in each of them.

A further impetus was provided to this transformation of the Sikhs when the head of the martyred Guru Tegh Bahadur was delivered to his son, the nine-year-old Gobind Rai in 1675. Guru Tegh Bahadur had given his life to protect the right of the Kashmiri pundits to practice their faith. The young boy, who was now called Guru Gobind saw what Guru Hargobind had seen before him: That the survival of the Sikhs now depended entirely on their skills in war, and he began working assiduously to hone this skill.

Guru Gobind Singh transformed the Sikhs into a well organized, highly skilled, and excellently trained group of warriors. The climax to this transformation came on that historic Baisakhi day of 1699, when he created the Khalsa. With an army made up of such brave men, the Sikhs became a formidable force. Little wonder then that Guru Gobind Singh was able to carry out such brilliant military campaigns.

Guru Gobind Singh is one of the most fascinating and remarkable personalities in Indian history. We see him first as a little boy, with a wisdom way beyond his tender years, advising his father that the most apt sacrifice that he could make to the cause of the Kashmiri Pundits was his own life. We see him as an adult with the multifaceted personality of the ideal Renaissance man. He was a brilliant military strategist and a general par excellence. He was an excellent administrator and an able leader of men. He was a polyglot with an outstanding command over Gurmukhi, Urdu, Persian, and Arabic. He was a great poet too. He had a deep interest in music and was considered a great musician.

This book is an attempt to relate the birth and growth of this great religion, Sikhism, through the life-stories of its ten Gurus. This work claims no originality; everything it contains has been culled from the sources listed at the end. It has been written solely for the young readers in a simple narrative form, so that they get to know more about Sikhism.

The only justification for retelling a story that has already been told so often is the firm belief that a story so beautiful and inspiring needs to be retold as often as possible. If a small fraction of the great charm of this story can communicate itself to the reader, the effort will not have gone in vain.

Part I

GURU NANAK
(1469-1539)

Chapter 1

BIRTH AND CHILDHOOD

Guru Nanak was born in Talwandi (now in Pakistan) in the fifteenth century. The village of Talwandi lay in Central Punjab, between the rivers Ravi and Chenab, in the direct path of the various invaders who came to India. The famous Turko-Mongolic conqueror Timur had destroyed Talwandi thirteen times by the time Guru Nanak was born in 1469, and each time, like the proverbial phoenix, Talwandi had risen again from its ashes. The last time it was rebuilt was in the fifteenth century under the supervision of Rai Bhoe, a Bhatti Rajput who had converted to Islam.

Rai Bhoe and his son, Rai Bular, who became the village chief when his father died, did a great deal for the development of the village and seeing this development, more and more people migrated to the village. They were attracted not only by the prospect of earning a better living, but also by the greater security that Talwandi now provided from foreign attacks. Amongst the families who came and settled down in Talwandi, was the Bedi family, which had migrated from a village close to Amritsar. During Rai Bhoe's time the family was headed by Shiv Ram. He was honest, hard-working, and good at handling money matters and keeping accounts. He was given employment by Rai Bhoe and was put in charge of the revenue accounts of the Bhattis. Shiv Ram's son, Kalyan Chand, who was an intelligent, hard-working boy, was trained by his father to follow in his footsteps. So when Shiv Ram died, Kalyan Chand (aka Mehta Kalu or Kalyan

Mehta), almost inevitably, became the Bhattis' accountant. The Bhattis paid their accountant well and the Bedis had one of the biggest houses in the village, their own fields, and a large herd of cows and buffaloes. Kalyan Chand had married Tripta, the daughter of Rama of Chahalwala, a village south of Lahore.

Most biographers and historians agree on the fact that Guru Nanak was born on Baisakh Sudi three (corresponding to April 15 1469), though the Guru's birthday is celebrated on the full moon (Purnima) of Kartik, occurring in November each year. On the night of Nanak's birth, Kalyan Chand was worried about his wife and the impending delivery. When it seemed that he would be able to bear the anxiety no longer, he heard the baby's cry. The midwife, Daultan, came out on to the verandah, the little baby cradled carefully in the crook of her arm and said, 'Congratulations Kalyan Chand, it is a boy.'

Soon after, he hurried to Pundit Hardyal's house. 'I have been blessed with a son, Punditji. And I have come to ask you to prepare his horoscope chart', Kalyan Chand said with some pride, as he bent to touch the pundit's feet.

The pundit after having prepared the horoscope, said to Kalyan Chand, 'Kalu, your son will sit under a canopy. Both Hindus and Muslims will respect him and his name will be famous on earth as well as in heaven. I will come to your house on the thirteenth day and name the child.'

As the village of Talwandi woke up to another day, the news of the birth of Kalu's son and of the pundit's predictions spread like wildfire. The next few days were exciting for the Bedi household. Several people from the village, and friends and relatives from neighbouring places came to congratulate them. On the thirteenth day, Pundit Hardyal returned and named the baby 'Nanak'. As a consequence, in later years, the village of Talwandi came to be known as Nankana Sahib.

In the early years of his life, there seemed little to mark Nanak as being special or different from other children of his age. But soon enough, he displayed traits of character and temperament that were unique and were to remain with him throughout his life: He was polite to everyone; he liked people for what they were; and always wanted to do things for others. Though he played games with the other boys, he was a quiet child, who preferred to be by himself, and seemed always to be lost in deep thought.

The village of Talwandi was small and much of the area around it was covered with a forest. Nanak loved to wander into the forest and he often met *faqirs* and *sadhus* and *sants* there, who would stop there for a few days before moving on. He was profoundly influenced by what they did and said. There was a high mound just outside Talwandi and he loved to sit on the top of it, and take a look at the countryside all around him. He noticed the changes that the different seasons brought, and enjoyed the various gifts of nature – a fact reflected in his sacred compositions, the Bani, in ample measure.

When Nanak was seven, his father, Kalyan Chand, decided that it was time for Nanak to learn how to read and write. He went to Pundit Hardyal and was given an auspicious date by the pundit on which to start the boy's education.

In Nanak's village there was a small school run by one Pandha Gopal, who was happy to accept Nanak as a pupil. Not only did he have a lot of respect for Kalyan Chand, he had also already heard about Nanak's polite behaviour. Nanak proved to be an extremely intelligent and hard-working pupil. He learnt the alphabets quickly and was soon ahead of the other boys in the school. The other boys were at first jealous of Nanak and made fun of him. But as Nanak always smiled at their teasing, and never got angry, they soon learnt to respect and like him.

Seeing Nanak doing so well in his studies, his teacher Gopal was sure that he would become a great man one day. Like Kalyan Chand, he too thought greatness lay in becoming an officer in the court of the Lodhi kings. So he began to focus on teaching Nanak arithmetic and accounts.

When Nanak was still a young boy, Talwandi came under the rule of Nawab Daulat Khan, who was at that time the governor of Sultanpur. Periodically, the governor used to send one of his officers to collect revenue from the Bhatti landlord of Talwandi, Rai Bular. While Nanak was studying with Gopal Pandha, the officer who used to come to collect the revenue was a Khatri by the name of Jairam. Rai Bular and Jairam soon became good friends.

One day, after the evening meal, Rai Bular said to Jairam, 'It is time, my friend, that you got married and started a family.'

'I too have thought of this, and my parents too feel it is time for me to get married. But I have not been able to find a suitable bride from a Khatri family,' Jairam said.

'What kind of girl are you looking for?' Rai Bular asked.

'I am looking for a girl from a good family, a girl who is good at household work, a girl who will respect and love my aged parents. She must also be a girl of intelligence and strength. Will you help me to find such a girl?' Jairam asked.

'I will try. There are many Khatri families in Talwandi. I am sure we will be able to find the girl you are looking for,' Rai Bular said. But in his heart Rai Bular already knew the girl who would be an excellent match for Jairam; this girl was

Nanki, the daughter of his accountant and old friend Kalyan Chand.

It was such an eminently suitable proposal that it was accepted immediately by both Kalyan and Tripta.

Nanak continued to attend Gopal Pandha's school, but he was not interested in learning how to keep accounts. He composed a poem for his teacher and when the teacher read it, he was very impressed and knew that there was nothing more that he could teach the boy.

However, Kalyan Chand was disappointed. Beautiful poems were all very good, but how could Nanak begin climbing the ladder of success if he did not learn practical things like keeping accounts, thought Kalyan Chand. After a few days, he came to the conclusion that his son's path to greatness might lie in studying ancient religious texts. So Nanak was sent to Pundit Brijnath Shastri, a famous Sanskrit scholar at that time. He had heard of the beautiful poem that Nanak had composed and was happy to have such a gifted boy as his pupil.

In the meantime, the day for his sister Nanki's wedding drew near. There was feasting, and the ceremony was performed according to Vedic rites. Rai Bular took part in the wedding as an important member of the family, and gave generous presents to both the bride and the groom. Then it was time for the *doli* to leave. For Nanak it was a poignant moment. He had always received special love and affection from his sister. She, before anyone else, had come to respect and admire her brother; and to recognize that there was something very special about him, and this had given him great emotional strength. And now she was going away ...

Nanki went away with her husband and the village

returned to its humdrum routine. Nanak returned to Pundit Brijnath Shastri and resumed his studies. He soon became fluent in Sanskrit, and knew many of the texts by heart. But he realized that he did not want to lead the life of a scholar. So, he said goodbye to his teacher and returned home, much to his father's disappointment. It was true, Kalyan Chand thought, that his son had learnt a great deal with Gopal Pandha and Pundit Brijnath Shastri, and it was also true that both of them admired and respected him; but obviously this was not enough to help Nanak achieve greatness.

Kalyan Chand made one last effort to provide some direction to his son's life. He took him to Maulvi Qutab-ud-Din, who taught Persian and Arabic. Both these languages were court languages at that time. Perhaps if Nanak showed interest in them and mastered them, Rai Bular would help him find a job either with the Governor in Sultanpur or with the emperor in Delhi. There was still hope that Pundit Hardyal's predictions would come true. Once again, Nanak proved to be a good pupil and learnt both the languages easily.

Nanak was now thirteen years old. It was time to perform the ceremony of the sacred thread (*janeu*). Once again Pundit Hardyal was asked to set an auspicious date on which the ceremony would be performed.

After the pundit had blessed the thread and reached out to put it across Nanak's shoulder, Nanak put up his hand to stop him. 'What are you doing with this thread?' Nanak asked.

'This is the sacred thread which marks the upper-caste Hindus. You are a high-caste Hindu. By wearing this thread you become a pure Hindu,' the pundit explained patiently.

'Can a person become pure only by wearing a thread?' Is

it not our actions that make us pure? The wearing of a thread will not make a difference. I will not wear it,' Nanak said.

The people in the courtyard were too shocked to say or do anything. Pundit Hardyal was confused, and angry with Nanak for creating this embarrassing situation.

He got to his feet, slipped into his wooden sandals and left Kalyan's house. Nanak sat on, quiet now, with a soft smile on his face. All around there were murmurs of resentment. No one had ever done this before – the pundit was angry; and Nanak had disgraced his family, his parents, and also his caste. One by one the guests left the house, not wanting to be part of this break with tradition, custom, and religion. The feast that was to follow the ceremony, did not take place. Kalyan was hurt and angry but he knew his son well by now, and realized that there was no point in scolding or punishing him. Nanak's mother, Tripta, was frightened at what her son had done. She was afraid that the gods would be angry with him, and that the priest would curse him.

Even if Nanak realized the enormity of what he had done, he did not show it. He continued to go to the Maulvi for his Persian and Arabic lessons. When he had become almost as proficient as his teacher, he decided that there was nothing more that he could learn from the Maulvi and gave up his studies.

Kalyan turned to his friend Rai Bular for help and advice, and the Bhatti sent for Pundit Hardyal.

'Punditji, our friend Kalyan Chand is very worried on account of his son Nanak. Do you remember what you predicted when the child was born?' asked Rai Bular.

The priest smiled his quiet, peaceful smile and said, 'Yes, I remember. And I say again: he will be a great man. But let him find his own path. Do not push him.'

'Yes, I think Punditji is right,' Rai Bular said. He had always liked the quiet boy and had often told his father to be gentler with him.

'If he does not want to study any more, do not push him. Let him start working at something,' said Rai Bular to his friend.

It was then decided that the boy would be encouraged to take on a job. Kalyan Chand returned to his home with a sinking heart. In spite of what Pundit Hardyal had said, he could not help thinking that no greatness could come to Nanak from doing any of the work that was available in the village. He felt Nanak could achieve greatness only by working at the court.

Chapter 2

SEARCH FOR AN OCCUPATION

Nanak had entered his fourteenth year, but his father Kalyan Chand had still not been able to figure out what work his son should take up. He knew that there was no point in asking Nanak to take up a task he did not like; he would only give it up after some time, just as he had given up his studies.

Kalyan Chand observed Nanak closely. Nanak was spending more and more time all by himself in the forest around Talwandi. This activity seemed to give him the maximum pleasure. The Bedis had a large herd of cattle, and taking them out to graze was an important task. Perhaps Nanak could take on the management of the herd. It would give him the chance to be by himself in the area around the forest. When this idea was discussed with him, Nanak was more than happy to take on the task.

Nanak took the cattle out to the common grazing grounds and into the forest. All day he would let them feed on the grass and the fresh leaves of the bushes, and in the evening he would drive them back home. Day after day he followed this routine. He was able to spend a long time alone with his thoughts. However, he loved the animals too and made sure that each of them ate well. He was no longer restless and his mother was happy to see this change in him.

From Kalyan Chand's point of view, there seemed to be a general improvement in Nanak's attitude. He performed his duties well; he spent more time at home with his mother and his father, and was friendlier with the villagers. He carried out other errands too for his father and performed them well. Kalyan Chand felt that his son was now ready to take on greater responsibility. He called the boy to him and gave him twenty silver coins.

'My son, you must go to the town of Chuharkana. It is market-day there today. Take your friend Bala with you. Buy some goods and then sell them at a slightly higher price here in Talwandi, and thus make a profit,' he said gently.

Nanak, in his new mood, was eager to please his father. 'I will do so, father,' he said and, accompanied by his friend Bala, he set out for the nearby town.

When they had reached the outskirts of the village, they came to a little path that led through the forest and was a short cut to the market town. In the middle of the forest, there was a clearing where various holy men camped when they passed through Talwandi. Nanak would often visit this place and listen to the holy men as they held their discussions and exchanged ideas. As a result, at a very young age, he had learnt a great deal about different religions and different religious movements. It was here that he met the Muslim scholar Sajjid Hussain and had first learnt about Sufism. Now too he stopped at the path which led to the clearing and after pausing for a moment or two, he said to his friend Bala, 'Let us take the path through the forest.'

'No,' Bala replied sharply, knowing that Nanak wanted to take the path not because it was the shorter way, but because he hoped to meet some holy men in the forest. If that happened, they would spend many hours there and would be late for their errand at the market.

'Let us take the main road,' Bala said. However, Nanak smiled at him and walked quickly down the path, and Bala had no choice but to run after him. Nanak had heard that there was a group of holy men in the forest who belonged to the Nirbani sect. He had never met any holy men from this sect before and was anxious to meet them.

The two friends came to the clearing in the forest and saw a large group of sadhus there. All of them were naked and stood in different postures, absorbed in meditation and prayer.

Nanak and Bala stood at the edge of the clearing, taking in this strange scene. However, Bala was impatient to get to the market. 'Let's go or we will be late,' Bala said, pulling at Nanak's sleeves.

'I will take only a few moments,' Nanak said and strode through the clearing and stopped before an elderly sadhu, who was obviously the leader. The leader's eyes were closed and his lips moved in silent prayer. At last, his prayers over, he opened his eyes. Nanak bowed to him and the holy man held up the palm of his right hand in blessing. Then he signalled to Nanak to sit down.

'Maharaj, why do you not wear any clothes?' Nanak asked.

'We are Nirbanis,' the holy man said, a gentle smile playing on his lips. 'We do not want anything that will bind us to this world. So we do not wear any clothes. We do not look for food too, and eat only when God sends us food,' he finished.

'And when did God last send you food?' Nanak asked.

'For me it was three days ago. For the other four men it has been eight days.'

Nanak was perturbed that these holy men should have gone hungry for so long. Perhaps God intended that he should be the instrument through whom they would be fed. He bowed to the sadhu, took his leave, and hurried to the market town.

When the duo reached Chuharkana, Nanak spent all his money on buying food items. He bought flour, oil, sugar, and many other things. He bargained fiercely and beat the prices down to a considerable extent. Bala was sure that when they sold their purchases in Talwandi they would make a good profit, and Kalyan would be very proud of his son.

The two friends took much longer on the return trip because they were burdened by the weight of their purchases.

They reached the clearing in the evening, and when Nanak took the load from his head and put it on the ground, Bala was happy to do the same. He was tired and was glad that Nanak had stopped to rest. As he wiped the sweat from his brow, he saw Nanak approach the leader of the Nirbanis and bow to him.

'Holy one, God has sent food for you and for all the other holy men of your group,' said Nanak. Bala was shocked beyond words when he heard this.

Nanak bowed to the holy men once again and, with Bala following, made his way out of the forest. When at last they reached the small mango grove just outside Talwandi, Bala stopped and said, 'Your father is going to be very angry because you have thrown away his money. He wanted you to make a good profit, but see what you have done.' He stopped to catch his breath and then went on, 'I will tell him the truth. I will tell him that if is all your doing; that I tried to stop you but you did not listen.'

Both friends were quiet. Their thoughts were on Kalyan's anger.

'You go ahead, Bala. I will stay here,' Nanak said. So Bala left his friend and made his way to the village. Because he loved Nanak very much and was afraid of what Kalyan Chand in his anger would do to him, he went quietly to Nanak's house and first told Nanki what had happened. It was only after this that he went to report it to Kalyan Chand. Fortunately Rai Bular was present when Bala related the story.

Kalyan was furious and said, 'Take me to where he is hiding.' They both hurried to the mango grove, followed by Rai Bular and Nanki. Kalyan Chand caught hold of Nanak and shook him hard.

'You waster, what have you done with my money?' He sounded so angry that Rai Bular was afraid he might strike the boy. He held his friend back.

'If the loss of twenty silver coins troubles you so much, I

will give you the money. But do not berate the boy,' Rai Bular said in a soft, gentle voice.

Kalyan was quiet for a while. But the whole affair had been too much for him: His dreams of his son's greatness now lay shattered.

'Greatness!' he said bitterly. 'Pundit Hardyal said my son would be a great man, and look what he has become! He cannot even be trusted with twenty silver coins,' he continued angrily.

Rai Bular put his arm around the boy's shoulders and spoke kindly to his friend. 'Pundit Hardyal was right. Tell me, my friend, what greater profit can a man earn than the merit he earns from feeding the hungry? He has invested your money wisely.' The Bhatti's words softened Kalyan's anger a little.

Nanak was upset at his father's anger. When his mother gave him his evening meal he refused to eat it. His mother said, 'You have earned so great a merit by feeding twenty hungry men. Will you not let me earn a little merit by feeding just one hungry boy?' She smiled and caressed his hair as she said this. Nanak felt the sadness lift from his heart at once. Despite his father's anger, he was glad that he had fed the holy men. He smiled at his mother and ate his food.

After the incident when Nanak had spent the money on feeding the holy men, Kalyan Chand barely spoke to his son. Though he did not scold Nanak, Nanki, who was on a visit to Talwandi, knew it was only a question of time before his anger erupted again. She was frightened by the prospect of what might happen. One night, while the men slept, she voiced her fears to her mother.

'I am frightened too,' Tripta said in a whisper. She added,

'I am also frightened by the thought that Nanak will, one day, go away from us. He spends so much time listening to the holy men who wander from place to place. I am frightened that one day, like them, he too will want to wander off on pilgrimages.' Her voice broke as she spoke and she began to cry softly in the dark. Nanki reached out and held her mother's hand.

Nanki finally found a way to resolve the difficult situation. Perhaps Nanak should go away from Talwandi for a while. He would thus be away from his father's anger and also from the influence of the holy men. Perhaps when the time came for her to go back to Sultanpur, she should take him with her. The more she thought on the matter, the more she felt it was the right thing to do.

When her husband Jairam came to Talwandi, a few days later, Nanki confided her plan to him. 'Yes, it is a very good idea. Nanak should come away with us. It will be good to have him with us in Sultanpur,' he said.

So the next morning, when Kalyan had gone to work and Nanak had gone for a walk, Jairam seated himself close to his mother-in-law. Tripta sat at her spinning wheel. Nanki, having prearranged it, left them alone and went into the kitchen.

'Mother, I have been thinking of Nanak. He spends too much time with the holy men,' said Jairam.

Tripta said with a sigh, 'Yes. Sometimes I am afraid that he will start going on pilgrimages with them and be away from home for great lengths of time.'

'If you permit, mother, I want to take him with me to Sultanpur,' said Jairam. The thread snapped and Tripta stopped in her spinning. Her son had never been away from her for a single day and the prospect of him going away now caused her much heartache. But at the same time, she knew that this was the only way to keep him from being influenced by sadhus and faqirs and to protect him from his father's anger.

'Yes, yes of course,' she said, still not looking up, afraid that Jairam would see the sadness in her eyes.

'You are his brother; you know what is best for him,' she said. She looked up at last, and smiled at her son-in-law, but he saw the tears glistening in her eyes.

'Do not worry, mother. It will only be for a short while. He will come back to you with his mind cured of all these thoughts and after having achieved something in life. Then his father will not be angry with him,' he said.

In the afternoon, Jairam carried his father-in-law's lunch to him. As Kalyan sat eating his meal, Jairam suggested that Nanak should go with him to Sultanpur.

'It is a good idea. I have not been able to do anything for the boy here. He might find some useful employment in Sultanpur and finally settle down. You must first go back to Sultanpur and see what chance there is of his finding a suitable job there,' Kalyan Chand said.

Fifteen days after Nanki and Jairam had left for Sultanpur, a messenger arrived with a letter for Kalyan. Jairam had spoken to Nawab Daulat Khan Lodhi and the Nawab had promised to help Nanak. The message said it was imperative that Nanak should come to Sultanpur at the earliest.

A few days later, Nanak set out on his journey to Sultanpur, accompanied by Mardana, who was Nanak's childhood friend. He belonged to a family of Dun Muslims, who were professional singers and rabab players. Nanak was fascinated by music and he spent many hours in the house of Mardana and thus became friends with Mardana.

Nanak never really returned to Talwandi again. He came back on short visits but it was never again to be his home.

Sultanpur was, at that time, a rich and prosperous town. This was mainly because of Nawab Daulat Khan. He had beautified the city and had built many gardens and grand buildings. He also brought learned people to Sultanpur, and thus the town became the home of teachers and scholars, who taught in the many Islamic schools that had been set up there.

Nanak and his companion, Mardana, were given a warm welcome on their arrival at Sultanpur, and the next morning Nanak accompanied Jairam to the Nawab's palace. As they were getting ready to leave the house, Nanki offered her brother a bowl of curd and sugar. Nanak said, 'I know you do this because you love me; you believe that this will bring me luck and the Nawab will give me employment. But sister, if merely by eating curd and sugar we could ensure good fortune, no one would need to work. No one would believe in God.'

There were signs of great wealth everywhere in the Nawab's palace: in the furniture, in the decor and in the clothes that the people wore. Nanak came into the Nawab's presence, and like Jairam, bowed before him in greeting, but when he looked up again he looked the Nawab straight in the eye.

'Come and sit beside me,' the Nawab said, pointing to the small stool by his side. 'Did you have any trouble on your way?' he asked.

'No sir, we had a comfortable journey.' The Nawab was pleased with the young man's manners. He liked the fact that Nanak was polite and well-behaved, yet there was no fear or deference in his eyes and voice – emotions that other people showed when they were in his presence.

The Nawab was a busy man. Yet he put all his work aside and sat and talked to Nanak for a long time. He remembered what Sayed Hassan, a Muslim scholar from Talwandi, who came to teach at one of the Islamic schools in Sultanpur, had told him about Nanak. Sayed Hassan had praised Nanak's knowledge and interest in religion. By the end of the meeting the Nawab had appointed Nanak as the officer in charge of his *modikhana.*

The modikhana was the Nawab's granary. It was a very important part of his office, because in those days farmers were given the option to pay their taxes either in either cash or in kind, and most of them chose to pay in kind, through grains. Part of the salary of the court officials was also paid in grains. So Nanak had to measure and record, not only the grains that came into the modikhana but also the grains that went out. Nanak had always been quick to learn and soon he was adept at his work. Nanki was happy that her brother seemed, at last, to have settled down.

The Nawab noticed how well Nanak worked and, in appreciation of his good work, gave him a house near the modikhana. The new house was a small one but Nanak was quite happy: he had never wanted anything more than a roof over his head. Nanki helped her brother settle into his new home; and Mardana, who moved in with Nanak, took charge of the household.

Soon Nanak's life established a pattern. He would wake up before the crack of dawn and go to bathe in the waters of the Bein, a rivulet that flowed close to Sultanpur. After this he would spend some time in meditation. Then he would come home and have his morning meal and go to the modikhana. The day would pass quickly in work. He was very sincere, honest, and hard-working, and recorded all transactions scrupulously. At the end of each month, he carried out a physical stock-taking to ensure that the stock of grains in the store tallied with the quantity entered in his account books. All through the day he would work and, in the evening, he would return home. Sometimes he would go to his sister Nanki's house and spend an hour or two with her.

Guru Nanak was about twenty-seven years old when he moved to Sultanpur. He had got married in the year 1487, and had been blessed with two sons. His father-in-law was Mulchand Khatri who lived in the town of Batala in Punjab. He had a daughter Sulakhni, who was said to be polite and soft-spoken. Both Jairam and Nanki had felt that she would make a good match for Nanak. It was during his stay at

Sultanpur that his sons, Sri Chand and Lakhmi Das, were born, in the years 1494 and 1496 respectively.

Sulakhni was as gentle as Nanak and made friends easily. Her best friend was Nanak's sister, Nanki. She was also very hard-working. From an early age she had helped her mother with the household chores and knew exactly what was needed to ensure that her own household ran smoothly. She had to prepare an evening meal without knowing how many people would be eating, because the number of people who came to participate in *kirtans* (devotional songs) led by Nanak, varied every day. She followed her husband's life; she woke before Nanak was awake, and made all her husband's guests feel welcome at her home.

Close to Sultanpur was a village, Malvian, and there lived a man named Bhagirath, who spent a great deal of time in the company of saints and holy men. He heard that Nanak, who looked after the Nawab's modikhana in Sultanpur, was a holy man. So he came to Sultanpur and attended the kirtan at Nanak's home. The kirtan touched his heart deeply and he was so influenced by Nanak's teachings that he took up abode in Sultanpur and became Nanak's first disciple.

Eleven years after Nanak's wedding, there was another wedding in the house – Mardana's daughter's wedding. Bhagirath was entrusted with the shopping. He went to Lahore for this purpose and came in contact with a trader named Mansukh. Mansukh was so impressed by what Bhagirath told him about Nanak that he too travelled to Sultanpur and became Nanak's disciple.

Professionally too, Nanak was doing well. The Nawab was very pleased with his work and showed him many favours. This aroused jealousy in the minds of some of the courtiers and they began to spread false tales about Nanak. They said that he was stealing from the modikhana and this was how he was able to feed so many people every evening. These rumours spread amongst the courtiers and some of the senior and trusted among them, took it upon themselves to complain to the Nawab that Nanak was misusing his position.

Nanak too heard these stories and, one morning, he went to see the Nawab about this.

'What is it, Nanak? What has happened?' he asked after greetings had been exchanged.

'There are people who say that I have stolen grain from the modikhana,' Nanak said, coming at once to the point. 'I would like you to have an audit so that the stores can be properly checked and accounted for,' he said and held out the keys to the modikhana.

'I do not believe these accusations,' the Nawab said. 'I know that you are honest, that you sometimes give out more grain than is their due, to the poor people. But I also know that you keep a careful account of all this and make it up at the end of every month. But yes, it is important that your name should be cleared and all these rumours should be laid to rest and the rumour-mongers shown up to be the liars that they are,' the Nawab said. He took the keys from Nanak and asked his treasurer to check the stores and the accounts. As was expected, everything was found to be in order.

A few days later, Nanak did not return home after his morning bath in the stream. When people went to look for him, they found his clothes on the river-bank but there was no sign of him. So they concluded that he had been drowned. The Nawab heard the news and came galloping to the spot, his officers riding close besides him.

'Get the fishermen's nets. Drag the waters. Hurry,' he shouted. While his orders were being carried out, he thought of Nanak. Nanak was a good swimmer, so it was unlikely he could have come to any harm. But perhaps Nanak had been so perturbed by the recent happenings that, lost in his thoughts, he might have swum into an unsafe part of the stream and been carried away by the current. Hours passed and, one by one, his officers returned.

'Did you find anything?' he asked each of them, and each shook his head in the negative. By now all his followers had gathered at Nanak's house. The men sat in silence, frightened by what was believed to have happened. Sulakhni was dazed with grief and her little sons broke into tears.

Nanki alone did not believe that her brother had died. She comforted Sulakhni and her nephews and assured them that nothing had happened to Nanak, and that he would soon be home again. This reassurance brought them hope and strength. 'You wait and see. Nanak will soon return,' she said. And on the third day, Nanak indeed returned.

What had happened was that while swimming in the rivulet Nanak had heard a voice – a voice with a strange dream-like quality to it. The voice told him that he must travel from village to village, and take his teachings to the common people. When he woke from the dream, he found that he had been meditating in the jungle. This was where he was found by the Nawab's servants, who had brought him back to town.

His disciples were very happy to see that their fears had been proved wrong. The Nawab too was very happy to see Nanak return safe and sound. The first words that Nanak spoke on that occasion were: 'There is but one God. There is no Hindu and no Musalman.'

This was the proclamation of Guru Nanak's new faith. He had also composed a few hymns while meditating in the forest.

Guru Nanak was now ready to go out beyond Sultanpur and spread his message to all the people who cared to listen to him.

Chapter 3

TRAVELS

Nanak set out on his journeys. His travels started in 1507 and lasted for nearly twenty-three years. He travelled to many far-off places in India, Lanka, Baghdad, Nepal, and Tibet. He put on a dress which was not the dress of the Hindu sadhus or the Muslim faqirs, but a combination of both. People would stop him and ask:

'Are you a Hindu or a Musalman?' people would ask him. And he would reply with a smile, 'There is no Hindu, there is no Musalman.'

On all his journeys he was accompanied by Mardana, the Muslim bard who played the rabab, a string instrument. During his travels he met many kinds of people – the rich and the poor, simple village-folk and learned scholars, and saints. He passed through small villages and big towns and cities. He visited many famous temples and mosques and places of pilgrimage. Everywhere he went, people found peace in his words of love and in his gentle, smiling face. In the evening he sang hymns in praise of God and people came to listen to his songs and to his teachings and learnt the lesson of love and kindness.

Nanak's travels can be divided into four major journeys. The first journey was towards the East. He is believed to have begun this journey by crossing the Beas and going first to what is now Amritsar. It was the month of Sawan (monsoon), the month when the sky is covered with dark clouds and the winds that blow are cool and fresh. Nanak came upon a beautiful spot. There was a large water-body, and all around it were thick groves of trees. Pleased by the beauty of the place, he stopped to rest under a tree. This was the spot at which Guru Arjan Dev, the fifth Guru, later built the Harmandir Sahib – considered the holiest Sikh temple. In the compound of the Golden Temple, the tree under which Nanak rested for some time still stands old and shrivelled, but very much alive.

From Amritsar, Nanak went to Lahore and then returned to Talwandi. He spent a few days with his parents, Rai Bular, and his old friends. Mardana too was happy to be with his family. Nanak was the centre of attention because he told many wonderful stories about life in the town of Sultanpur.

'How are my grandsons?' Tripta asked her son as she sat beside him while he ate his food.

'They are fine,' Nanak said. 'Sri Chand is with Nanki in Sultanpur and Lakhmidas (also known as Lakhmi Chand) is with Sulakhni in Batala,' he added.

'Do you not miss them?' Tripta asked again.

'I travel at my soul's command,' Nanak replied, looking straight into her eyes. 'I cannot let earthly bonds tie down my feet,' he said. His mother watched him as he ate, her heart full of love; and as she watched, tears sprang. She knew that her son was a saint and already people had begun to call him Guru. But she could not help feeling a deep sadness at the thought that he had to leave his wife and sons while he followed the dictates of his spirit. Kalyan Chand too came, at last, to be reconciled to the path his son had chosen to follow. He listened with pride when Nanak spoke to the people who came to see him. There was great wisdom in the answers he gave to their questions. And in the evenings, when Nanak sang his hymns in praise of God, Kalyan Chand too felt close to God. At last he knew what Pundit Hardyal had meant when he had predicted that Nanak would be a great man.

Nanak spent time with Rai Bular, the Bhatti, who had sensed his greatness long before anyone else, and was happy to be with him again.

Soon it was time for Nanak to resume his journey. His parents knew that it was God's will that he must go, and so they made no effort to hold him back.

Nanak and Mardana left Talwandi and reached the town of Saidpur, and Nanak stopped at the door of Lalo's house. Lalo was a carpenter and was, at that time, working in his courtyard. He saw a shadow fall across his doorstep and looking up, saw Nanak. He came forward to greet him. He saw the glow on Nanak's face and folding his hands, bowed his head in greeting. Nanak reached out and took Lalo's hands in his own. The carpenter's hands were hard and calloused and Nanak knew that here was a man who earned his living by the sweat of his brow and the labour of his hands.

'I am a tired traveller. Will you give me a place to rest?' Nanak asked.

'All that I have is yours. You have done me great honour by coming to this humble abode. But I belong to the lowest of the low-castes and you will be defiled by staying in my house,' Lalo said.

'There is no low-caste, there is no high-caste,' Nanak replied and stepped into Lalo's house.

Malik Bhago was the most important official in Saidpur. He worked as the revenues collector for Nawab Daulat Khan. It was his son's birthday, and he had arranged a great feast for all the sadhus and faqirs, and for all high-caste Hindus. Through this feast he thought he would earn merit in the eyes of God. There were many who came to the feast, and Bhago was sure that God would reward him for having fed so many worthy people.

'Did all the holy people of the town come to my feast?' he asked one of his servants after the feast was over.

'All, your honour, except one,' the servant replied.

'Who is that?' Bhago asked, surprised.

'It is the strange faqir from Sultanpur, who goes by the name of Nanak.'

'And why did he not come?'

'It seems sir, that he prefers the simple food in Lalo's house.'

'Lalo, that low-caste carpenter? Go and summon him to my presence.' Bhago was truly angry now.

When Nanak arrived, Bhago spoke to him in anger, 'What is so special about the food of the low-caste Lalo that you would rather eat that simple fare than all the rich dishes served at my feast?'

'There is no low-caste and no high-caste. Our caste, our place in this world, is determined by our actions alone,' said Nanak. He then went on to prove to Bhago and all the assembled people that Lalo's bread was special. 'Lalo works hard with his own hands and earns very little. Yet he was ready to share his bread with others, even though he might himself go hungry. Bhago earns his money by exploiting the poor. When he shares it with others, it is with a motive: he thinks he would earn favour with God. Lalo's bread was full of the milk of human kindness, whereas Bhago's full of the blood of the poor,' said Nanak.

Nanak stayed for many days in Saidpur, and made many disciples, among them Malik Bhago. When Nanak left Saidpur, Lalo took upon himself the task of propagating Nanak's message of love, brotherhood, and equality.

Nanak and Mardana next crossed Punjab through the famous town of Harappa and came to the town of Tulamba (now in Pakistan's Punjab province). Near the main gate of the town was a rest house run by a man named Sheikh Sajjan, who pretended to be a holy man. He dressed in white and spent a lot of time in prayer. He wore a *tilak* on his forehead, which was the mark of Hindus and a rosary around his neck. He had built a mosque and a temple near his rest house. As a result, both Hindu and Muslim travellers came to his rest house and he looked after all their needs. But a fact that was unknown to the people was that whenever a particularly rich traveller came to his inn, Sheikh Sajjan would kill him in his sleep and steal all his money and his belongings.

Nanak and Mardana too came to Sajjan's rest house. Nanak's face had a glow, but Sajjan thought the glow came from eating rich food and living a life of indolence. So he concluded that Nanak must be a very rich man. He fed Nanak and Mardana well and gave them special attention. He expected Nanak to go to sleep after dinner and thus provide him with the opportunity of carrying out his malicious intentions. But instead of going to sleep, Nanak decided to conduct kirtan and he invited Sajjan to attend. Sajjan had no option but to accept the invitation. The music touched his heart and the words made him see his own evil ways. He fell at Nanak's feet, told him of his evil deeds and begged to be forgiven. He gave away everything he had, and spent the rest of his life in the service of others.

Nanak travelled next to Kurukshetra and then to Panipat where he spent a few days in discussing religious matters with the Sheikh of Shah Sharaf. He then went on to Delhi and from there, travelled to Haridwar. Here he saw many people, who first bathed in the river, then stood and prayed and offered water to the rising sun by throwing it towards the east.

'Why are you throwing the water towards the sun, my friend?' he asked a young man who stood in the river close to him. 'I am offering this to the spirits of my ancestors. It is to quench their thirst,' the young man replied.

Nanak stepped into the river, bathed, and then turning his back to the sun, began to offer water towards the west. All the people who were standing on the river bank were amazed to see this.

'What are you doing, strange man?' they said. 'Have you gone mad? Why are you throwing water in that direction?'

'Why,' Nanak answered, smiling softly, 'My land is near Lahore; and Lahore, as you know, is towards the west. There has been a drought there, the land is dry and my crops will be ruined. So I am irrigating my land.'

They all laughed at Nanak and Nanak pretended to be angry.

'Why are you laughing at me?' he asked.

'You are truly mad,' they said between peals of laughter. 'How can the water you offer here, reach as far a place as Lahore?' they asked.

'How far is the land where your ancestors live?' Nanak asked.

'It is forty-nine and a half crore *kos* away,' a learned pundit replied.

'Well, if the water can reach a spot which is forty-nine and a half crore kos away, it can surely reach my farm, which is only 250 *kos* away from here,' Nanak said.

From Haridwar, Nanak and Mardana travelled eastward, through the lower ranges of the Himalayas. They passed through Almora in Himachal Pradesh, where people used to offer human sacrifice to their goddess at that time. Nanak knew that if he was to make the people give up this custom, he would have to spend some time with them, and teach them the lesson of love for each other. In the beginning the main priest at the goddess' temple was suspicious of him. He thought that Nanak would try to undermine his position among the people. But Nanak did not talk about religion at all. He went quietly among the people, bringing help and comfort wherever he could. Gradually, the people began to think kindly of the stranger who had come to live amongst them.

The days slipped past and soon it was the day for the next sacrifice. A young seventeen-year-old boy was being offered as sacrifice. He was bathed, and dressed in new clothes, and made to kneel before the goddess; the priest said all the special prayers that needed to be said on the occasion. The large crowd of people waiting for the sacrifice felt that the goddess would be pleased with it, and would bless them with prosperity, happiness, and a bounteous harvest.

At the last minute, Nanak stepped forward from the crowd. 'Stop,' he said to the priest. The crowd turned to look at Nanak. They respected him and they were sure that he would not have stopped the ceremony without adequate reason.

'Why do you offer this sacrifice?' he asked the priest.

'To please the goddess,' the priest replied.

'Your goddess is your mother: She is kind and gentle and you are all her sons and daughters. Do you think the pain and suffering that is caused by human sacrifice would please her? Do you think she would be happy to see one of her children being killed? Your religion teaches you to love one another like brothers – to treat your neighbour's pain and suffering as your own. Your religion says that there can be no happiness, no success if it is based on someone else's tears. Why then should you take part in causing such pain and suffering to another? Think of what the boy's mother would go through if he were to die. You are all like her, you would suffer with her,' Nanak said. The priest was won over by Nanak's arguments and actively supported Nanak's campaign against human sacrifice, and the people soon abandoned this horrific practice.

Nanak stayed for some time in Gorakhmata near Pilibhit (now in UP), the seat of the Nath Yogis. There, many people became his followers, and in later years, the place was renamed Nanakmata.

From the hills, Nanak and Mardana came down to the Gangetic plain, and travelled along the river: They passed through Ayodhya – the birthplace of Sri Ram; then through Allahabad where the Ganga and Jamuna meet, and came finally to Benaras. Here, they were the guests of a very learned pundit by the name of Chatur Das. Both Nanak and the pundit would hold long discussions on religious and spiritual matters; and both left wiser and richer with these exchange of thoughts. Nanak and Mardana now travelled on to Bodh Gaya, where Lord Buddha had attained enlightenment. It had by then become less important as a centre of Buddhist learning and had become more a place of pilgrimage.

From Gaya the travellers went on to Patna, and then to Bengal, moving forward to Assam. There is to this day, a temple at Dhubri on the Brahmputra River in Assam, which marks Nanak's visit there. From Dhubri, Nanak and Mardana travelled to Guwahati, Manipur, Imphal and Dhaka and down to the Bay of Bengal and then to Puri. Here the people did not like Nanak at first, but as they listened to his hymns and his teachings, they realized that he was a true Guru. He taught the people that God did not live in the stone and wooden statues they worshipped, but in their hearts. At Puri, Nanak also met the famous Bhakti saint, Chaitanya Mahaprabhu.

It was at Puri that Guru Nanak composed and sang his famous hymn, *aarti*, in Raag Dhanashree in 1510.

Mardana had by now become homesick and wanted to return to his family and friends. To spare him any more pain, Nanak started on their homeward journey. As they travelled through Central India, they came across a man-eating tribe. Nanak stayed for some time with this tribe and weaned it away from cannibalism.

They then travelled towards the south; through the thick forests and across the desert of Rajasthan and came to the river Sutlej. They crossed the river at Pakpattan (now in Pakistan), and spent some time here meeting with Sheikh Ibrahim – the descendant of the famous Sufi saint, Sheikh Farid.

They came at last to Talwandi. Tripta and Kalyan were overcome with joy to see their son again after twelve years.

Then, after some days, Nanak visited Sultanpur. He was greeted warmly by Nawab Daulat Khan, Nanki, and Jairam, and his son Sri Chand. Jairam sent a message to Batala and soon Sulakhni and Lakhmidas returned to Sultanpur, and for a little while the husband and wife, and the two sons were together again.

For nearly six years (from 1511-1517) Guru Nanak was content to be among his loved ones. Then the restlessness came upon him again, and saying goodbye to his family and friends, he set out on his second journey. According to Professor Sahib Singh, a prominent Sikh scholar and an authority on Sikh history and religion, Guru Nanak commenced his next journey on September 1517.

In the first leg of his journey, the Guru crossed the Sutlej, at what is now Goindwal (in Tarn Taran district of Punjab), and came to Bhatinda. He stayed there for a short time and then when on to Sirsa, where he spent a few months with some Sufi saints before going south to Bikaner. He also spent time with the monks at a Jain monastery there. He next stopped at Ajmer and visited the shrine of Khawaja Moin-ud-Din Chisti, and reached Pushkar at the time of the annual fair that is still held there. He passed through many towns and reached Rameshwaram, where he crossed the sea to Sangaldeep, Sri Lanka. (According to some biographers, the Guru's visit to Lanka formed part of his first Udasi. *)

Sri Lanka was then under the rule of a king named Shivnath. One of Guru Nanak's merchant disciples, possibly Mansukh or Bhagirath, had made many trips to Shivnath's capital city and the king had been impressed by the disciple's simple religion, and wished to meet his Guru. At last the king's wish was granted and Guru Nanak and his followers set up camp in a grove outside the capital. The King came

---

*The four journeys undertaken by Guru Nanak at various stages of his life are as Udasis. In another context, Udasis are a sect started by Sri Chand, Nanak's elder son when he did not get the gaddi. Their primary belief is that salvation can be achieved thorough renunciation – including the renunciation of family and loved ones.

and greeted the Guru, and was accepted as a disciple along with the queen.

Guru Nanak crossed the Palk Strait (the strait linking Tamil Nadu and Sri Lanka's Mannar district) and travelled along the western coast passing through Tanjore, Trichinopoly (it covered the present-day districts of Tiruchirappalli, Karur, Ariyalur, and Perambalur), and Palghat. The Guru passed through many important towns like Nasik, Baroda, Somnath, Madhopur, Junagarh, Porbander, Dwarka, and Bhuj. He stayed for sometime at Onkaar on the banks of the Narmada. Guru Nanak went finally to Pakpattan and after spending some time with his old friend Sheikh Ibrahim, he came back to Talwandi.

Because of Nanak's teachings which had spread all over Punjab, Talwandi had become famous. Now, when Nanak returned and Kalyan Chand saw the large number of followers that his son had garnered, he knew he had been wrong to doubt the path Nanak had chosen as a boy. Tripta was very happy to see her son, but got little time with him because she was kept busy looking after his followers. The happiness of Nanak's return to Talwandi was shadowed by the fact that his mentor, Rai Bular, was very ill. Every day the Guru spent many hours with him, comforting him. Rai Bular wished to hear his hymns and thus Nanak sang for him. A few days later, Rai Bular drifted off to sleep while Nanak sang his favourite hymn for him. It was a sleep from which he never woke up.

After a few days Nanak returned to Sultanpur after five years amidst great rejoicing.

This time too, Nanak's stay in Sultanpur was a brief one. When he expressed his desire to set out on his third journey, Nawab Daulat Khan, his old employer, pleaded with him to stay on.

'Stay here with us, Nanak. Be done with your travelling. We need you here. Stay here and bring the true message to my people.'

'I cannot stay till my soul tells me to. I hear an inner voice telling me to go and I must obey it,' said Nanak, and set out on his third journey.

His first stop was at Pakhoke (in Amritsar), where his wife, Sulakhni, and their sons were staying, and he spent some time with them. He was attracted to a spot across the river Ravi and wanted to set up a dera there. Ajit Randhawa of Pakhoke, who had become a disciple of Nanak, gave the Guru the land, and a village was set up there, which he named Kartarpur. Word spread that the Guru had set up a permanent home there and people flocked to Kartarpur to meet him. The village prospered and more and more people came to live there. The Guru's parents and family also came to live in Kartarpur, as did Mardana's family.

After staying for a few months at Kartarpur, the Guru set out on his third journey, accompanied by Mardana. Nanak travelled to Sialkot, then on to Jammu and then to Kashmir. He met many pilgrims on their way to the cave temple of Amarnath. One of these pilgrims was a very learned Brahmin by the name of Brahm Das, who was greatly respected for his learning. He was not only a devoted Brahmin, but always sought to learn more about other religions as well. He noted Guru Nanak's strange dress and began to question him. Guru Nanak's dress while on his Udasis had features of both the Muslim faqir and the Hindu sadhu. This dress appeared strange, but it was Guru Nanak's way of emphasizing the fact that he was neither a Muslim nor a Hindu. They spent some days together in discussions on the essence of life and religion, and Nanak's views greatly impressed Brahm Das. There is now a Gurdwara at Mattan (in Jammu and Kashmir), which stands at the spot where the Guru and Brahm Das had met.

From Srinagar, Nanak went on to Ladakh, where there is a Gurdwara called Patthar Sahib, which has been built to commemorate Nanak's visit to the place. From here he followed the upward course of the river Indus into Tibet, where he stayed at a monastery for a few days. The head Lama was so pleased with his teachings that he accompanied him to Mansarovar, the holy lake. Nanak then went on to Nepal and Sikkim. From Sikkim he came back, following, as closely as possible, the route that he had taken on his way out. Nanak thus came back to Sultanpur in 1518.

His brief stay in Sultanpur was a sad one, because during this time, both his sister Nanki, and his brother-in-law, Jairam, passed away. The couple had no children, and it was Nanak who performed their last rites. It was also the last time that he met Nawab Daulat Khan.

Guru Nanak stayed for a few days in Kartarpur. People asked for his advice and listened to his teachings and his hymns. They were soothed by the Guru's words, and they returned to lead their lives as per the Guru's directions. But soon his soul prompted him to move again, and hence he set out on his fourth and last journey.

This time the Guru travelled north to Multan (now in Pakistan), then to Sukhur (now in Sindh province of Pakistan). Then he travelled south along the river Indus till he came to Thatta (also in Pakistan). From here he went west to Hinglaj (an important Hindu pilgrimage place in Balochistan, Pakistan). Here he met a group of pilgrims on their way to Mecca. He joined them and crossed the Arabian Sea with them. Nanak was dressed in blue robes, a colour that is sacred to the Muslims and carried everything that a Muslim pilgrim on his way to Mecca carries: a staff, a prayer mat, the holy book Quran, and a spouted pot for performing his ablutions. The boat brought them to Jeddah in Saudi Arabia, and the pilgrims travelled with a caravan towards Mecca. Nanak sat outside his tent, talking to all the men who would listen to him. Some were suspicious of him, and thought he was trying to turn them away from their own religion and convert them to a new religion. Others understood what he was saying and respected him, and slowly he came to be looked upon as a great teacher by the pilgrims.

When they reached the outskirts of Mecca, Nanak stopped for the night at a mosque. He was very tired from his travels and after saying his prayers, he went to sleep. He did not know that his feet were pointing towards the Kaaba, the holiest shrine of the Muslims. Because he was tired and weary, he slept till late in the morning. When it was time for the morning prayers, one of the attendants of the mosque discovered the traveller fast asleep, with his feet pointing towards the Kaaba. The attendant was so upset by what he considered to be an insult to God, that he went quickly up the steps and brought Qazi Rukn-ud-din, to witness this act of sacrilege for himself. The qazi was very angry too. He struck Nanak with his staff and shook him awake.

'Wake up. Look at the terrible sin you have committed. You have pointed your feet towards the place where God resides, God will be very angry with you. You must rub your face in the dirt and beg him to forgive you,' said the qazi angrily.

'You are right O qazi. 1 have indeed insulted God and deserve to be punished. But I am an ignorant man and to avoid making this mistake again, I would be grateful if you could point my feet towards a direction in which God does not reside.'

The qazi was taken aback by Nanak's request. He understood what Nanak was trying to tell him: God was omnipresent and His home was everywhere, so it was wrong to designate any one place as the house of God. While he was at Mecca, the Qazi and Nanak met often and later became good friends.

From Mecca, Nanak travelled to Medina and then on

to Baghdad on to the banks of the Tigris in Iraq. There is a stone slab outside Baghdad, with an inscription on it, which tells us that Nanak had been to Baghdad. The Guru set up his camp near a tomb outside the city. In the evenings he would conduct kirtan, and many people came to hear him and appreciated the beauty of his hymns. But many others became angry because in the orthodox form of Islam, music was not allowed to be used in worship. The anger spread and one day a large group of men came to stone Nanak to death. But when they came close they saw him at prayer and the prayer he was singing was the *azaan* – which summons all the faithful Muslims to prayer – the stones fell from their hands and, one by one, they knelt, and joined in Nanak's prayer. They understood now that here was a saint who respected all religions.

From Baghdad Nanak travelled to Iran. From there to Kabul and Jalalabad and over the Khyber Pass to Peshawar. He crossed the Indus into the Punjab and went to Saidpur to visit his uncle who lived there.

This was also the time when Babur invaded India. He had captured Sialkot and also Saidpur. The people of Saidpur had put up a strong resistance and this had angered Babur. As a result he was excessively cruel to the people of Saidpur. Many were killed and many taken prisoner. Nanak was also amongst the prisoners. While in prison, he conducted prayer meetings there too. The prison warden would listen to Nanak everyday and finally came to the conclusion that he was a great saint.

'Your Majesty, we have committed a sin. Baba Nanak is a saint and we have made him a prisoner,' the warden said to Babur.

Babur thought for a while, and then said, 'If this is true, we must ask his forgiveness. I will go to see him myself.'

Babur visited the prison, and asked Nanak a number of questions, and from the answers Babur was convinced that Nanak was a holy man. He bowed to him and said, 'Forgive me, O Holy One. I did not know what I was doing. As from this moment you are free, as are all your men.'

'These are all my men,' Nanak said, pointing to all the prisoners. 'I cannot leave the prison without all of them,' he added.

Babur smiled, 'You are truly a great man.' Then, turning to his officer, he said, 'Release all the prisoners.'

'Ask me for something, so that I may know you have forgiven me,' Babur said.

'I seek nothing, but if it will make you happy to do something for me, then return all the wealth and property of the people of Saidpur that has been confiscated by you, and also all that has been looted by your soldiers,' Nanak said.

This was done and soon afterwards Babur returned to Kabul. Nanak stayed for a few days in Saidpur in the year 1521, and then returned to Kartarpur.

It was that lovely time of the day which in English they call 'dusk' and in Hindi *goudhuli bela*.

Nanak's wife, Sulakhni, sat near her cooking fire, lost in thought as she waited for her sons to come home for their evening meal. It was winter, the darkness set in early and there was a chill in the air. But she sat close to the fire and did not feel the cold. She thought of her sons and how different they were from each other. Sri Chand, the elder, now twenty-six years old, was saintly like his father. He had no need for things. His clothes were those of a hermit, simple and plain, and just enough to cover his body. He ate little and that too only the simplest of food. He was always praying or reciting from the holy books. While he was a boy, he had lived with his aunt, Nanki, and when he had shown some interest in religion, it had made Nanki proud and happy. 'He is just like Nanak,' she would say and because she loved her brother so much, she encouraged Sri Chand to spend more time in learning about religion. Sri Chand grew up and became a sadhu.

'Like father, like son,' Sulakhni said to herself with a smile. Then she checked herself from pursuing this chain of thought. She told herself, 'Be honest; he is not like his father.' Sri Chand did not care about worldly things and spent a lot of time in prayers. In this, he was like his father. But in many ways he was very different. She had watched him once, while he was in discussion with some other holy men. When one of them disagreed with what he said, his eyes flashed and his face became ugly with anger, and he raised his voice at the other sadhus. He was proud of his knowledge and this pride made him arrogant. She had watched her husband too when he held his discussions with other holy men, and though they did not always agree with him, she had never seen anger or pride in her husband's eyes. 'No, Sri Chand was not like his father. But then neither was their younger son, Lakhmidas,' thought Sulakhni.

She had kept the younger son with her and watched him grow. Every time he had shown interest in matters connected with religion or holy men, her heart had filled with fear. She was afraid that he would take after his father and she would lose him too. So she did everything to keep his mind fixed on worldly things. In this she was helped by her parents. They were always giving him new things – new clothes, new toys, new shoes, and all kinds of rich food to eat. He grew up with no interest in God or in prayers. She had succeeded in keeping him with her, but had paid a heavy price for this success. Her son had grown up to be a selfish, materialistic young man who thought only of himself, and showed no feeling or consideration for others. So, in a way, she had lost him too. If it had not been for Kalyan Chand and Tripta, her life would have been lonely. Like her, they too spent their days waiting for Nanak's return. She smiled to herself as she thought of the soft quiet lives that the old couple led and of the love that had grown between them and her.

As she waited for her sons' return, she heard footsteps coming down the long quiet street that led to her home. Her head came up with a start. The sound seemed so familiar. But it couldn't be: So many times during these long years of waiting she had thought she had heard this familiar step. Yet when she had run to the door to look for Nanak, there had been no one there. She heard the sound again. The blood rushed to her head. Yes, there could be no mistaking it. Even after all these years, she remembered the sound of Nanak's footsteps. She got up and ran to the door, and there he was, thin and gaunt; dressed in those strange clothes, his cheeks hollow, his beard now streaked with grey. He smiled at her and she fell at his feet and shed tears of joy.

'Sulakhni Puttar, who is it? Who has come?' And the weak, tired voice of Nanak's mother, which was normally only a whisper, now came loud and clear with a strength that only hope can bring.

Nanak drew Sulakhni up, put his arm around her shoulder, and together they went into the house to meet his parents.

It was a joyous homecoming. As news of Nanak's return spread through Kartarpur, people flocked to the Bedi house to meet their Guru.

Nanak was happy to meet his sons again, but they were so different from him, from everything that he believed in, that they were like strangers to him. He was a stranger to them too because he had spent so little time with them while they were growing up.

Nanak never put back on his sadhu's clothes again. He wore the ordinary clothes that all common, middles-class men wore. He started the day, as he had always done, by having a bath and then spent a few hours in prayer and kirtan. The Guru's compositions, the Japji Sahib and Asa-di-war were recited in the morning. Mardana, who had played the rabab for so many years while Nanak sang, continued to play even here in Kartarpur. He was joined by his son Shahzada, who had become as good a musician as his father. Large groups of people came to listen to the kirtan. Then Nanak ate a simple meal and went to work in the fields. These fields were all part of the area that had been gifted to him by his disciple Ajit Randhawa. Some of these fields had been cultivated by a few of Nanak's followers, who had settled down in Kartarpur. Other fields remained fallow. Now Nanak began to cultivate these fields. He worked in the fields himself and this set a good example for all the other people who lived in Kartarpur and they too worked hard and enjoyed the fruits of their labour.

In the evening there was a discourse or a discussion on religion and then there was kirtan, where the Guru's compositions – *sodaru* or *aarti* would be sung. Then all those who had attended the prayers, sat down and ate the evening meal together.

The number of pilgrims who came to Kartarpur grew steadily. People who came from far-away places had no place to stay because the people of Kartarpur had already taken in as many guests as they could.

One day Nanak sent for one of his disciples who was a master builder.

'I want to build a *dharamshala* – a place where all the people who come from outside Kartarpur can stay in comfort. The dharamshala must have a big hall where our meetings can be held when the sun is too hot or when it rains, and of course you must also build the *langar*,' said Nanak.

Word of the project quickly spread and by the time the master builder had finished making his design, cartloads of bricks, lime, and wooden beams had already been brought to Kartarpur by the Guru's followers. By the time work on the digging of the foundation began, an army of men had descended upon Kartarpur. By the end of the year the dharamshala was ready. All the followers now had a place to stay. There was enough covered space for the religious meetings, and the big langar served meals twice a day to all who came. His disciples now brought vegetables and grain and food for the langar and there was always plenty of everything.

More than a year had passed since Nanak's return to Kartarpur and his life had become so settled that people felt that he would not go away again. Sulakhni too believed that he would stay always with her and stopped looking at him with worry and fear. In the mornings and evenings, when he went in and spent some time with his parents, they were at last content.

One day, while Nanak was tilling the fields, Sri Chand came running to him. 'Father, come quickly. Mother wants you at home.' Nanak felt the fear in his son's voice and knew that something was wrong, but he did not ask anything.

There was a crowd of people near the door and in the courtyard. They all stood there in silence and when they saw Nanak they made way for him. He went into the room and saw that his father had been lowered to the ground. His mother cradled her husband's head in her lap. Kalyan Chand's breath came in long gasps and his whole body shook as he breathed. He looked so weak and thin and tired that Nanak knew the end was near. Kalyan Chand raised his head as he saw Nanak come into the room and tried to smile. Then he held out a trembling hand to his son and Nanak, bending down, clasped it in both of his; and thus – his head cradled in his wife's lap, his hand held firmly by his son; Kalyan Chand breathed his last.

There was a deep silence for a moment and then some of the women who stood outside the room began to weep. But Nanak did not weep, nor did Tripta. Nanak gently closed his father's eyes, then taking his father's head from his mother's lap, he helped her to her feet and led her from the room.

The next few days were taken up by the funeral ceremonies.

Through all these days, Tripta sat in silence – not weeping, not speaking, eating only a few morsels and that too when she was forced to eat. There was no outward sign of sorrow on her face as she sat praying, always praying. 'What is it, mother? Why have you become so quiet?' Nanak asked one day.

Tripta replied in a clear and strong voice, 'I must prepare myself – I have to go join your father. I cannot leave him alone for long.' And the day after all the ceremonies related to Kalyan Chand's last rites were over, Tripta too passed away peacefully in her sleep.

Gradually, over the months, the people in Kartarpur became one community. Those who were farmers tilled the land but the grain was shared by all. Those who had skills like the potters, the weavers, the carpenters, and the masons used them in the service of the *sangat*. The women worked in the langar. They cut and cooked the vegetables and made the chapatis, and men who could make no other contribution, served the meals and washed the utensils. Those who had medical skills treated the sick; and those who were learned or had musical abilities, joined Nanak in the discourses and the kirtan. All the members of the community, those who stayed in Kartarpur and those who came to visit, served the sangat in one way or other.

During his travels, Guru Nanak had set up centres in many places, some of them very far away, and he had left these centres in the charge of his followers. Now his followers came from these centres to Kartarpur to learn more from their Guru, and take back new strength to their own centres. Kartarpur, the city of the Creator, thus became the centre of the Sikh world.

Many of the Guru's disciples became famous and earned

respect not only for their learning but also for their good, kind deeds.

One of these disciples was Bura. He had been a young boy of twelve when he first met the Guru. He belonged to a family of Randhawa Jats and lived in the Amritsar district. Like Nanak, when he was young, Bura too took the family cattle out to graze. Like Nanak, he too liked to spend his time in deep thought about religious matters. Once when on his travels Nanak stopped in a jungle just outside Bura's village, Bura greeted the Guru with great respect and brought him refreshments. When it was time for the Guru to move on, Bura asked for a boon. Nanak smiled at the young boy.

'What is it that you seek?' asked Nanak.

'Oh, holy one, I seek to be freed from the cycle of birth and rebirth,' said Bura.

'You are too young for such thoughts. From where did this idea come to you?' Nanak wanted to know.

'When Babur's army came to our village his soldiers camped in this jungle. They took whatever they wanted from the villagers. Then they cut the corn in the fields. They cut the ripe corn with the unripe corn and made no distinction between the two. Watching them I realized that death also makes no distinction between the young and the old,' said Bura.

The Guru hugged the boy and said, 'You are not a child,' he said. 'You speak with the wisdom of an old man.'

So Bura came to be known henceforth as Bhai Budha. When the Guru set up his home in Kartarpur, Bhai Budha, too, moved permanently to Kartarpur. He was respected for his wisdom and his kindness and people came to him with their problems. He lived to the ripe old age of 125, and was fortunate enough to work with five successive Sikh Gurus.

Another famous disciple of Guru Nanak was Moola Keer. He lived a simple life according to the Guru's teachings. He worked hard during the day and spent his time in reciting the Guru's prayers and hymns in the evenings. He was an honest man and he spent most of his savings in looking after the Sikhs – as the followers of Guru Nanak came to be known – who stopped at his home on their way to Kartarpur. One day a Sikh, while resting in his house, saw Moola Keer's wife putting some money and jewellery away in her cupboard. The Sikh waited till everyone in the house had gone to sleep and then he stole the jewellery and the money from the cupboard and put it in his bag. Early next morning he woke up Moola Keer and asked him to open the gate as he was in a hurry to resume his journey. While they were walking to the gate, the bag fell to the ground and the jewellery and money fell out. Moola did not say a word. He put the money and the jewellery back in the bag and gave it back to the Sikh.

The Sikh was so ashamed of what he had done, that on reaching Kartarpur, he confessed his crime to the Guru. The Guru sent for Mola Keer and when he was ushered to his presence, the Guru asked him, 'This Sikh told me of your strange behaviour. Why did you give the jewellery and money back to this thief? You should have caught him and taken him to the *kotwali.*'

'He is a Sikh,' Moola replied in a quiet voice. He then continued, 'If I had handed him to the police, everyone would have come to know and people would say that a Sikh had done something that was evil. This would have brought disrepute to all Sikhs.'

The Guru was pleased by what Moola said and asked him one last question. 'On his return from Kartarpur this Sikh will stop in your village. Will you take him into your house?'

'Yes master. I will take him into my house and give him food and shelter and serve him as well as I can. You have taught us that we must hate the sin, not the sinner. There is nothing in my heart that I hold against him,' Moola said without hesitation.

Perhaps the most well-known of the Guru's disciple was Lehna. He came from the village which is now known as Sarai

Nanga in Muktsar district. From Sarai Nanga he had moved to Khadur. He had been a great worshipper of the Goddess Durga. Then he had heard Nanak's hymns and had come to Kartarpur. He was twenty-eight-years old, and served the Guru and the Guru's sangat with great devotion. For Lehna the Guru's word was a command and the service of the sangat was a form of worship. Though all members of the sangat were equal, Lehna was respected by all the others because of his great spirit of service. Ever since he had returned from his journeys, Nanak knew that neither of his sons could be his successor – Sri Chand lived a life of renunciation while Lakhmi Das was too materialistic. He chose Lehna as his successor. He brought him to the banks of the Ravi and embraced him, and said, 'From now on you will be known as Angad, which means one who is a part of my body.' Then Guru Nanak placed five copper coins before Angad and bowed to him. Thus Angad became the second Guru of the Sikhs and came to be known as Guru Angad Dev.

In 1530 Nanak made one last journey. It was a short journey across the Ravi to Achal, a small village in Batala district of Punjab. There was a very old and famous temple in Achal dedicated to Lord Shiva's elder son, Kartik, and during Shivratri a big fair would be held in the town. During this fair many holy men came to Achal and held debates and discussions on subjects connected to religion. When Nanak was sixty-one-year old, he too came to Achal to take part in the Shivratri fair. By now his fame as a Guru had spread far and wide, and there were many of his disciples amongst the crowds of people thronging the fair. As Nanak neared Achal, news of his coming spread and people came out to greet him. Some asked him for his blessings, while some others asked for his advice. Most of them stayed to listen to his kirtan and his teachings. This aroused the jealousy of a few of the sadhus. They argued with him and tried to belittle him in the eyes of the crowd.

'You were a sadhu for twenty-three years and you wore the sadhu's dress and travelled far and wide. Now you have given up the sadhu's attire and returned to your home and started working in the fields. The sadhu lives on a far higher plane than the farmer and others who work with their hands. You have demeaned yourself by giving up the sadhu's life,' said one of the sadhus. But Nanak only smiled.

'Tell me, O holy one, what do you do when you are hungry? Where do you get your food from?' asked Nanak.

The sadhu was surprised by this simple question. 'Everyone knows that we earn nothing. The only food we eat is what we get when we go begging,' he answered.

'And who gives you this food?' Nanak continued.

'The householder, of course,' replied the sadhu.

'And the householder is one who works with his hands: the farmer the labourer, the weaver, the potter, all of them. Then I think the householder is greater than you. You become a sadhu and then go with your begging bowl to the householder. You would starve to death if he did not give you anything to eat,' said Nanak at last.

Listening to such debates, many people at the fair were converted to Nanak's teachings. He was a simple farmer himself and what he taught was a lesson that even ordinary people, who lived ordinary lives, and worked with their hands, could understand. On the last day of the fair, Nanak said goodbye to the other holy men and to his disciples; and with Mardana by his side, returned to Kartarpur.

When Mardana was seventy-six-years-old, he fell ill. Many famous *hakims* and *vaids* came to treat him, but to no avail. Nanak was always by his bedside. He caressed Mardana's hair and this brought comfort to Mardana and he drifted off into an exhausted sleep. And still Nanak sat by his side. He looked closely at his friend's face and saw him as he had been when they had first returned to Talwandi – surrounded by an admiring group of friends, as he told them amusing stories about their life in Sultanpur. He saw him as the rather plump young man who had gone with him on that first journey. He had not been happy to go because he loved good food, but on their journey, he often had to go hungry. Nanak smiled as he remembered that Mardana had always been hungry; had always asked for food. Through all his long journeys, Mardana had travelled with him in sun and rain and snow, over hills and plains and mountains, to regions that were strange and unfamiliar. He had looked after Nanak in every way, attended to all his needs and found joy in that service; and through it all he had learnt to laugh at all their troubles. Then, when they sang their hymns, he played his rabab with such feeling that those who listened to it were moved by the music. He had been with the Guru for so many years that he had become part of the Guru's way of life and his teachings.

All these memories came rushing one after another through Nanak's mind as he looked at his companion who was sleeping.

'God, be merciful to my friend. He is a good man,' he prayed silently.

Even though the illness continued to weaken him physically, yet with each passing day, Mardana seemed to become more and more at peace with himself and with his fast-approaching death.

Early one morning, he opened his eyes and saw the Guru still sitting by his side, the way he had sat when he went to sleep.

'Master, my time has come,' he said, without fear.

'So be it, I will build a tomb over your body so that you will be famous,' Nanak said.

'No,' he said with a sad smile. 'My spirit is attempting to

find release from this cage of bones and skin and flesh. Do not seek to hold it in a prison made of stone,' he said and paused for breath. 'And as for fame: I have all the fame in the world that I need. In years to come, whenever people talk of you – as I know they often will – they will talk of me too,' said Mardana.

Nanak held his friend's hand in both of his and squeezed it gently. In Mardana, he had found the respect and devotion that a disciple gives to his Guru; the love a friend gives to a friend; the support and affection that a brother gives to a brother.

Mardana closed his eyes and it seemed that he was asleep again. Then suddenly, he opened them wide and said, 'Go, go Master. It is time. It is time for the morning prayers.' His eyes fixed on his Master's face – Mardana left this world. Nanak closed his friend's eyes and drew the sheet over his face. Someone in the room began to sob, and Nanak saw that it was Shahzada, Mardana's son. He drew him into an embrace and consoled him. Then he went quickly to bathe so that he could be in time for the morning prayers.

In the evening, Nanak began his discourse like every other day. When it was time for kirtan he remembered that Mardana was no more. Who would give the music for his song? He looked, as he had always looked, when he began his song, towards the spot where Mardana usually sat. He saw Shahzada, sitting in his father's place, ready to start playing his rabab. Nanak smiled and began singing.

The years rolled by. The number of those who believed in Nanak and his teachings grew every day. People all over Punjab began to live the way Nanak had taught his Sikhs to live. They were freed from the empty customs and rituals that they had been forced to observe in the name of religion.

Nanak heard the voice of God calling out to him and knew that his time upon earth was now nearly over. He went to the banks of the river Ravi and lay down under a tree. Word spread quickly that the Guru's end was near. His disciples hurried from far and wide for one last *darshan* of their Guru and he was constantly surrounded by his disciples. The end came peacefully on 27 September 1539, and Guru Angad Dev took over the leadership of the Sikhs.

Chapter 4

Teachings

Guru Nanak did not claim to be an incarnation of God or even a special messenger of his. He claimed only that he was a teacher, trying to teach people how they could live good, simple lives, which would bring them closer to God.

The appeal of Nanak's teachings was instantaneous, and almost from his first sermon he was able to win disciples. Thus, by the time he died, he had built up a strong community of Sikhs, not only in Kartarpur, but also at other centres all over India.

The reasons for the great and instant appeal of Nanak's teachings are easy to see. The two major religions being followed in the Punjab were Hinduism and Islam. Hindu scriptures were taught in Sanskrit – a language which had been popular in ancient India, but which by then had become archaic. In fact all the sacred books of the Hindus are in Sanskrit and most people could not understand them unless they were interpreted by a scholar or a priest. Islam was taught through old Arabic, the language in which the Quran is written. No one in the Punjab used either of the languages, and as a result it was beyond the comprehension of the average man. When Nanak composed his famous hymns – which contained all his teachings – he did so in the language spoken by the people of Punjab at that time. Nanak used the colloquial dialect of North Punjab and interspersed dialects from other regions while writing his hymns. However, the language used by the people of Punjab has evolved greatly in the intervening centuries between then and now.

They could be understood even by an illiterate person. As a result, people naturally veered away from the older religions – which they found difficult to understand – and towards the Guru's teachings, which they were able to understand on their own.

Another factor that brought an immediate appeal to Nanak's teachings was his use of music. Music formed the medium of his teachings. All his hymns are set to various *ragas* of Hindustani Classical music and, to this day, they are sung in the raga in which they were composed. Music has always been an integral part of Indian culture and of the Indian way of life. It is also a well established fact that people will respond more readily to a song than to a speech. So when Nanak began his discourses with the singing of beautiful hymns, he found many willing listeners; who, overwhelmed by the beauty of the songs, stayed on as a captive audience to listen to his sermons.

The starting point of all of Nanak's teaching is his concept of God. He says that there is one God who is without form, who is not born and so cannot die. As such, when we worship God it is not necessary to deify pictures or statues. By doing this we are not worshipping God, because God is formless. *Ik Onkar Satnam*, Nanak's first composition and the opening phrase of Guru Granth Sahib (*mool mantra*), explains these points beautifully. It goes, *Ik Onkaar Sat Naam Kartaa Purakh Nirbhay-o-Nirvair Akaal Moorat Ajoonee Saibham Gur Parsaad Jap…* (He is the One Universal Creator God. His name is truth. He is creativity personified. He has no fear, no hatred. He is the image of the undying. He is beyond birth and self-existent).*

Nanak went on to say that God was Truth. By saying this, he made God a standard by which men could judge their own

---

*Translation source: *http://www.desidime.com/*

actions and behaviour. If God was Truth, then to behave in an untruthful manner would be to go against God. Behaving in an untruthful manner included telling lies, stealing, being dishonest in conduct, and doing things that hurt other people.

Since it is difficult for an average man or woman to understand the concept of God as formless or a force that is omnipresent and omnipotent, it becomes essential for all of us to have a 'Guru'. It is the Guru who will help the disciple to understand God and love Him. It is the Guru who will give his followers strength so that they are able to bear all the sorrow and pain that life brings to them. It is the Guru who shows us the path of Truth. He is like the captain of a ship who will guide us carefully through shoals and the troubled waters of life and bring us safely to God.

Because the Guru plays such an important part in our pursuit of God, we must obey him in everything and follow his teachings and his instruction with complete and unquestioning faith.

Again and again, Nanak stressed the importance of the role of the Guru in the disciple's life and the need for the disciple to have total trust and faith in the Guru. At the same time Nanak also stressed that we must never forget that the Guru is only a teacher who shows us the path to God. He is not God. As a result we must follow his teachings, listen to his advice, but must never make the mistake of worshipping him.

Nanak says that all men must choose a Guru. This would imply that after one Guru's death his disciples would have to choose another Guru. In conformity with this concept, Nanak appointed Angad as his successor during his lifetime.

Nanak preached a complete adherence to the Guru's instructions. So after his death, his followers became Angad's followers. Angad could now carry on Nanak's work. So by appointing a successor, Nanak introduced a very special feature to the new religion. Each Guru, in imitation of Nanak's example, would choose his successor during his lifetime. This ensured that the leadership of the Sikhs remained unbroken. Because of this, Sikhism became a strong and unified religion. This saved Sikhism from breaking up the way other sects, like the Kabirpanthis and Vaishnavas, broke up into splinter groups, after their respective Gurus' death.

Guru Nanak taught that it is essential for every man to perform the duties of a householder. Earning a living, getting married, bringing up one's children, looking after one's parents, all these were duties that everyone must perform according to the Guru. No real good could be achieved by giving up the world and going to the mountains to live alone and pray. Man must live amongst the impurities of the world and yet try to remain pure; just as the lotus remains pure even though it grows in stagnant water. True prayers, Nanak said, were good actions and good actions can only be performed towards other men. If we take *sanyas*, we will not get a chance to perform good deeds for others and, no matter how much we close our eyes in prayer, no matter how many mantras we recite, our prayers will not be true prayers. We must live amongst men, perform our duties to the best of our ability, and always strive for the good of our fellowmen. Only by following this path, can we come close to God.

Nanak lived the life of a householder himself in the later part of his life. He lived with his wife and sons, and worked in the fields. When the time came to choose his successor, he chose Angad who was also a householder with a wife and children. From this simple act it followed that all the Sikh Gurus would be householders and that an ascetic would not become the Guru. This meant that all the Gurus lived the same life that their followers lived and shared in their joys and sorrows. The human side of their personalities and their lives made them greatly loved by their followers.

Nanak believed in the equality of all men. In Hindu society, caste and religion have always walked side by side. But two

Bhakta saints from the South – Ramanujan and Ramananda – said that it was possible to have a society without the caste system. The Muslims too had no caste system and Punjab had been familiar with the idea of casteless society since the Eleventh century. Nanak's mind was influenced by both the Bhaktas and the Muslim saints. He taught that by treating the lower castes as untouchables we were hurting them. When we do things which hurt other men, we are moving away from the truth and from God. So all men, irrespective of their caste, must be treated equally. We must give a man of the lowest caste the same respect that we would give to a man of the highest caste. Nanak preached that all his followers must sit side by side; with no consideration of their wealth, social position, or their caste; and become one united sangat by praying together and taking part in kirtan. And with the passage of years the langar became a visible representation of Nanak's most important teaching. By eating together, his followers put aside all distinctions of caste, creed, and wealth and reiterated their faith in their Gurus' teachings: All men are equal and belong to one caste and one race – humanity

Nanak was against empty rites and rituals. A Muslim could not be a true Muslim by just praying in the mosque, fasting or going on a Haj to the Kaaba. A Hindu could not be a good Hindu by merely hosting feasts for holy men, performing *yagnas* and other rites, or going on pilgrimages. A true Muslim and a true Hindu must be kind, honest, truthful, polite, and good at heart. True religion is a way of life. He summed up this way of life by saying that people should work honestly, pray sincerely, and be charitable.

Nanak built a bridge between the Hindus and Muslims, but in so doing he created a new community of people who had their own way of living. Nanak's followers lived the way their teacher had taught them to, and their way of life was different from that of the Hindus and Muslims of the time. They had a separate place of worship (which came to be known as gurudwara) and did not go to the temple or the mosque anymore. Their way of worship was also different. They did not bow before stone idols or repeat Sanskrit prayers. Nor did they turn west, towards Mecca and pray in Arabic. They sang Nanak's songs and prayed in their own mother-tongue, Punjabi. Even their greetings to each other were no longer Hindu or Muslim greetings, but the Guru's greeting of 'Sat Kartar' or 'True Creator', which later became 'Sat Sri Akal'.

It is often said that most of Guru Nanak's teachings, his ideas, have been taken from other religions and other religious leaders. This may be true, but he gave to all these ideas a new form, which was his own. He made his ideas tools through which human personality could be developed. So powerful are his teachings that they have remained strong and clear even five hundred years after his death. They have helped the Sikhs to overcome every difficulty that they have faced. The cruelty of the Mughal government, and the great military strength of Ahmad Shah Abdali in the eighteenth century, could not eliminate the Sikhs because they had Nanak's teachings to give them strength. Nanak's teachings brought out the best in his followers and gave them the strength to face and survive all hardships.

The Guru, who was capable of giving such great strength to his followers, has left behind a memory of gentleness and love. He has often been described as meek and gentle. He did not try to impress people with his spiritual strength by performing miracles and used only personal example and gentle persuasion to win followers. He was also a great poet and used his poetry and music to reach the hearts of his people. His poetry ranks among the great works of literature of the world. He was truly one of the greatest teachers the world has ever known.

Chapter 5

THE JANAMSAKHIS

Most of what is written about Guru Nanak has been learnt from the Janamsakhis. The Janamsakhis are stories from the Guru's life. These stories have been put together in a chronological form and, when we read them, it is like reading a biography of the Guru. There are many such sets of stories, but the more important ones are the Bala Janamsakhis, the Puratan Janamsakhis, the Meherban Janamsakhis, and the Janamsakhis that are supposed to have been written by Sewa Dass and some others.

In modern times, Janamsakhis do not enjoy the same importance they did till about a hundred years ago. Till then people believed implicitly in everything that these stories contained. Now the readers feel that many of these stories and the details contained in them are not altogether authentic. The first of these sets of stories was written more than a hundred years after the Guru's death. Till then they were handed down from father to son by word of mouth. As a result, each time these stories were retold, the story-teller modified or changed the story a little. By the time they were written, the stories had become very different from the way they had been told originally. Also, these stories were told by people who were not highly educated and they were told to simple village-folk who were, at best, semi-literate. To impress the villagers – who believed in magic and miracles – the writers brought in these elements into their stories. It is well known that the Gurus were against performing miracles or showing off their spiritual power.

So when the Janamsakhis tell us about the Guru performing miracles to impress his followers, we naturally doubt their authenticity. Yet, we cannot reject the Janamsakhis altogether. They are very important, because each of these stories is an illustration of some aspect of Guru Nanak's teachings.

There are many interesting stories about the Guru in the Janamsakhis. However, it is possible to relate only a very few of these here.

When the Guru disappeared while he was bathing in the river, many believed that he had been drowned. When he reappeared and said he had heard a voice, many believed that a miracle had taken place. But when Nanak said again and again, 'There is no Hindu, there is no Musalman,' many believed that he had lost his reason. News of what Nanak had been saying was brought to the qazi, the head of all the Muslims in Sultanpur.

'Your holiness, this kafir is saying over and over again: There is no Hindu, there is no Musalman. What does he mean?' the people asked the qazi.

The qazi was very angry. He felt that if Nanak kept saying there is no Musalman, many Muslims would believe him and stop performing all the rituals that they should, as devout Muslims, be performing. He went to see Nawab Daulat Khan, the Lodhi ruler of Sultanpur about this. 'Lord, this madman must be stopped immediately. He is preaching dangerous precepts,' the qazi said. The Nawab could see that the qazi was angry, so he did not interrupt him. 'He can say what he likes about the Hindus but he has no right to make comments about Islam. How can he say that there is no Musalman?' asked the qazi.

The Nawab loved Nanak dearly and he had been very happy when Nanak had reappeared. But he had heard about the strange things Nanak was saying and now that the qazi had come to him, he knew that he had to do something to stop Nanak. So the Nawab sent for Nanak.

'Tell us, Nanak, what do you mean when you say there is no Hindu, there is no Musalman. Are not the qazi and I followers of Muhammad?' asked the Nawab.

'There is no Hindu, there is no Musalman.' Nanak repeated. 'There are only true followers of God. We must be firm in our faith, our hearts must be clean, and we must not have any greed or pride. We must not be troubled by life or death. We must accept the will of God. We must be unselfish and kind to all. Only then can we call ourselves true Musalmans,' he added

This made the qazi even angrier. 'And what are you?' he shouted at Nanak.

Nanak only smiled and in his soft, gentle voice said, 'I am neither a Muslim nor a Hindu.'

'Why?' asked the qazi.

'Because I try to live according to the teachings of all religions. To me all religions belong to God,' said Nanak.

The qazi felt this was a good opportunity to trap Nanak. 'It is time for offering the Friday *namaz*. If to you, all religions are one, join us in prayer in the mosque.'

'That I will do with pleasure. I will follow when you lead the prayer,' said Nanak.

So the Nawab, the qazi, and the Guru set off for the mosque. The qazi took his place at the head of the congregation. During the namaz, when all the other worshippers knelt, Nanak remained standing. The qazi saw this from the corner of his eye and, the moment the namaz was over, he turned to the Nawab and said, 'See, my lord. This man is a liar and a cheat. He said all religions are equal and he would join us in namaz. But he did not do so. He must be punished.' The qazi spoke very angrily and a crowd of people collected around him.

'Tell me my friend, what do you have to say to this?' the nawab asked Nanak.

Nanak did not reply to the nawab's question. He turned,

instead, to the qazi. With a smile on his lips and a twinkle in his eyes he said, 'You are a man of God, in the house of God, and you have just led a congregation of a thousand men in prayer. I know you will tell the truth. Tell me what was on your mind while you prayed?'

The qazi thought for a while, then he saw Nanak looking at him and the smile from Nanak's lips had spread to his eyes. The qazi knew he must tell the truth. 'I was thinking of my mare.' He spoke softly but the silence around was so complete that everyone could hear him. 'My mare gave birth to a foal last night. It was a difficult birthing, but all went well and I now have a beautiful foal. The stable is next to an open well and I was worried that the foal may fall into the well. This would be a great loss to me and so my mind was on my mare and her foal,' said the qazi.

'So tell me, O learned one. Does prayer consist only of kneeling and bowing and reciting a few words?' asked Nanak.

'No,' said the qazi, now understanding why Nanak had not joined him in prayer. 'Prayer is to control the mind, so that when you praise God, you think only of Him and of nothing else. You are right, Nanak, while my body was bowing to God, my mind and spirit were full of other things,' the qazi added.

In another story from the Janamsakhis, Nanak and Mardana were on their first journey. It was the beginning of monsoon and they travelled in the heavy rain. From the forests at the foothills of the Himalayas, the two travellers moved slowly down to the Gangetic plain. They stopped to rest in little villages and in the evenings, if it was not raining, Nanak conducted kirtan in the courtyard of his host's house. His fame spread quickly and people came from far to listen to his songs and to hear his teachings. Amongst the people who came was a shopkeeper from a nearby town. At first he came because he had heard so much about the Guru and wanted only to see who this strange holy man was. But once he heard Nanak's teachings, he became a disciple and came every evening without fail. The moment he closed his shop, he would rush home, spend a few moments with his family and then hurry to the village where Nanak dwelt. He knew the Guru would soon move on and he did not want to miss a single day of his kirtans. He spent hours not only in the service of the Guru, but also in the service of other members of the sangat. In this service he found more happiness than he had ever known before.

One morning he was a little late in opening his shop. As he walked up the steps, he was humming one of Nanak's hymns. His neighbouring shopkeeper had already opened his shop and called out to him, saying, 'You seem very happy these days, my friend. Your business must be thriving.'

'Yes, my business is very good these days, but it is the business of the mind and spirit,' the shopkeeper replied.

'What do you mean?' asked the other shopkeeper.

'I go everyday to listen to the teachings of my Guru and he has brought me great wealth of the mind and the spirit. He has brought me close to God,' said the first shopkeeper

'Take me also to meet your Guru, perhaps he will make me rich as well,' said the other shopkeeper.

'You can come whenever you choose. You can come this evening when we close our shops,' the Guru's disciple offered.

But in the evening the second shopkeeper turned to pleasures of the flesh and did not go with the Guru's disciple.

Every day he would call out to his friend to take him to his Guru and every day he would give in to temptation and stay back. So the Guru's disciple led the life of a saint, serving his Guru and the other members of the sangat, showing kindness to everyone, spending his spare time in prayer. The second shopkeeper led a selfish life in which he thought only of his pleasure and his thoughts, words, and actions were full of sin.

One day, the second shopkeeper was waiting for some friends under a tree just outside the town. As he waited and with nothing better to occupy him, he picked up a stick and began to dig up the earth. He saw something shining in the soil he had dug up and, on picking it up, found it was a gold coin. He ran home and brought a pickaxe and began to dig, sure that he would find more gold. At last his pickaxe struck something hard. He dug up the loose soil with his hands and found a big earthen jar buried in the ground and was sure that he had found buried treasure. He held the jar in his lap and loosened the lid, but when he opened the jar, he was disappointed to find that it was was full of ash. He turned the jar over and emptied all the ash. Then, very carefully, he rummaged through the ash, a little at a time, so that he would not miss anything. But there were no more gold coins to be found and he was very disappointed. But then he consoled himself with the thought that one gold coin was better than none at all.

He returned to his shop. Soon he saw his friend and neighbour coming to open his shop. The Guru's disciple walked with a limp and his left foot was bandaged.

The second shopkeeper called, 'What has happened to you?'

'Today, while returning from my Guru's village, a thorn went into my foot. It went in deep and when I pulled it out, my foot began to bleed. I had to have it bandaged,' said the disciple.

Hearing this, the second shopkeeper began to laugh, and said 'You are the one who talked about wealth and look at the wealth each of us has got. You, who are good and kind, have been given a thorn in your foot while I, who lead a life of sin and debauchery, have been given a gold coin. I wonder how your Guru will explain this.'

The Guru's disciple smiled and said, 'Come with me this evening and you can hear what he says.'

So, that evening the second shopkeeper, at last, came into the Guru's presence. He listened to the kirtan and to Nanak's teachings and when the sangat moved away for the evening meal, his friend led him up to the Guru and introduced him saying, 'Master, this is my friend and neighbour. His shop is next to mine and he has a question to ask you.'

The Guru listened to the question, looking carefully at his disciple as the other shopkeeper spoke. Then he smiled and turned to the speaker and said, 'You are right. You can think of the gold coin as a reward and the thorn as a punishment. But let me put it another way. I say that you were destined to find a big jar, full of gold coins but because you lead a life of sin, the coins in the jar were turned into ash and you found only one coin. Your friend was destined to be impaled on a sharp stake but because of his good deeds, the stake was reduced to a small thorn. Man's life is made up of the actions he performs. If his actions are bad, even the good that comes his way is reduced. If his actions are good, even the harm that comes his way is reduced.'

The Guru next went to the sangat at Prayag which is now called Allahabad. Here the three rivers – the Ganga, the Yamuna and the mythical Saraswati – meet. This point is considered very holy and special merit is attached to bathing in the *sangam* at Allahabad. It is felt that by doing this all of one's sins can be washed away, especially on days that have been designated for this purpose. On these days, the banks of the river are crowded with thousands of people all waiting to bathe in the river, at the time which the priests have declared as most auspicious. People come from all over the country to Prayag to bathe in the holy waters.

When the Guru reached Allahabad, the biggest of these holy fairs – the Kumbh Mela – was in progress. It is held once in twelve years and marks the special configuration of the stars during the month of 'Baisakh', and commemorates the spilling of a few drops of the holy nectar (*amrit*) at this spot, when the Gods carried it away from the *rakshas*.

For fifteen days during the mela, every bit of open land is covered with camps of holy men and pilgrims. Each group says its special prayers and practices its own customs. But at the appointed time, they all come to the sangam to bathe.

The Guru arrived on the banks of the holy river and set up his camp. Mardana played the rabab and the Guru sang a song in praise of God. The music was so sweet, Nanak's voice was so strong and pure, and the words of the song so beautiful, that crowds of people gathered around to listen.

'Who is this holy man?', a whisper went around the crowd. 'We have not seen him here before,' they agreed.

Then someone answered, 'He is Nanak, the great Guru from Punjab. He travels far and wide to bring his teachings to people even in distant lands.' So in a few days Nanak had drawn many followers to his teachings. There was a *mahant* who had his camp close to Nanak's camp. His jealousy was aroused when he saw that his followers were abandoning him to listen to Nanak's teachings. He began to say nasty things about Nanak, but no one would listen to him.

Guru Nanak sat in meditation. Suddenly he heard a great commotion around him. It was *Brahma muhurta* (a period of one and a half hours before sunrise), the time which is considered most holy by the pundits for a bath in the holy waters. So it was thought that anyone who bathed in the sangam at Prayag at this time would become so pure that he would surely go to heaven when he died.

Everyone ran to the river to bathe but Nanak sat on, lost in his thoughts. One by one the pilgrims and the holy men returned, sure that their dip in the holy waters had made them so pure that they would go to heaven. When the neighbouring mahant returned he saw that Nanak had not taken a bath and the auspicious time had passed. He felt this was his chance to belittle Nanak and win his followers back. He stood outside Nanak's camp and called out loudly, 'Look at this foolish man. He has come all the way to Prayag but at the auspicious time he has not bathed in the river.' He repeated these words many times and soon a large crowd collected. Nanak's new disciples were surprised that their Guru had been so careless. They had thought that like all of them, he too had come to Prayag to bathe in the holy waters to wash away his sins.

'Why should I have bathed in the water at this particular time?' Nanak asked the mahant in a clear and strong voice.

'You know why. You need to bathe in order to wash away your sins. You know that anyone who bathes in the river at this time becomes pure, as all his sins are washed away by the holy waters,' the mahant shouted in anger.

'We cannot become pure by merely washing our bodies. We can become pure by making a place for God in our hearts. If our minds hold evil thoughts towards other men, if we are ready to cheat and to steal, how can the mere washing of our bodies in the holy waters make us pure? We will be like a brass utensil which has been polished from the outside till it shines, but which is filled with poison inside. Saints are pure and holy, even when they do not bathe; and sinners remain sinners, even if they bathe four times a day,' said Nanak.

Now, let us move towards the fourth story. When Guru Nanak set out on his journey to Lanka from Prayag, he passed once again through Lahore. This time word had already reached Lahore that the Guru was coming. In Lahore, there lived a very rich merchant by the name of Duni Chand. Once a year, Duni Chand performed memorial ceremonies for his dead father. It so happened that during that particular year, these ceremonies were being performed at the time when Nanak came to Lahore. Among these ceremonies was a grand feast for Brahmins and holy men. When Duni Chand heard that Nanak the Guru was coming to Lahore, he personally escorted the Guru to his house and offered him great hospitality. Nanak saw signs of great wealth around him, and Duni Chand himself boasted about his great riches.

The Guru stayed with him for a few days. He took part in all the ceremonies and Duni Chand and the Guru got to know each other well. One evening the Guru took out a needle and gave it to Duni Chand. 'Duni Chand, you have been a very good host and you have looked after me very well. You are now my dear friend and I have great trust in you. This needle is important to me. Please keep it with you, keep it very carefully and after our deaths, when we meet in the next world, give it back to me,' said Nanak.

Duni Chand went back to his room quite confused. He did not understand why the Guru had given him something so ordinary as a needle to look after carefully and carry into the next world.

At night as he was getting ready to go to bed, his wife asked him, 'What is it that is troubling you? I have never before seen you with such a serious look on your face.'

'You know Guru Nanak?' Duni Chand asked.

'Who does not know him?' his wife said with a smile.

Duni Chand took out the needle and said to his wife, 'He gave me this needle. He told me it was important to him, and asked me to look after it very carefully; and when we meet in the next world, to give it back to him. I cannot understand why he has asked me to look after a needle in this way.'

Duni Chand's wife was a wise woman. She smiled at her husband's confusion.

'It is so simple, my husband. Will you be able to take this needle with you when you die?'

Duni Chand thought about the question for a moment

and said, 'No, of course not. I will not be able to take it with me when I die.'

'And where will all your wealth go? If you are not able to take a small thing like a needle with you, will you be able to take your whole wealth with you?' asked Duni Chand's wife.

Duni Chand understood at last what the Guru was attempting to teach him. The food he had fed to Brahmins and holy men would not cross the barriers of death and reach his father, just as all the money he had collected would not go with him when he died. What would go with him were his good deeds. Far better to feed the hungry than to feed the Brahmins; far better to use his money to help the poor than to keep it locked up in the hope of carrying it into the next world.

Duni Chand opened up his treasure chests and used all his money for the welfare of the poor after this. Nanak has talked about death in his Janamsakhis. Perhaps the most beautiful Janamsakhi is the one about Nanak's last moments on this earth.

Nanak lay under a tree on the river-bank just outside Kartarpur. Angad sat with Nanak's feet in his lap, his heart heavy not only with the grief of the approaching end but also with the burden of the responsibilities that he would soon have to carry.

All day, people from distant places came to see their Guru one last time. Sometimes, Nanak would close his eyes and sleep, sometimes he would be awake, but he did not see any of his followers. His breathing was heavy and the end was very near. A wind struck up and shook the leaves of the trees. Some of the dry leaves rattled as they struck each other.

Nanak opened his eyes and looked up at the leaves. Then he looked at Angad and smiled. And Angad understood the meaning of that smile – that the old leaves must fall and make place for the new; just as the old must leave the world to make place for the young. Then the Guru's eyes became clouded again and he seemed to lose awareness of the world around him, and of the people who sat by his side.

A murmur started amongst the Guru's Muslim followers, who sat on his left. At first Angad could not make out what they said. Then, as their voices became louder, he heard the words clearly, 'He is ours, our *pir*, our holy man. So when he dies, his body must be handed over to us so that we can give it holy burial.'

The Hindu followers who sat on the Guru's right were very upset by this claim. 'No, no. Nanak was born a Hindu. His father's name was Kalyan and his mother's name was Tripta. In his teachings there is a great deal that he has taken from the Hindu way of life. Besides, he has never said that he is a Musalman. So how can you say he is yours? He is our Guru and his body will be ours so that we can give him the funeral rites that all true-born Hindus need in order to go to heaven,' protested the Hindu followers.

The Guru opened his eyes and chuckled softly and Angad held up his hand and the quarrelling disciples fell silent. 'You are both right,' he said, looking first towards one group and then towards the other. 'I belong to both of you. But there is a way to solve this difficulty. Each of you must bring flowers, lots of flowers, and put them beside me. The Muslims must put their flowers along my left side and the Hindus must put them along my right. Then tomorrow when it is time for my funeral, you must look carefully at your flowers. If the Hindus' flowers are fresh, then I belong to the Hindus and they can cremate my body; and if the Muslims' flowers are fresh then I belong to the Muslims and they may do with my body as they wish,' said Nanak. By now, he was tired; he closed his eyes again and drifted off to sleep.

The Guru's commands were obeyed and both Hindus and

Muslims brought flowers and put them down as the Guru had directed. Then they sat down to wait out the night. Some of them slept, others looked at the Guru's face by the fluttering light of the oil lamps that burned near his head, afraid of what they saw in that sleeping face. The breathing became softer and softer. It was how only a little while before dawn. It was the time that the Guru described as *amrit vela* – the time of nectar – the Guru's favourite time of the day.

The Guru awoke one last time. In a very faint voice he asked his followers to pray. He himself said one last prayer, then drawing his sheet over his face he went into eternal sleep.

All through the morning the disciple sat beside their Guru in silence. Then in the afternoon when it was time for the funeral ceremonies, the Hindus and Muslims both carefully examined the flowers they had brought. The Muslims looked at their flowers and found they were still as fresh as when they had brought them. When the Hindus looked at their flowers they too found that they were as fresh as when they had been plucked. Both sides looked at each other in wonder. Even in his death the Guru had underscored the lesson he had taught all through his life. All men are equal. There is no Hindu. There is no Musalman. There are only decent men, like the Guru, who have made their lives as beautiful and fresh and sweet-smelling as flowers with the good deeds that they have performed and spread the perfume of their deeds far and wide.

Part II

GURU ANGAD DEV TO GURU TEGH BAHADUR

(1504–1675)

Chapter 6

Guru Angad Dev
(1504–1552)

It was five o clock in the morning. Lehna had got out of bed, bathed and now sat under the tamarind tree in his courtyard to meditate and pray. This had been his habit for so long that, Khivi, his wife, no longer knew when he got out of bed.

Usually Lehna was so lost in his prayers that he did not notice when the birds began to twitter. But now he was not able to concentrate and was aware of the beginning of the day and the first flutter of birds' wings. This had happened often in the recent past and at first he had ascribed it to the restlessness that always possessed him at the approach of the *Navratras*. He was an ardent devotee of the Goddess Durga and during the Navratras, he led a pilgrimage to her temple at Jawalamukhi (in Kangra, Himachal Pradesh). The excitement of the impending pilgrimage had always made him restless. But then he remembered that the previous year, when the head priest of Jawalamukhi had finally brought him into the presence of the goddess, he did not feel the deep glow of happiness that he had always felt. There was a feeling of inadequacy, a feeling that there should have been something more at the end of the pilgrimage.

Now, sitting under the tree in his courtyard, he felt the same sense of inadequacy and knew that his inability to concentrate on his prayers was caused by something more deep-rooted than by the excitement of the impending pilgrimage. This realization made him uneasy and afraid. Then, from his neighbour's courtyard, he heard a soft clear voice, raised in song. It was a strange hymn but the words gave him peace and strength and when the singer finished his song, Lehna was not afraid or restless any more.

All through the morning he helped his father. His father, Pheru, was a rich trader with a variety of business interests and there was a great deal of work to keep Lehna busy. But as he worked, his mind kept going back to the hymn and he wondered who had composed it. By mid-morning he could not bear not knowing any more: he knew he had to find the answer to this question. He excused himself from his work, and went to his neighbour Jodha's house.

'Tell me the name of the hymn you sang this morning and the name of the poet who wrote it,' Lehna said, coming straight to the point.

Jodha had just sat down to his mid-day meal and he looked up at his neighbour and smiled and said, 'It is the *mool mantra* written by my Guru, Guru Nanak of Kartarpur. Come and join me in my meal.'

'Thank you,' Lehna said, 'but I must go. I have work to do.'

Lehna's work was to persuade the members of his party to stop at Kartarpur on their way to Jawalamukhi. But his friends did not agree. If Lehna had not been the leader of the group, he would have broken from them and gone to Kartarpur on his own. But as the leader, he had certain duties and responsibilities which he could not give up, and so his visit to Guru Nanak had to wait.

Two days later, like the other pilgrims, Lehna too tied bells to his wrists and his ankles and they went on their way to the Devi, singing and dancing. But each time he clapped his hands and stamped his feet and sang *Jai mata di*, he would hear a soft, sweet voice in his head: *Ik onkar, sat naam, karta purakh*. Even when he came to the temple and went into the presence of the Goddess, it was Jodha's voice that kept ringing in his ears.

It was a strange, emaciated Lehna who returned to Khadur. The other pilgrims reported that he had eaten very little, only nibbled at his food when they had forced him to eat. He had behaved in a strange, uncharacteristic manner by keeping very much to himself all through the pilgrimage.

Lehna stayed at Khadur only for two days after his return. Then, while everyone was asleep, he mounted his horse and rode to Kartarpur. He reached the Guru's *dera* just before dawn. As Lehna rode into the dera he noticed a strange silence, everything was still and quiet. He got off his horse and tied a cloth around the horse's hooves to muffle their sound, so that it would not intrude upon the silence. He came, as quietly as he could, to the centre of the dera and as he did so, he heard a strong beautiful voice break into the same hymn that Jodha had sung. *'Ik onkar, sat naam, karta purakh...'* He was overcome by the beauty of the voice and of the hymn. He let go of the horse's bridle and fell on his knees. He lowered his forehead to the ground and wept, and knew at last that this is what he had been searching for; he knew that he had come home.

After the morning prayers, Lehna went up to a Sikh disciple who seemed to be some kind of a leader because so many of the other disciples showed deference to him.

'I am Lehna from Khadur,' Lehna introduced himself. 'I have come to have darshan of the Guru and to serve him,' he added.

'You are more than welcome, Lehna of Khadur. I am Bura Singh but people call me Bhai Budha,' said the disciple.

Within a few days it was as if Lehna had always lived in Kartarpur. Wherever there was work to be done, Lehna was the first to reach out and attempt to do it. No task was too lowly, too menial for him.

With Lehna's unstinting and devoted service, it was only a matter of time before the Guru noticed him.

Lehna had always been very fond of children. In Kartarpur, too, Lehna found great pleasure in being with the children. For a little while, before the evening prayers, he would join the children in their play and the whole dera would echo with the children's laughter and people would stop and smile and shake their heads and say: 'What a child this stranger is!'

The Guru had noticed the stranger's presence, had seen with what dedication and sincerity he applied himself to every kind of task. One evening, as he left his home to go out for the evening prayers, he was greeted by the loud laughter of a group of children, laughter that was so joyous that it made him smile.

'Bhai Budha,' he said turning to his trusted disciple, 'what is it that makes our children so loud in their happiness?'

'Master, they have found a new playmate.'

The Guru nodded and said, 'Yes, so I hear.'

The little group walked towards the central prayer area. By the time they came to where the children had been playing, the children had all gone. Lehna stood there by himself and as he saw the Guru approach he bowed low, waiting for him to pass. But the Guru did not pass by. He stood near Lehna and put his hand on Lehna's head.

'Who are you and from where do you come?' Guru Nanak asked in a gentle voice.

For a moment Lehna stood there not daring to speak. The Guru had put his hand on his head, the Guru had addressed him. He felt such a deep joy that he was afraid to speak and thus break the spell. But the Guru waited and Lehna knew that he must answer.

'I come from Khadur and my name is Lehna,' he said, his voice so low it could hardly be heard.

'Your Lehna, your debt, was here, with me, and that is why God has brought you to Kartarpur.'

The days slid quietly into months and the months into years and Lehna worked each day to pay his debt to the Guru by working with tireless devotion in the service of the sangat, the assembly of devotees and disciples. Each night, he went to bed happy in the thought that he had done the most that he could do, the best that he could do. He sought no reward, no special mark of affection from the Guru. Soon everyone in the community knew that he was special because of the special quality of his service and, in many small ways, the Guru also showed special marks of favour for his devoted follower.

Lehna had always shown consideration and love for his parents, his wife and his children. Even though he was away from them, he did not forget them. He wrote to his father as often as he could. Pheru had always known that his son was different from the sons of the other traders, because he had always found greater pleasure in giving than in receiving. So it did not come as a great surprise to him that his son now spent all his time in the service of others with no thought for himself. Khivi, too, knew that there was something special about her husband. She missed him and when his letters were read out to her, tears would come to her eyes. He was a good man, her husband, and what he was doing must be good. So like Sulakhni, Guru Nanak's wife, before her, she prepared herself to wait out the time till her husband's return.

Sometimes Pheru would accompany Jodha on his visits to Kartarpur to see how his son was faring. On these visits, Pheru listened to the Guru and was influenced by his teachings. Occasionally he invited his daughter-in-law to go with him and even though their stay in Kartarpur was limited to a few days, Khivi was happy to be with her husband again.

Lehna had been in Kartarpur for three years now, and it was an established fact that he was one of the Guru's chosen disciples. One day, after the morning prayers, the Guru sent for Lehna.

'You have paid your debt to me well,' the Guru said, referring to their first conversation three years ago. 'But there are other debts you still have to pay: the debt to your father, the debt to your wife and children. You must return to Khadur to settle your affairs.'

The story of Lehna's service and of the favour he had received from the Guru had travelled to Khadur before him. When the news spread that Lehna had returned, all the people came out to greet him. There was love and affection for a good, kind man who had been away for three long years, but there was also respect for the man who had come so close to the master.

People came to him for advice and they also came to listen to his teachings, Guru Nanak's teachings, and they joined him when he sang Guru Nanak's hymns. Lehna spent this time in arranging his affairs and when he was sure that he had made sufficient provision for his father, his wife, and his children, he said goodbye and returned to Kartarpur.

He reached Kartarpur late in the evening and found that the Guru was still out in the fields. There were three bundles of freshly cut fodder that still lay in the field, waiting to be carried home. 'I'll send a servant to carry this as soon as I get home,' Lakhmi Das said. However, Lehna didn't wait and lifted the bundles onto his head, one upon the other, and made his way back through the fields. The fodder was wet, dripping wet and the muddy water flowed from his head down over his neck to his shirt and soon the shirt was covered with smudges. It was a beautiful shirt made of 'boski', soft Chinese silk that Khivi had bought from a travelling salesman who passed through the village. On the day of his return to Kartarpur, he had worn this special shirt. And here it was now, sticking to his back, soiled and dirty. But he did not notice this. He was happy to be performing a service for his Guru. It was Sulakhni who noticed the dirty shirt. The moment she saw Lehna approaching the house with the load of fodder on his head, she took Guru Nanak aside.

'How could you do this?' she asked. 'How could you allow Lehna to carry this load and dirty his clothes with mud?'

'When the mud comes from such willing and selfless service, it does not remain mud – it becomes saffron. And when the load of fodder is carried by Lehna it is no longer a load but the halo of God's blessing,' Guru Nanak said. Sulkahni looked at Lehna, so humble and meek, and then she looked at her proud and arrogant son and she knew the truth in Guru Nanak's statement.

A few months later the monsoon broke in a strong, heavy rain. For hours on end the rain came down, heavy and strong. A report was brought to the Guru that one of the newly built walls in the dharamshala had given way, and the Guru hurried to see the extent of the damage. Part of a wall had indeed given way.

The Guru saw that if it was not attended to immediately, there was danger of the entire wall coming down, and the roof caving in.

'Son, this must be attended to immediately,' he said to Lakhmi Das.

'Yes, father. But none of the masons could be found. Don't worry father. I will find a mason and have it attended to first thing in the morning,' Lakhmi Das assured his father, while stifling a yawn. The Guru did not say anything more and returned home. But Lehna slipped away quietly into the darkness and brought two labourers back with him. The mason was away on a visit to a neighbouring village and would not be back till the next morning. Lehna organized all the material – the bricks, lime, and sand for the mortar. Hour after hour he struggled through the night, rebuilding the wall as best as he could.

By the time the Guru stopped at the site on his way to morning prayers, the damaged part of the wall had been sufficiently built to avert any more danger to the building. Word of this incident spread through the community and it was clear to everyone that Lehna was the chosen one, and most people knew, without anything being said, that he would be the next Guru. But there were some who felt that Sri Chand, Nanak's elder son, who was a very pious man, should be the next Guru. Sri Chand was not an ambitious man, but a particular group of disciples tried to poison his mind against Lehna.

Guru Nanak, in his wisdom, saw that he must act to keep the peace in Kartarpur. He called Lehna, Sri Chand, Lakhmi Das, Bhai Budha and his other senior disciples to him.

He addressed Lehna and said, 'Bhai Lehna, you have shown over these long years that you are the flesh of my flesh and the blood of my blood. You are my *angad*, part of my *ang*, my body. Because you are my *angad*, you must continue the work that I have begun. Come Bhai Budha, come forward and apply saffron paste on Angad's forehead,' said Guru Nanak. Then he put five copper coins and a coconut at Lehna's feet and bowed to him. Guru Nanak bowed to Lehna, and he was ordained as the second Guru of the Sikhs – Guru Angad Dev.

The Guru had appointed his successor during his lifetime to make sure that there would be no opposition to the Guru later on.

To avoid any trouble between Guru Angad and his sons, Guru Nanak decided that Guru Angad should go back to Khadur. Without his physical presence, the opposition to his anointment would slowly melt away. As always, Guru Angad bowed to his master's wishes and returned to Khadur.

Guru Angad laid great importance on a proper education for children. Apart from studies, Guru Angad realized that children should also be physically strong, apart from being good at studies, and insisted that they should take part in sports. He asked their teachers to organize competitions and he himself gave away prizes to the winners. He said that physical fitness was necessary because you could only have a healthy mind if you had a healthy body.

Guru Angad was happy in Khadur, happy that he was able to bring the teachings of his Guru to the people. At the same time he missed his Guru very much and his deepest wish was that the Guru should send for him. Then, at last, the Guru did send for him and he returned to Kartarpur with joy in his heart. But the joy turned to sadness when he realized that his Guru was dying. He was with Guru Nanak when Guru Nanak breathed his last. Then he took leave of Mata Sulakhni and of Sri Chand and returned to Khadur. This is what his Guru had wanted him to do and he knew that this was the only way he could avoid any differences coming up between him and the Guru's family.

At Khadur, he continued the Guru's work. Some of Guru Nanak's chief disciples, like Baba Budha, now came to Khadur to follow Guru Angad and they saw that the lamp Nanak had lit in Kartarpur now spread its glow in Khadur. Khadur now became the centre of the world for the Sikhs. Guru Angad realized that what held his followers together were the teachings of his Guru and these teachings had come to them in the form of Guru Nanak's hymns. He began to collect all the hymns composed by Guru Nanak in order to set them down on paper. These hymns had all been composed in the language of the people, in Punjabi. Guru Angad felt that they could not be written in the Arabic script which was the script of the Quran, or in the Devnagri script, the script in which the holy books of the Hindus were written. Some historians suggest that he chose thirty-five suitable letters from different scripts and developed the Gurmukhi script in which he wrote Guru Nanak's hymns. Others are of the opinion that the script was already in existence and Guru Angad only improved upon it. Guru Angad collected all his guru's hymns and wrote them down in the new script. He made copies of this collection and gave them to each of the centres of the

Sikhs, so that his followers could read these hymns and learn them by heart.

The Guru himself did not write as many hymns as Nanak, but the few *shlokas* he wrote are now a part of the Guru Granth Sahib.

At this time an old man by the name of Amar Das came and joined the sangat at Khadur. He had been a Vaishnav, but was in search of a Guru. He joined the community in Khadur and spent his life in the service of others.

Guru Angad took care to give all respect to Mata Sulakhni and to Sri Chand. He made frequent trips to Kartarpur to pay his respects. He did everything in his power for Sulakhni and for Sri Chand and in this way they too came to love and respect him. They refused to listen to those who tried to poison their minds against Guru Angad and thus the guru was able to avoid a split among Nanak's followers.

Guru Angad had a very rich follower named Gobind, who was involved in a property dispute with his relatives. It was a very valuable piece of property and Gobind prayed silently to his Guru for help and promised that if he won the case, he would build a new town for his Guru. As luck would have it, Gobind did win the case and all the property became his. He was a true disciple and did not go back on his word. He came to the Guru for his blessings and asked for the Guru's help to build the new township. The Guru could not leave Khadur, so he asked his favourite disciple, Amar Das, to go and supervise the building of the new township. So the town of Goindwal was built. Gobind built a beautiful *haveli* and once again came to his Guru and begged him to come and live in Goindwal. Since the Guru was not in a position to leave Khadur, he asked Amar Das to take up residence at Goindwal.

When Guru Angad had first brought the teachings of Guru Nanak to Khadur, he had run into opposition from a group of *tapasvis* (ascetics) who had set up a dera in Khadur. The chief of these was Shiv Nath. Shiv Nath had opposed Guru Angad in every way, but Guru Angad had quietly gone about his work and had soon gathered a large following. This made the tapasvis angry because they had been very powerful in the village, but now their followers were slowly deserting them and becoming the followers of Guru Angad. One year there was a severe drought in Khadur and the surrounding area. The people came to their Guru and begged for his help. 'You are a man of God, and if you pray, God will grant your prayers,' said the people. 'It is the will of God, The rain will fall only when God decides that it must fall,' the Guru said.

The villagers felt that the Guru could make the rain fall if he so wished and they were not happy with the Guru's answer. Some of the older villagers remembered that when they had been the followers of the tapasvis, Shiv Nath had sometimes performed miracles for them. Now the villagers felt that the Guru having failed them, Shiv Nath might still be able to work a miracle and bring the life-giving rain to relieve them of their suffering. When he heard what they wanted, he taunted them saying, 'So now that you are in trouble, you have remembered me. Go back to your Guru, whom you follow, and ask him to help you. Ask him to make the rain fall. Go.'

The villagers returned sadly to their homes. But the hot dry days continued. Those who could afford to move, left the village and went to live in other towns and villages. But most of the villagers could not afford to do this and were compelled to stay on in Khadur. Soon it was clear that unless the rain came soon, they would all die and they went again to Shiv Nath and fell at his feet and cried.

'We are sorry, O tapasvi. Forgive us. We will never desert you again.' The tapasvi thought he could now have his revenge on Guru Angad.

'All right, I will help you. But there is one condition. You must drive this so-called Guru out of your village,' said the tapasvi.

It was a difficult situation for the villagers. They had all been followers of the Guru and they all knew in their hearts that he was a great and pious man. How could they tell him to leave the village? But their suffering was great. They knew they knew that without the rain they faced certain death and they believed that Shiv Nath could work a miracle and make this happen. So, after a great deal of discussion, it was decided that a group of five would go and request the Guru to leave the village. But when they reached the dera, they came to know that the Guru had already left Khadur already and set up camp a few miles away after learning of their quandary. The villagers went back to Shiv Nath. He organized a great yagna and recited many special mantras. He took generous offerings from the villagers and performed all kinds of rites. He promised that the rain would fall the next day, but the next day came and went and there was no rain. The days stretched into weeks and still there was no rain and the villagers realized that Shiv Nath could not make the rains fall. They realized that their Guru had been right; no man could interfere with the will of God. They were all very ashamed of what they had done and they went to the Guru and begged forgiveness. As was to be expected, he forgave them readily and returned to Khadur. A few days later the rain came and the people went wild with joy.

Like Guru Nanak, Guru Angad knew that he must appoint his successor during his lifetime, so that there would be no trouble or dispute after his death. He announced that Amar Das would succeed him. Once again Baba Budha anointed the new Guru. Like Guru Nanak, Guru Angad also realized that his family was not happy with his choice, especially his son Datu, who had hoped to be the next Guru. To avoid any conflict between his family and Amar Das, he asked Amar Das to set up his dera in Goindwal. A few months later, surrounded by his devoted followers, Guru Angad breathed his last. The year was 1552 and Guru Angad was forty-eight-years old at the time.

Guru Angad remained the Guru of the Sikhs for thirteen years. During his tenure he set up many centres. He organized a system of collecting the offerings from each centre and then distributing them to the centres according to each centre's need. In this way the expenses of running the langars and the schools, even by the smallest centres, could be met. He knew that if the children were given a good education and made sound of body and mind, they would have good all-round personalities and grow up to be very useful members of society. This is why he persuaded all Sikhs to send their children to school. He insisted that education must be in the children's mother tongue, so that the children would have a sense of identity and would be proud of their heritage.

During his stewardship the new faith was strengthened and the following increased considerably.

Chapter 7

Guru Amar Das
(1479–1574)

It was still an hour before dawn, but Amar Das could lie in bed no longer. He was restless and his mind refused to be still. For the major part of his sixty years, he had always woken up at dawn and joined his father in prayer. Then over the years, as he grew older, he went often to the holy towns of Haridwar and Kurukshetra, sometimes once a year, sometimes even twice. He spent a lot of his time and money in helping the poor, the sick, and the needy. He was respected by all the village-folk because he never spoke loudly, never lost his temper, and always worked for the good of others. But in the last few years, his visits to the holy towns, his bathing in the holy waters of the Ganga, and even his acts of charity had not brought him much peace. On his last trip to the Ganga, he had met a monk, a *brahmachari*. They talked of many things, about life and religion, and the monk was impressed by Amar Das' knowledge and learning. They spent a lot of time together. So when they were returning from Hardwar, it was only natural that Amar Das should invite the monk to stop for a night in his home in Basarke in Amritsar.

After the evening meal, they climbed up to the terrace where their cots had been laid. They talked late into the night and just as they were about to fall asleep, the monk asked, 'You are so wise and know so much about religion. Who is your Guru?'

'I do not have a Guru,' replied Amar Das.

'What?' the monk said in surprise. 'You do not have a Guru? Then all my trips to the Ganga and all my fasts have come to nought because I have lived with you and eaten food with you,' he added. The monk left the house at once and hurried back to Haridwar to bathe again in the holy Ganga. He had committed a 'sin' by being with a man who had no guru and needed to wash away his sins.

Amar Das was very upset by this incident. It had been three nights since the monk had left in anger and all the three nights he had not been able to sleep. Perhaps this was the reason why he had not found peace even after twenty years of bathing in the Ganga. Without a guru, his search had been futile. Now, unable to stay in bed any longer, he got up, and very carefully, one step at a time, he felt his way down the staircase. He was halfway down, when he heard the voice of Bibi Amro, his brother Manak Chand's daughter-in-law. She was the daughter of Guru Angad Dev of Khadur. She had won the hearts of her husband's family through her kind, gentle ways and had brought to her new home, the Sikh way of life and the teachings of both Guru Nanak and Guru Angad Dev. The first light had now broken and he could see the dim outline of the girl's figure as she swept the courtyard of his brother's house. She was afraid of disturbing the other members of her family so she sang her hymn in a soft voice. But in the stillness before dawn, Amar Das could hear each word clearly. He stood where he was, moved by the sweetness of the voice and the beauty of the words. This was not the first time that Amar Das had heard Bibi Amro singing this hymn. But Amar Das had been secure in his beliefs and had not wished to change and so he had not listened to her words properly. But now, after the monk's rebuke, he was full of doubt. Now he listened to her words. In the beauty of Bibi Amro's song he saw a path along which he could continue his search.

The song finished. It was now light. Amar Das hurried into his brother's courtyard and fell at Amro's feet. She covered her head and face and quickly drew back. 'What are you doing Babaji?' she asked.

'I bow before the voice that spoke through you. I bow before the truth and wisdom of these words. Bibi take me to your Guru at once.' Perhaps both Amro and Manak Chand knew in their hearts that this was a very special moment, and they gave in to Amar Das' wish. A short while later, Amro and Amar Das set out on the journey from Basarke to Khadur Sahib. They came, at last to Khadur, to the Guru's presence. Amro went in to bring the news of Amar Das' arrival to her father and the Guru, out of respect to a man who was almost twice his age, rose to his feet and went forward to embrace him. But Amar Das would have none of this. He fell at the Guru's feet and said: 'I come as a humble disciple, Guruji. Give me a place at your feet.'

He was true to his word. During the twelve years that followed, all that he sought was a place at the Guru's feet. He worked like any other humble servant of the sangat. In spite of his advancing years, he worked hard, and watching him, the Guru would often smile. In Amar Das' humility and spirit of devotion, he saw himself, the young Lehna, who had worked selflessly in the service of the Guru at Kartarpur. He saw the same spirit, the same light, a spirit and a light which he had not seen in any one else, not even in his own sons.

It was difficult for Amar Das to accept the new way of life. One by one, he had to give up beliefs that he had held dear for so long. The Guru said there was only one formless God but like all true Hindus, he had believed there were many deities, each of whom was a form of God. He himself had chosen to worship one of these deities, Lord Vishnu. The Guru taught that because God was without form, it was wrong to worship idols. Amar Das had worshipped idols all his life. Wherever he had gone, he had looked first for the idol so that he could offer his prayers. The Guru taught that there was no merit to be earned by going on pilgrimages and bathing in holy waters. He himself had spent a lifetime going to Haridwar and bathing in the waters of the Ganga.

And yet, painful as it was to give up all his beliefs, Amar Das did not hesitate. He did as the Guru taught because the Guru was above everyone. He filled his mind with the Guru's words, his days with the Guru's service, and there was no place for anything else.

When Choudhary Gobind built the Guru Mahal in Goindwal and asked Guru Angad to come and live in it, the Guru told Amar Das to go in his place. He also told Amar Das to bring his family to Goindwal. In this way Amar Das could now also perform the duty which Guru Nanak had asked all his followers to perform, the duty of the householder.

Though he lived in Goindwal, Amar Das would get up very early in the morning, go to Khadur and spend the whole day in the service of his Guru and of the sangat. There was one particular service that he found special pleasure in. Every morning, he carried fresh water from the river for the Guru's bath. For years he had never failed in this service. His Guru needed to be at the prayer meeting at dawn and before that he needed to have the water for his bath. So Amar Das woke up three hours earlier to bring the water to his Guru on time.

Then one morning, on a dawn that was darker than any other, Amar Das or Amru, as he was called by some, missed his way in the dark, lost his footing and stumbled into a pit that a weaver had made for his loom. Somehow he was able to save the precious water from spilling. The rain had made the ground slippery and he could not step out of the pit without spilling the water and thus called out for help.

The first light had broken in the sky and the Guru waited for Amar Das and because Amar Das had never been late before, the Guru was sure that something bad had happened. He walked quickly towards the river. He came to the weavers' huts and picked his way through them and then he stopped. Very clearly he heard Amar Das' cries for help. Then, from the hut nearest to him, he heard the weaver say to his wife, 'Someone is calling for help.'

'It must be Amru the homeless, wandering around in the dark. Go back to sleep,' the woman said to her husband.

The Guru reached the pit, drew the pitcher of water from his disciple's head and set it on the ground. He rescued Amar Das from the pit and held him in his embrace for long. He then sent for Bhai Budha. Then the Guru bathed Amar Das with the water that had been so carefully brought for him. He dressed him in new clothes and asked Bhai Budha to anoint him. He himself bowed before him and addressed him, 'Home of the Homeless, the honour of the unhonoured, the support of those without support.' Thus was Guru Amar Das ordained as the third Guru of the Sikhs at the age of seventy-three. He set up his centre at Goindwal. A few months later, Guru Angad breathed his last and all the Sikhs now looked to Guru Amar Das for guidance and came to Goindwal to seek his blessings. Two rules that Guru Amar Das had laid down at the very outset were: All those who came to see him must first eat food in his langar, the rich along with the poor, the high-caste with the low-caste; the second rule was that no woman was to observe purdah.

Once Goindwal became the headquarters of the new Guru, the town began to grow very quickly. People came to meet the Guru and seek his blessings and decided to stay on in the town. Goindwal was located at an important point on the road from Lahore to Delhi. Because of this, there were many travellers on the road, and the town became an important trading centre. So many buildings were being constructed that there was not enough wood and the Guru sent his nephew Sawan Mal to Haripur to obtain wood, which could then be floated down the Beas. Sawan Mal brought the teachings of the Gurus to the people of the area around Haripur. Eventually the raja of Haripur and his queen became the Guru's disciples.

One day a band of devotees came from Lahore and among them was a very handsome young man. His name was Ram Das but people called him Jetha. Jetha impressed everyone, not only by his good looks but also by his pleasing manners. He stayed in Goindwal and spent his days in the service of the sangat. He worked so hard that everyone noticed it; the Guru noticed it too but made no comment.

At about this time the Guru ordered the building of a *baoli* – a large well at Goindwal. This could be reached by climbing down eighty four steps. His followers could cleanse their bodies by bathing in the baoli before they came to prayers. The Guru also named Baisakhi (April 13), Maghi, the first day of the Indian month of Magh, and Diwali as the three days on which his followers should come from far and near to the Guru's dera.

The Guru had taken personal interest in the construction of the baoli and would spend hours in supervising the work. He saw Jetha working from morning till night, sometimes carrying the mud away like a common labourer, sometimes carrying the mortar for the bricklayers. Always there was a smile of joy on the young man's face, but still the Guru did not say anything.

By now there were hundreds of disciples who came to Goindwal everyday and the Guru realized that the number of his followers had become very large and there was need to set up a proper organization.

He divided the northern region into twenty-two units; and each unit was called a *manji*. The name was used because Gurus sat on a manji or cot when they met their visitors. Each manji was headed by a faithful disciple, who gave guidance to all the Sikhs in his area. The Guru also trained a band of 146 followers, of whom 52 were women, to attend to the spiritual needs of his followers. These apostles or *masands,* as they were called, could organize prayer meetings, spread the teachings of the Guru and collect offerings. As a result, the Guru's teachings were spread far and wide, and this increased the number of the Guru's followers even further. Ever since Sawan Mal had brought the Guru's teachings to the hill people, and the raja of Haripur had become his disciple, many Rajputs too had joined the ranks of the Guru's followers.

One day the Guru received a message that one of his followers, a young Rajput from the hills, had died from snakebite. As was his habit, he put everything aside and went to the youth's home to try and comfort the family. He gave all the comfort and solace he could to the boy's mother and father.

Then he looked around and saw the boy's wife. She was dressed as a bride. She wore a red suit and her bridal jewellery, and on her hands and feet were the marks of fresh *mehendi*. When she finally looked up at the Guru, there was fear in her eyes. He recognized her now, and remembered the time she had come to Goindwal, three years ago, as a new bride. She had come, with her husband's family, to his house to seek his blessing. When she had bent down to touch his feet, he had stopped her and drawn her up and looked into her face. She had met his eyes briefly and then looked down again. In that brief moment he had seen fear in her eyes, fear of being in a new place, of being among strangers. He remembered clearly what had happened next. He had given her the silver coin that he gave all new brides and new-born children as a token of his blessings. Then, as she had turned to go he had stopped her. 'Do not be afraid. You may be a daughter-in-law in the home that you are going to, but in my home you will always be my daughter.' She had looked quickly into his eyes again and this time the fear in her eyes was gone. Then she had turned and followed her husband out of the house. Now here she was, a young widow, being compelled by her family to commit sati.

No, the Guru decided, this could not be, not here in his dera. He took the girl's hand and raised her to her feet and led her out of the house. The family members, too surprised to react, parted and made way for the Guru. As he walked past the father of the dead boy, the Guru stopped and addressed him.

'Remember, you brought the young girl to my house as a new bride three years ago?' asked the guru. The father-in-law did not look up.

'I said then that though she was your daughter-in-law, she was my daughter. With the death of your son she is no longer your daughter-in-law. That tie has been broken. She remains my daughter and I have come to take my daughter home.'

Even though a terrible tragedy had been averted, there was still great sadness that hung over the girl's life. Widows were looked down upon; they were regarded as unlucky and not allowed to take part in any function. They had to dress in white and eat the simplest of food. The Guru felt strongly about this, he felt it was cruelty that society inflicted on the unfortunate women. When he found a suitable man amongst his followers, he encouraged him to marry the young widow. So word went forth in the community about the marriage that was to be held. All preparations were made but no pundit could be found to perform the ceremony. It was against their religion, they said, no one had ever heard of a widow being remarried. The time came for the wedding and still no pundit would come forward. Finally the wedding was performed by the Guru himself. Instead of Sanskrit shlokas and mantras the Punjabi hymns of the Guru were recited and the two became man and wife. Happiness returned once more to the girl's life.

The Guru gave instructions that prohibited the practice of sati among his followers and the remarriage of a widow was to be regarded as an act of virtue. He said that pundits were no longer required for performing religious ceremonies, and any Sikh could perform these ceremonies. The ceremonies themselves no longer consisted of reciting Sanskrit prayers, which no one understood, but the singing of the Gurus' hymns, which everyone knew and understood.

The Brahmins were angry with the Guru because he had broken the caste barriers by insisting that everyone eat together. He had also done away with the practice of sati and encouraged widow-remarriage. Also, he had undermined their importance by saying that religious ceremonies could be performed without them. They put their heads together and sent a deputation to emperor Akbar's court. The Brahmins complained that the Sikhs, under their Guru, were destroying the Hindu religion and doing everything against the rules of the religion. Akbar gave the Brahmins a patient hearing.

'I cannot take any action till I have heard what the Guru has to say in answer to these charges,' said Akbar. He sent a message to the guru asking him to come to his court at Lahore. Guru Amar Das was too old to make the journey and sent Bhai Jetha as his envoy. The only advice the Guru gave Jetha was that he must answer all questions carefully, honestly, and without fear.

When Bhai Jetha reached the emperor's court, he was treated with great respect and given a very special welcome. He was told of the complaint that the Brahmins had made and he gave satisfactory answers to all the charges that had been made against his guru and his teachings.

'Caste is not important. It is our deeds that are important. A low-caste *shudra* can be a very good man because of his good deeds, and a high-born Brahmin can be a sinner because of his evil deeds. God is without form. It is wrong to make idols of him and to worship these idols. If it gives comfort to visit holy places and bathe in holy waters, we may do so. But we must remember that the best way to wash our sins is to understand our own deeds, to see where we have done evil and vow to be good and kind in the future. We must insist on good thoughts and good actions and not on empty rituals and the observance of strict rules regarding our food or our ceremonies. Any practice which reduces other human beings, especially women, to the level of subhumans and does not allow them even the right to read the holy books, cannot be a practice that is sanctified by any religion,' thus spoke Jetha in front of Akbar.

Akbar was very impressed by what Bhai Jetha had said and dismissed all the charges against the Guru and the Sikhs. He sent Jetha back to Goindwal with presents for the Guru and a promise that he would come to the Guru to seek his blessings.

When the emperor reached the dera he was asked, like all other visitors, to partake of food in the langar. The normal langar fare was put before him.

'Is this what the Guru eats?' he asked one of the attendants.

'No, Your Majesty. The Guru eats only *ogra*,' replied the attendant.

'Then I must eat only *ogra*. What is good enough for the Guru is good enough for me,' said Akbar.

So a small helping of the dish cooked from coarse unseasoned rice was put before the emperor. As he ate, he noticed hundreds of pilgrims who were being fed in the langar and was greatly impressed by the organization and by the Guru's generosity. After he had eaten, the emperor was brought to the Guru, who greeted him with affection. They talked together for a long time about religion and about spiritual matters. At last it was time for the emperor to leave. He thanked the Guru for his blessings.

'I would like to do something for you to show my gratitude,' Akbar said before he left.

'The Almighty fulfills all our needs,' the Guru replied.

'The need is not yours, O Guru,' Akbar said in all humility. He further added, 'The need is mine. I feel the need to do something for you and for the dera. I would like to give you a jagir and the income from this land could be used to help meet the expenses of the langar.'

'The langar looks after itself,' the Guru replied. 'The faithful bring what they have to offer and what they bring is cooked and distributed. Nothing runs short; nothing is saved for the next day, each day we start afresh and God always provides.'

The emperor was confused. As he had said, the need to give was really his need. Then he saw Bhai Jetha and Bibi Bhani sitting a little away from them. He remembered Bhai Jetha well and he also knew that he was married to the Guru's daughter, Bibi Bhani.

'Your daughter is my daughter,' he said, happy that he had found a way out of the dilemma.

'I would like to give a present to my daughter,' he added.

'So be it, that I cannot forbid,' said the Guru.

A few days later, a band of officials from the Mughal Court came to the dera with the registration papers of a piece of land, as a gift for Bhai Jetha and Bibi Bhani.

For long it had been in the Guru's mind that the Sikhs should have a permanent centre of their own. Tradition too demanded that before the new Guru was anointed, he needed to have set up his own centre. The Guru knew that Jetha, when he became Guru, would have to move out of Goindwal, just as he himself had to move out of Khadur, and Guru Angad Dev had to move out of Kartarpur. So he called Jetha and asked him to set up a new township on the land that had been gifted to him.

At about this time, Guru Amar Das feeling that his end was near called Bhai Budha and other prominent Sikhs, including his sons, Mohan and Mohri, to him. He declared that Jetha, who would henceforth be called by his original name Ram Das, would be the next Guru. Bhai Budha applied the saffron tilak as an act of anointment and Guru Amar Das placed the coconut and the copper coins at Ram Das' feet and bowed to him. Everyone present, bowed to Ram Das, who now became the fourth Guru of the Sikhs.

Guru Amar Das died in 1574 at the ripe old age of ninety-five. With his typical humility, just before his death he said that his followers should not observe the rites and customs of mourning that are meant for the dead. They should only recite God's name, and as true Sikhs, submit to the will of God.

He had become the Guru at the age of seventy-three, an age at which most men say they have done with life and are happy to live in retirement. But in the twenty-two years that remained to him, he achieved a great deal. His teachings were simple: 'Do good to others by giving good advice, by setting a good example, and by always having the welfare of mankind in your heart.'

He reorganized the administration of the Sikh community so that the word of the Guru could reach more people. He set up twenty two centres for the Sikhs so that they could get immediate help for all their problems from the nearest centre and not have to wait till they came to him.

He championed the cause of women. He took them out of purdah, forbade the practice of sati and encouraged widow remarriage. He said that women were in every way equal to men and fifty two of his apostles were women.

The Guru was a great poet; he composed 907 hymns and reached out to his followers with his poetry and that of the first two Gurus. These are great achievements, but we must also remember Guru Amar Das, the third Guru of the Sikhs, as a model of kindness. Whenever there was any pain or sorrow in the home of one of his followers, it was as if there was pain and sorrow in his own home, and he would abandon everything and go to comfort the one who was suffering. He fulfilled Guru Angad Dev's prophecy in more than ample measure. He was truly 'the home of the homeless, the honour of the unhonoured and the support of those without support.'

Chapter 8

GURU RAM DAS
(1534–1581)

In Lahore in 1534, there was a well-known locality called Chuna Mandi. Lahore was a flourishing city and there were always new buildings coming up and because, in those days, *chuna,* or lime, was used in the mortar for construction, the *chuna-mandi* also flourished. There were hundreds of shops and as many godowns. But there were also hundreds of little houses on both sides of the narrow lanes, houses that were built one against the other like rows of matchboxes. In these houses lived many lower middle-class people: many of them connected with the lime trade and others because they could not afford to pay the rents in more upmarket localities.

In one such house lived Hari Das, a khatri of the Sodhi sub-caste, and his wife Anup Devi. They were both very simple people and always worked for the good of others. They were quite content and happy with their lot in life. But they had not been blessed with a child. At first they thought it was only a matter of time, but as the years passed, they began to feel that God did not want them to have a child. They tried to accept the will of God with good grace. Anup learned to live with the taunts that her mother-in-law heaped on her, and with the fun that her neighbours poked at her childless state. She lavished her love on all the children of the area, and Hari Das, too, found comfort in giving to others' children the love that he would have given to his own.

But in their heart of hearts, neither Hari Das nor Anup Devi ever gave up hope. On quiet evenings, when they sat side by side, the same thought would pass through both their minds. They would sit there imagining their child playing in the courtyard. They prayed continuously that this dream would come true. At last, by God's grace, twelve years after they had been married, a son was born to them. He was a very handsome child, fair and healthy, with sharp features and big clear eyes. He was named Ram Das, the servant of God, though they called him Jetha, the first-born.

Everyone loved Jetha. All the women, who had made fun of Anup's childlessness, now looked for a chance to play with this happy, cheerful infant. They looked for excuses to come to Anup's house so that they could hold the baby for a little while. Jetha grew into a handsome boy, unspoilt by all the attention that was lavished on him. Though he always answered everyone with a smile and spent time with anyone who stopped him or spoke to him, he was happiest when he was in the company of holy men. Long before he could understand what they were saying, he would sit in their company and listen to their discussions with interest. It became a joke in his family and among his friends. Every time he was missing or someone was looking for him, a friend or a family member would call out, 'Go to the banks of the Ravi where the holy men camp, you are sure to find him there.' Before he was in his teens, he was familiar with most of the Hindu religious texts, the Vedas and the Upanishads, and knew most of the shlokas and mantras by heart. But knowledge of the holy texts alone does not fill your stomach, especially if you are from a middle class family like that of Hari Das.

Hari Das and Anup would sit side by side at the end of the day, waiting for their son to return from his visits to the holy men. While they waited, they would worry about his future. It would have been all right if he was going to school. But after the first few years of formal education, once he had learnt to read and write, Jetha had stopped going to school. Instead, he spent all his time listening to holy men the way Guru Nanak had done years ago. And like Kalyan Chand, Guru Nanak's father, Hari Das too worried about his son's future. But when Ram Das did return, at last, from his visits with the holy men, it was impossible to be angry with him. He showed great care and concern for his parents and everyone around. Young as he was, he found pleasure in helping other people and taking upon himself work that others were not willing to do. When they saw this, his parents would smile with affection and pride. Yet, at other times, their worry about his future would return and they often talked about this to their friends and relatives.

It was their neighbour who suggested a possible solution. He too was a simple man and earned his living by selling roasted gram. 'Give Jetha some roasted grams to sell,' he told Hari Das and Anup Devi. 'It is the simplest thing for him to do and for which no special skills are required. He is very hard-working and once he understands that work can be turned into money, everything will be all right. He will stop spending his time with holy men,' suggested the neighbour.

So Anup Devi prepared a big bag of roasted grams and gave him a small metal container with which to measure the gram out when he sold it. Ram Das was accompanied by his neighbour, who showed him a busy corner in the market, where he would find many customers. Jetha did, indeed, find many customers. His gram was sold out soon enough and, for the next few days, he came home to his parents every evening with the money that he had earned.

Hari Das was happy because he knew that this was only a beginning. As his son grew older, he would apply his mind to other trades and would do well. Then, a few days later, while he was selling his gram, Ram Das heard that there was a group of holy men camped on the banks of the Ravi and he felt he must go to meet them. When he reached the camp, he saw that the sanyasis had not eaten anything the whole day. Without a second thought he gave his entire gram to the hungry sanyasis and came back even happier than when he had made money by selling his gram. He had no way of knowing that years ago, another boy had felt this happiness too. Guru Nanak had also made a true profit by feeding a group of hungry sadhus.

Guru Amar Das had many followers in Lahore. With each passing year the number of his followers increased and Ram Das often heard people talking about the Guru. He heard them talking about his teachings and about the great dera in Goindwal, and he wanted to go and visit the Guru. With his parents' permission, he joined a group of devotees who were on their way to Goindwal.

Ram Das, at once, won the hearts of everyone around him with his polite behaviour and his great spirit of service. He worked from morning till night and always had a smile on his face. People around him became very fond of him and it seemed as if Jetha had always lived in Goindwal. When it was time for the band of devotees to return to Lahore, Jetha stayed on. He sent a message to his parents that he was well and asked for permission to stay on in Goindwal.

Bibi Bhani, the Guru's youngest daughter, had now reached marriageable age and her mother, Mansa Devi, was worried about finding a suitable boy.

'What kind of boy do you want for our daughter?' the Guru asked, when she voiced her concern.

Mata Mansa Devi looked up and saw Jetha standing at the door. She saw his good looks and remembered his pleasant manners and his selfless devotion to the Guru and his kindness and his humility.

'Someone like him,' she said pointing to Jetha.

'Why someone *like* him?' the Guru asked. 'There can be no one like him. So if you like Jetha so much, why not Jetha himself?'

'Yes, I know our daughter will be happy with him,' Mansa Devi said.

For Jetha, his Guru's wish was his command. The Guru sent him home to Lahore to seek his parents' permission. Hari Das was proud that the great Guru had found his son worthy to be his son-in-law, and so he readily gave his consent. Thus, Jetha and Bhani were married.

Even after his marriage, there was no difference in the life that Jetha led at Goindwal. He still worked with the same spirit. All day he would work and, at night, when he was sure the Guru was asleep, he would slip quietly into the courtyard of the Guru's house where the Guru slept. Jetha would press the Guru's tired legs and massage the soles of his tired feet. The Guru would smile to himself in the dark and think of the very great love that this disciple had for him. At last, the Guru did give an indication that he recognized Jetha as being a special devotee by sending him as his envoy to Akbar's court.

But it was only shortly before his death that Guru Amar Das formally announced that Jetha would be his successor. Jetha was anointed by Bhai Budha in 1574 and he became the fourth Guru of the Sikhs, Guru Ram Das. In keeping with Guru Amar Das' wishes, Guru Ram Das started the building of a centre of the Sikh religion. He had already started work on a tank, which later came to be known as Amritsar, while Guru Amar Das lived and after the latter's death, he came to live there and a town was built around the tank.

The construction of the tank was a major project and it took many years to complete the construction. Sikhs, moved by love for their Guru and for their religion, came from far and near to help with the work. Bhai Budha, too old now to work himself, would sit in the shade of a *beri* tree near the tank from where he would supervise the work that was being done.

A great deal of money was required to buy building material and to run the langar for the large number of devotees who had come to work on the project. The Guru's treasury had been exhausted and the Guru wondered what he could do to keep the construction going.

He invited his most faithful devotees to a meeting. Through his masands or apostles he made a direct appeal to his devotees in each manji. There was an overwhelming response to this appeal. Money now came in regularly and never again did the Guru have to worry on this account. The holy tank, which later came to be known as Amritsar or the pool of nectar, began to take shape, and near its banks the devotees built a house for their Guru which was called Guru Mahal.

As the township grew, the Guru encouraged traders to settle there. This suited the traders because of the town's proximity to Lahore. With the revenue from traders, the Guru was able to send his missionaries to all parts of India. Gradually the town of Ramdaspur or Amritsar, as it came to be called later, became an important commercial centre and soon rivalled Lahore in importance. More than its commercial importance, Amritsar became, in later years, the centre of the Sikh world, and Guru Amar Das' dream was fulfilled.

Guru Ram Das had many followers but one of the most important disciples was Bhai Gurdas.

Bhai Gurdas was the son of Guru Amar Das' younger brother, Datar Chand. Guru Amar Das had taken on the responsibility of his education and the boy had come to live in Goindwal. He was a very intelligent and devoted disciple, and did a lot to spread the Gurus' teachings. Guru Ram Das recognized this special ability and sent him to Agra to set up a centre there.

Like the first three Gurus, Guru Ram Das was also a poet. He wrote many hymns and prayers which were later included in the collection of sacred writings. One of his poems, Var Gauri, gives some details of the life of Guru Amar Das.

The Guru had three sons: Prithi, Meherban, and Arjan. Prithi proved to be greedy and selfish while Meherban was an ascetic and had cut himself off from worldly matters. Over the years, Arjan showed total obedience to the Guru's wishes. He proved, through his spirit of service, that he was worthy of treading the path that Nanak had first trod. At the appropriate time, the Guru declared that Arjan would be the next Guru. The aged Bhai Budha applied the tilak and Guru Ram Das put five copper coins and a coconut at Arjan's feet and bowed to him.

Shortly afterwards, in 1581, Guru Ram Das passed away at Goindwal. The fourth Guru died at the age of forty-seven. He had been the Guru for seven years. He knew that the most important task before him was to strengthen the practices that Guru Amar Das had begun. Like Guru Amar Das, Guru Ram Das made sure that everyone who came to visit him first ate at the common langar. By doing this, he made the practice of eating together at the langar an essential part of the Sikh religion.

He made sure that all religious ceremonies were performed in Punjabi, the language of the people and said that no pundit or priest was needed for this. Perhaps in memory of the wedding ceremony of the Rajput widow that Guru Amar Das had performed, Guru Ram Das wrote a very beautiful hymn, especially for weddings, and this hymn provides the base for all Sikh weddings.

Guru Ram Das strengthened the organization of the Sikh religion. He was in regular touch with the manjis and because of his personal interest in the administration, the manjis functioned efficiently and this encouraged more and more non-Sikhs to join the sangat.

Guru Ram Das was a very quiet and humble man and his dealings with people were always mild and gentle. This is probably the reason why, during his stewardship, there was no conflict with either the Muslims or the Hindus. This was also the reason why he was able to maintain cordial relations with with the sons of the third Guru, who had been passed over in the succession to the gaddi *or* guruship.

Once Sri Chand, the elder son of Guru Nanak, visited Amritsar. He had become old by then. Guru Ram Das treated him with great respect and stepped down from his gaddi to greet him. Sri Chand was pleased to see how widely his father's teachings had been spread through the efforts of his three successors. Any bitterness he may have had at not being made the second Guru, was now put aside. Yet, before he left, he could not help making a joke at the Guru's expense.

'Everything is well. And I am truly happy to see your wonderful work. But tell me, Ram Das, why do you keep such a long beard?' asked Sri Chand as he indicated towards the Guru's long, flowing beard which reached down to his waist. The Guru folded his hands and bowed to the saint and said, 'I keep it so long Babaji so that I can clean the feet of holy men like you, with it.'

He bent down and wiped the dust from Sri Chand's feet with his flowing beard. Sri Chand was moved to tears; he drew the Guru up and held him in a tight embrace. Then he drew away and held Ram Das at arm's length and looked closely at his face and then into his eyes.

'The light of my father shines in your face and in your eyes,' he said in a quiet, steady voice. 'Such humility is a very special gift from God. I can see, now, why you are the Guru and not I,' he added He put his hand on Guru Ram Das' head in blessing, then turned and strode away from the dera.

Chapter 9

GURU ARJAN DEV
(1563–1606)

Guru Amar Das' house in Goindwal was always filled with the sound of children playing and having fun. The Guru had many grandchildren and they filled the house with their noise. The Guru loved all his grandchildren dearly and always found time to play with them and listen to their stories.

One day, the Guru had some important visitors, a group of religious leaders who had come to discuss certain issues with him. While they were all involved in their discussions, Arjan, Bibi Bhani's youngest son, came crawling into the room. When he saw his grandfather, he made a happy gurgling sound and came crawling towards him. The Guru picked him up, kissed him on the forehead and took him on his lap. Arjan lay in his grandfather's lap, happily sucking his thumb. Here his mother Bibi Bhani found him, when she came looking for him. But when she reached out to take him away, the Guru shook his head and Bhani understood that she must leave the baby there. She turned and went back to her work. After this it became a common sight to see the baby Arjan in his grandfather's lap.

The Guru ate very frugally. His usual meal was *ogra,* a dish made from coarse rice and dal. Since he did not want any of his disciples to feel compelled to follow his example, he usually ate alone in his room. On one occasion his food was brought to him while he was busy writing, and Bibi Bhani left the covered *thali* and went quietly away. When the Guru did, at last, turn to have his meal, he was surprised and amused to see that Arjan had already uncovered the *thali* and was eating the ogra. The Guru sat back and smiled and watched the child while he ate. When his little stomach was full, he looked towards his grandfather and saw the Guru smiling at him.

Arjan grew up, and was very devoted to his parents. When his father became Guru, he spent as much time in the Guru's presence as he could. For him the Guru was now no longer merely his father, but had become his Guru too. Young as he was, he knew that the first rule of his faith was complete obedience to his Guru. He found great happiness in being with the Guru and in carrying out the Guru's wishes. He helped with the building of the holy tank and understood how important it was to his father. He listened while his father talked to Bhai Budha and Bhai Gurdas and understood that his father had great plans for the future of the Sikhs. Like all the earlier Gurus, Guru Ram Das too composed beautiful hymns. From him, as from his grandfather, Guru Amar Das, Arjan got the inspiration to compose poems and hymns himself.

Arjan's life, as we have seen, was centered on the Guru. As he grew from being a boy to a young man, his need to be with the Guru grew as well.

Guru Ram Das' time and energy were spent in building the holy tank and making plans for the temple. As a result he was never able to move out of Amritsar, even for the shortest of times. Whenever there was work to be done outside the dera, he always asked one of his senior disciples or one of his elder sons to attend to it. He understood Arjan's need to be always with him and very rarely asked him to go on these errands and this was resented by Arjan's eldest brother, Prithi Chand.

Prithi Chand had seen the wonderful work that was being done on the holy tank and the large offerings brought to the treasury by the masands and had met the important people who came to greet the Guru. He realized that the Guru's position was one of great power and authority. Quite early in life, he began to consider that this position would one day be his. As he grew older, he convinced himself that since he was the Guru's eldest son, he must be the next Guru. Now he saw that his father kept Arjan close to him and he became jealous of Arjan. His suspicious nature convinced him that this constant proximity to the Guru would assure Arjan the premier position in their father's affection and could, one day, lead to Arjan usurping the succession that was rightfully his.

At this juncture, the Guru's cousin, Sahari Mal, came to visit him with an invitation to his son's wedding. The Guru was too busy in his work to be able to attend and he looked for someone he could depute to go in his place. Since it was a family affair, it would be best if one of his sons attended. Prithi was the eldest and he sent for him and asked him to attend the wedding.

Prithi stood for a moment, in silence, his eyes fixed on the ground, determined not to provide Arjan with another opportunity to come closer to the Guru.

'Father, I cannot go.' Everyone was shocked by his words. 'I will stay here and work for you,' he added.

'This is also my work. By going to the wedding you will be serving me,' the Guru said. But Prithi shook his head in the negative.

'No. Representing you at a wedding is something that anyone can do. As your eldest son, it is more meet for me to stay by your side and assist you in more important and serious matters. I will not go to the wedding.'

The Guru knew what was in Prithi's heart and smile at the mistake that Prithi was making: Succession to the gaddi had never been by the rule of primogeniture, and merely by staying on in the dera, Prithi would not be sure of securing the position of the next Sikh Guru for himself. In fact the succession had always gone to the one, who through his conduct and his actions had proved himself to be the most suitable. By his refusal to attend the wedding, Prithi had in fact, broken the basic tenet of the Guru-shishya relationship – the tenet that demands implicit obedience to the guru's will on the part of the disciple. He had in fact taken the first step towards proving his unsuitability to be the next Guru.

'Please yourself. It does not matter,' the Guru said.

He turned then to his second son and asked, 'Meherban, my son, will you go in my place?' In this instance too the Guru knew what the answer would be even before he had posed the question.

Meherban was a recluse and did not enjoy taking part in functions like weddings. He would not make this sacrifice even to please his father.

'Father, you know I do not enjoy taking part in such functions. Why don't you send Arjan?' suggested Meherban. The Guru then turned to his youngest son. The boy's eyes filled with tears at the thought of being separated from his Guru even for a few days. But he had learnt his lesson well – No matter what the personal pain, he must carry out the Guru's bidding. He came forward and touched his father's feet and turned away.

'And stay for all the ceremonies. Don't come rushing back after a day or two,' the Guru said in an affectionate tone.

The boy turned back to face the Guru. This time there were no tears in his eyes, no fear of the pain that he would have to bear in the coming days.

'I will not return till you send for me, Guruji,' Arjan said. Once more he bowed to the Guru and then turned and went away to attend the wedding.

The story goes that Arjan was very unhappy being separated from his Guru and he wrote two letters to his father, giving expression to his pain. Both these letters were received by Prithi, who, as was to be expected under the circumstance, made sure that they were not delivered to the Guru. The Guru was worried about Arjan: It was strange that Arjan should have stayed away for so long without sending any news. At last, Arjan wrote a third letter to his father and the messenger was instructed to deliver this letter only to the Guru. The Guru immediately wrote back to say that his son should return and it was only after receiving this letter that Arjan returned home.

The years passed and with each passing year, Arjan gave further proofs of his unselfish devotion to the Guru and his dedicated service to the sangat. It was clear to all that he, more than any other disciple, had understood well the teachings of the Gurus before him. So it was no surprise that when Guru Ram Das realized that his end was near, it was Arjan whom he proclaimed as his successor. Once again it was Baba Budha who was called upon to apply the saffron tilak on his forehead. On 1 September 1581, at the age of eighteen, Guru Arjan Dev assumed the mantle of the fifth Guru of the Sikhs.

For the first time the Sikhs had a Guru who had been born and brought up in the Guru's household. He had listened to the teachings of two Gurus before him – his father and his grandfather, and had seen how they conducted the affairs of what had by then become a huge organization. He also understood the tasks that lay ahead of him.

The foremost task was to complete the construction of the holy tank that his father had started. The second was the construction of the sacred temple, what is now known as the Golden Temple, which had been the dream of both his father and grandfather. He knew that he had to give to the Sikhs a centre to identify with, that was as important as Banaras and Haridwar were to the Hindus, or as Mecca and Medina were to the Muslims.

Guru Arjan began by making the tank bigger. He wanted to pave the tank and build side walls, a task for which specially baked bricks were needed. Bhai Bhalo, a Sikh from

Malwa region, was sure that he could give the Guru the kind of bricks that were needed for the purpose and set up the first of many brick-kilns. Wood was required for these kilns. Once again Sikh disciples were sent to the neighbouring hill states to get the wood, and word of the Guru and his teachings spread further and further into the hills, and many of the rajas came down to visit Ramdaspur (or Amritsar), and to seek the Guru's blessing.

Prithi Chand who had still not accepted Arjan as the Guru, sought to turn the Sikhs against his brother by spreading false stories about him. The Guru heard of this but was too busy with the new project to pay any attention.

While the tank was being enlarged and paved, work on the temple's design had also begun. The Guru kept an open mind and discussed all the details with his disciples. At first it was felt that the temple should be built at a height, like the mountain shrines of the Hindus. In this way the temple would be seen from miles around, and would inspire awe in all those who looked up at it. But the Guru convinced everyone that the temple they were going to build was not like any other temple. He said that the temple should be built at a lower level than the land around it. The Guru was a very humble man and felt that the temple should inspire humility and reverence, and not awe. If the temple was built at a lower level, everyone who came to visit it would have to go down to enter it and, in so doing, would feel humbled, which was the right frame of mind to be in, while entering a place of worship.

There was also a great deal of discussion as to the number of doors the building should have. Many different ideas were presented. Finally, the Guru voiced his opinion, 'There should be no doors. The temple should be open from all four sides so that it is always ready to receive anyone who wishes to enter it,' he said.

The designs were completed and work was started in 1588. Guru Arjan Dev asked Hazrat Mian Mir, a great

Muslim saint, to lay the foundation stone. Hindus, Muslims, and Sikhs worked side by side to build the temple. As the temple took shape, people saw that it was an admixture of the architectural styles of both Hindu and Islamic buildings.

Though the Guru's followers gave generously of their money and their labour, the project was of such an enormous scale, that at one stage, work slowed down. Hired labour was needed, and for this, more funds were needed. Guru Arjan Dev realized that the Sikhs should have a fund from which money could be taken whenever it was needed. This would help, not only the construction of the temple but any other community work that the Sikhs might undertake in the future. He gave instructions that all true Sikhs should contribute one-tenth of their income for the service of the community, and this contribution was called *Daswandh*. The masands were instructed to collect this contribution and bring it with them to Ramdaspur on the first day of the month of Baisakh.

The temple was at last completed in 1604. The holy tank was filled with water and given the name of Amritsar or 'the lake filled with divine nectar', and in course of time, the town around it also came to be called Amritsar.

After the temple was completed, the Guru decided to go on a tour of the Punjab. This tour lasted for five years, and during this tour he built three new townships, Tarn Taran, Kartarpur (not to be confused with Guru Nanak's Kartarpur), and Hargobindpur. Of these, Tarn Taran became a very important pilgrimage centre in its own right. During these five years, Guru Arjan Dev brought thousands of people into the Sikh fold.

Guru Arjan Dev returned to Ramdaspur in 1595. Immediately on his return, he came face to face with a fresh crisis caused by his elder brother. Prithi Chand had composed a hymn and used Nanak's name at the end, the way all the Gurus did. Guru Arjan Dev realized that if Prithi could do this, anyone could do it and in times to come, no one would be able to tell which hymns had been composed by the Gurus, and which were by imposters claiming to be the Gurus.

The Guru knew that this could lead to a great deal of confusion and the only way to avoid this was to make a collection of all the hymns composed by the first five Gurus. This would be considered the authentic and definitive collection of the Gurus' hymns and all confusion would be avoided.

The Guru gave this task utmost priority. He discussed the matter with Bhai Budha and Bhai Gurdas, and it was decided that Bhai Gurdas would help him in completing this great project.

On Guru Ram Das' death, Bhai Gurdas had returned from Agra. During the construction of the great temple, he had made himself useful in every possible way – especially in dealing with all the correspondence connected with the project and in maintaining the accounts. He had impressed the Guru with his intelligence, his scholarship, and his ability to work diligently. Thus he had come to be recognized as a prominent member of the community; next only to Bhai Budha.

The first task was to collect all the compositions of the first four Gurus. Guru Arjan Dev had his father's compositions with him and knew that he could get the compositions of the first three Gurus from his maternal uncle, Bhai Mohan, at Goindwal. As a child, he had been present when Guru Amar Das had asked his son Mohan to make a collection and if he could get this collection, it would make his task easier.

He sent Bhai Gurdas with a request to Bhai Mohan for the loan of this collection. Bhai Mohan, even though he lived in Goindwal, lived the life of a total recluse. He did not meet anyone or see anyone and rarely spent time even with his wife and son. Bhai Gurdas was lucky to be granted a meeting with the recluse and to present Guru Arjan Dev's request to him. Bhai Mohan considered the Guru's request for a few moments and then shook his head in the negative.

'No. These hymns were given to me by my father. My son, Sahas Ram, has written them down in two *pothis* (volumes) and these pothis are the most valuable and sacred possessions I have. I will not part with them.'

When Bhai Gurdas returned with this message, Guru Arjan Dev smiled and said, 'Baba Mohan is not one to deny a sincere request. I will go to him myself.'

By the time the Guru reached Goindwal, Bhai Mohan had again retreated to the upper room of his house, on the river Beas, and was lost in meditation. The Guru sent all his attendants away and took up his position in the street below Bhai Mohan's window. Day after day he sat there, waiting for the moment when his uncle would notice him, and day after day there was no response. While waiting, the Guru composed a beautiful hymn in Raga Gauri and sang it in his beautiful, clear voice. The hymn was addressed to Mohan, which is one of the names given to Lord Krishna. Bhai heard the hymn and his heart softened at the sweet humility of Guru Arjan Dev. He came down to the street, bowed to the Guru, and handed over the pothis to him.

Apart from the Goindwal pothis, there were, at that time, other collections of the Gurus' hymns, which had been collected and preserved by other Sikh devotees. Guru Arjan Dev tried to collect as many of these as possible. One of the most important of these was a volume presented to the Guru by a Sikh, Bakht Arora of the Hassan Abdal area (now in Pakistan). Guru Arjan Dev also went to Kartarpur and Khadur and got collections of the works of the earlier Gurus from Sri Datu, son of Guru Angad Dev. Then the Guru sent messengers and important disciples like Bhai Piara to far-off places to collect the compositions of the saints whose teachings were similar to that of the Gurus.

When the Guru had collected all the material possible,

he went with Bhai Gurdas to Ramsar, a mile away from Harmandir Sahib (or the Golden Temple), the temple built by him in the holy tank. Here, in the centre of a thick grove of beri trees, tents were put up and the Guru and Bhai Gurdas began their monumental work. All the hymns that the Gurus composed had been composed to be sung at the sangat, and each Guru had indicated the raga in which the particular composition was to be sung. Guru Arjan Dev took this as a starting point. There were altogether thirty *ragas* that had been used for the different compositions. So he arranged his compositions according to the ragas. The Japji, containing the mool mantra, *Ik Onkar Satnam*, was kept at the beginning, at the head, and all the other compositions were arranged in thirty groups, according to the ragas to which they were to be sung.

All the Gurus took the title of Nanak when they became Guru and wrote their hymns under the pen-name of 'Nanak'. This meant that there was no way of knowing which Guru had composed a particular hymn. However, Guru Arjan Dev felt that there should be some indication as to the authorship of the various hymns. So he gave each Guru the title Mahala or 'Home of God' and a number. So Guru Nanak was designated as Mahala Pehla or the first home of God. Guru Angad Dev as Mahala Dooja or the second home of God and so on ... The hymns in each raga group were then arranged in the chronological order of their composition. At the end of the book, Guru Arjan Dev included the compositions of the Bhakta saints like Kabir, Guru Ravidas, Namdev, Baba Sheikh Farid, and many others.

Bhai Gurdas, who was a great poet in his own right, worked as the scribe for the original granth or collection of hymns by Sikh Gurus. For a year Guru Arjan Dev and Bhai Gurdas worked at their task and the holy book of the Sikhs, called the Guru Granth Sahib, was at last completed. When we look at the original copy we see that the Guru had studied every page again and again, even after Bhai Gurdas had set it all down. Some compositions were considered unsuitable, and were hence excluded from the final draft. The original Granth, in rich leather binding, is preserved and kept at Kartarpur. It is now in the custody of the Sodhis, the descendants of Dhirmal, Guru Arjan Dev's grandson.

The granth, at that time referred to as the Adi Granth, was installed with great ceremony in the Harmandir Sahib at Amritsar. At the installation ceremony, the Guru asked Bhai Gurdas to recite some passages from the book. Later he appointed Bhai Budha, now an old man, as the first *granthi* or custodian of the book, and it was Bhai Budha who read from the book everyday at the morning and evening prayer meetings.

Bhai Budha was one of the first Sikhs to listen to Guru Nanak's teachings. He had been invited to anoint all the Gurus, right from Guru Angad to Guru Arjan Dev, and had been by the side of all the Gurus during their stewardships.

Because the granth contained all the teachings of the Gurus, it soon became a symbol of the Gurus. This fact was emphasized by the instruction given by Guru Gobind Singh to the Sikhs. After him there would be no Guru in flesh and blood. All the teachings that the Sikhs needed were contained in the Guru Granth Sahib, and that they must regard it as their Guru. This instruction of the Tenth Guru is repeated after prayers when the Sikhs recite together:

'*Sab Sikhan ko hukam hai, Guru manyo Granth*'
(We command all Sikhs to hold the Granth to be the Guru).

The Adi Granth was from then on called the Guru Granth Sahib.

Since the granth is now considered the Guru, the text has remained exactly the same as when Guru Arjan Dev wrote it down, except for the addition of Guru Tegh Bahadur's hymns by Guru Gobind Singh.

Thus we see that by compiling the Adi Granth, Guru Arjan Dev did much more than what he set out to do originally. He gave the Sikhs a holy text which finally became a focal point for all Sikh communities, no matter where they were based. The Guru Granth Sahib is now given the same respect that would be given to a living Guru.

All major religious ceremonies of the Sikhs consist in making a complete reading of the Granth Sahib either in forty-eight hours non-stop, or in small parts spread over a week or ten days. At the closing of this ceremony, sacred hymns are sung, and *prasad* is distributed. No event of any importance in a Sikh's life can take place without the presence of the Guru Granth Sahib.

However, Prithi's hostility towards his younger brother remained unabated. He used the Adi Granth to try and create more trouble for the Guru. Through some influential officials, he complained to emperor Akbar about the holy book. The officials complained that the book contained passages which were decidedly anti-Islam in tone. Akbar did not, at first, believe this because his own experience of Guru Amar Das and of Sikhism had shown him that Sikhism was a very tolerant religion, and taught respect for all religions. It was unlikely that the fifth Guru would preach against Islam or write anything derogatory about the Muslims. But the complaints were made persistently and repeatedly, and at last Akbar decided to conduct an inquiry into the matter.

As it happened, Akbar had to make a trip to the North. He stopped outside Amritsar and sent a message to the Guru asking to see a copy of the Adi Granth. The holy book was brought to him and Bhai Budha and Bhai Gurdas read out a few of the hymns. Then Akbar asked some other learned men like Sahib Dyal to make random readings from the granth.

Akbar found that apart from the writings of the Guru, the Granth also contained the writings of poet-saints, both Muslims and Hindus, from all parts of Northern India. He found that all the hymns were very beautiful and expressed his own beliefs that each religion should respect all other religions, and that religious practices should be simplified. Akbar was delighted with the Guru's work. He followed the Sikh practice of bowing before the holy book and made an offering of fifty one gold *mohurs*. He also gave robes of honour to Bhai Budha and Bhai Gurdas and sent presents for the Guru. In spite of Prithi's hostility, Guru Arjan Dev bore him no grudge and invited him to come and take charge of the langar at the Harmandir Sahib.

The death of emperor Akbar and the starting of his son Jahangir's reign marked a radical change in the attitude of the Mughals towards the Sikhs.

Many Muslims had become followers of the Sikh Gurus, and this had annoyed the Muslim religious leaders. While Akbar was alive, they had not dared set up an opposition to the Sikhs. But after Akbar's death, these religious leaders came out openly against the Sikhs. Jahangir did not have the spirit of religious tolerance that his father had, and in his keenness to to win over the Muslim religious leaders, was ready to support their viewpoint. Most of all he himself was jealous of the growing influence of Guru Arjan Dev and the Sikh religion. He wrote in his diary that he was aware that many Hindus and Muslims were following the teachings of the Guru.

From this it was clear that he was only looking for an opportunity to suppress the Sikh religion, and this opportunity came a few months after he became emperor. His son Khusrau had been Akbar's favourite and many people at the court had felt that Khusrau would make a better emperor than Jahangir. Shortly after Jahangir's accession to the throne, Khusrau revolted against him. While he was trying to collect a strong enough army to fight against his father, he visited Guru Arjan Dev in Amritsar and asked for the Guru's blessing. The Guru was a man of peace and could not help the prince in his war against his father, but he gave him his blessings, just as he would have given his blessings to anyone who came to his dera. But this innocent and harmless act was to lead to trouble between the Sikhs and the Mughals. Khusrau was not able to build up a strong enough army and was defeated and arrested by his father. Jahangir decided to punish all those who had helped his son and to crush the Guru as well. Jahangir wrote in his diary: 'I fully knew his (the Guru's) heresies and ordered that he (the Guru) should be brought into my presence, that his houses and children be made over to Murtaza Khan, the Governor, that his property should be confiscated and that he should be put to death with torture.'

The Guru received the emperor's summons with complete equanimity. He had no illusions about the fate that awaited him and was quite reconciled to it. Before he left in answer to the emperor's summons, he sent for Bhai Budha and gave instructions that his son Hargobind should be ordained as the next Guru of the Sikhs.

Mian Mir tried to intervene on the Guru's behalf, both with the emperor and the governor, but they both turned a deaf ear to his pleas. Many of the Guru's disciples wished to accompany the Guru to Lahore because they knew that this could be the Guru's last journey and wanted to be with him. The Guru dissuaded them from going with him. Accompanied by a handful of attendants, Guru Arjan Dev made the short journey from Amritsar to Lahore and presented himself at the court of Murtaza Khan, the Governor. Murtaza Khan ordered that the Guru be chained and taken to a dark, airless dungeon in the fort where he was treated like a common prisoner. His fine clothes were taken away and he was given a coarse, dirty robe to wear. His only food was dry *rotis* and water. But he did not notice these things as his mind was occupied in constant prayer.

Next day the governor ordered that the Guru be brought into his presence.

'Do you deny that the traitor Khusrau came to your dera to ask for help?' asked Murtaza Khan.

'No, I do not deny it.' the Guru replied in a strong clear voice.

'Do you deny that you applied tilak to the traitor's forehead and treated him with every mark of respect?'

'No, I do not deny it,' said the Guru once more.

'The emperor Jahangir has ordered that for your role in the mutiny, you must make a public apology and pay a fine.' The Guru shook his head in the negative to this. 'I had no role to play in the rebellion. The prince came to me like many other people come to me. I gave him my blessings in the same way that I give my blessings to all the people who come to my dera. I did not give him any assistance. So I cannot apologize or pay a fine,' he said.

'The emperor's orders are clear. If you do not apologize and pay the fine, you will be put to death,' said Murtaza Khan. The Guru knew what Jahangir was trying to do. By making him apologize and pay a fine the emperor was trying to place the Guru and the Sikhs in a subordinate position. If the Guru gave in, the Sikhs would always be at the mercy of the emperor. If he apologized for something he had not done, or paid a fine, he would be recognizing the authority of the emperor over the Sikhs. The building of the Harmandir Sahib and the compilation of the Adi Granth had forged a strong, independent identity for the Sikhs. The emperor sought to undermine this identity. 'No, I cannot apologize or pay a fine, not even if you put me to death,' the Guru said.

Murtaza Khan looked down at the Guru from his throne. The Guru met his gaze without flinching, and it was the governor who had to look away. He knew that the Guru had not helped Khusrau and he also knew that the Guru would not give in. He would have to carry out the second part of the emperor's orders and put the Guru to death.

'Take him back to the dungeon,' he ordered. Murtaza Khan sent for his chief executioner, who was a specialist in torture. He was able to invent newer and more horrible means of torture every time he had to deal with a victim. It was said that he could make people say whatever he wanted them to say after just five minutes of torture.

Now he came into his master's presence, bowed low and waited for his master's orders.

'You have heard of the so-called Guru who is imprisoned in the fort?' asked Murtaza Khan.

'Yes, Master, I have heard of him,' the executioner replied.

'The emperor has a special interest in this man. He wants him to die a horrible death. But before he dies, he must apologize for what he has done and beg forgiveness,' said Murtaza Khan. 'I will do my best, my lord. I have never failed you, 1 do not think I will fail you now,' said the executioner.

The executioner put his mind to the task and came up with an ingenious solution. It was the hottest time of the year, so the torture would be through heat. Out in the burning sun, on a little hillock, he dug a pit which was covered by a plate of iron. He lit a huge fire under the plate. Once the plate became red hot, the Guru would be made to sit on it.

Town criers were sent around the city to make announcements about the torture and the people were ordered to come out and see how a traitor would be punished. Long before the sun rose on 30 May 1606, a huge crowd had collected around the place of execution. Every rampart of the fort, the roof of every house and every tree-top was occupied by the people who had come to see the torture. There were soldiers everywhere to keep the people under control and to see that no one interfered with the proceedings.

Then, when the day was at its hottest, the Guru was brought forth from the dungeon. Because of the shackles on his hands and legs, he had difficulty walking. Yet he carried about him an air of dignity and pride and there was no sign of fear on his face. There was only peace and a soft glow and it was as if he was going to address his sangat and to lead them in prayers and not walking out to meet his death. A way had been cleared for him through the crowd, and at last he came at last to the base of the little hillock. He paused for a moment and then climbed up the steps that had been made for him. When he reached the top, the jailers unlocked the shackles. The Guru looked briefly at the iron plate and then down at the people swarming around and smiled. A murmur went up from the crowd and then a group of women began to wail. The Guru held up his hand and the wailing was stilled. The executioner threw a few drops of water on the plate. The water hissed and turned to steam immediately. He signalled to the guards. Two of the guards brought the Guru forward. One last time, the Guru looked around at the people. A hush descended on the crowd. There was complete silence, the silence of people waiting in fear. Then he took the few steps that were needed to get him to the iron plate. He sat down cross-legged on the plate and closed his eyes and his lips moved in prayer.

There was a change in the attitude of the crowd. There was still total silence. But now it was the silence of respect and admiration for the great courage of the Guru.

The Guru showed no signs of pain or discomfort. There was a joy singing in his heart. What he was doing was for his God and for his people. The more his tormentors made him suffer, the greater would be his sacrifice. The more he suffered, the stronger the resolve of his people would become.

The executioner was angry. He had been sure that his victim

would scream with pain and beg for mercy, admit his sins and ask for forgiveness. But this had not happened. Instead this strange Guru sat through the terrible pain without a cry.

The executioner looked up at the fort. He knew that Murtaza Khan was up there in the highest chamber of the fort. He also knew that if he failed, instead of the promised reward, his own life would be in danger. He looked again at the crowd. He could see that many of the people were crying openly, many of them had folded their hands in prayer and many were now kneeling down, their foreheads touching the ground in homage to the great man. He knew he had to act quickly. If he allowed this to continue, more people would express open sympathy for the Guru and some of them might even take it upon themselves to attempt to free the Guru, and Murtaza Khan would have an open revolt on his hands.

The pit had been filled with sand over which the wood was burning. One side of the pit was open and it was through this that more and more wood was being added to keep the iron plate. The executioner summoned two of the guards. They used shovels and drew up the hot sand, which they poured over the upper part of the Guru's body. A loud cry went up from the crowd. A few even ran to the base of the steps where they were stopped by the guards.

There was no change of expression on the Guru's face. His lips still moved in prayer, and there was such peace and calm on his face that it touched the hearts of all the people who watched him being tortured. The executioner became more and more frustrated. He ordered more wood to be put into the pit, more sand to be poured over the Guru's body. Yet there was no cry from the Guru; no protest, no expression of pain. On and on the torture went. For the crowd which watched, they knew that the Guru's superhuman strength could only have come from having complete faith in God.

As the torture continued, even the executioner began to have doubts. He was sure now that the Guru was a saint, because only a saint could have lived through so much, only a saint could have borne such great pain without a cry. Had he been right to torture a man of God? God would be angry with him. He had orders to carry out. His master Murtaza Khan would have been angry with him for not carrying out his orders. But was Murtaza Khan's anger a more terrible thing to face than God's anger?

At last the day of agony came to an end. The sun sank low on the horizon and the breeze that blew up from the river brought a marginal relief from the heat of the day. The torture was called to a halt. The Guru put on his robe and covered his bruised body. Preparations were made to take the Guru back to his prison. Before he came down from the hill he turned to his tormentors.

'My body is covered with blood and sand and secretions from my blisters Give me permission to wash it all clean in the waters of the river,' he said quietly.

They had all seen the agony the Guru had been put through. They had all been touched by his great strength. Now they were moved by the humility of his request. There could be no harm in letting him bathe in the river. The Guru was led to the river bank, the crowd following at his heels.

The guards stopped at the top of the flight of steps which went down to the river bank. The Guru drew off his robe, and people saw his body covered with blisters. The Guru went down the short flight of steps and lowered his bruised and battered body into the waters of the Ravi and swam a short distance. In spite of his great courage and forbearance, the torture had been too much for him. Even the effort to swim became too great. The waters closed over his head and his soul surrendered its earthly frame.

The Sun had sunk over the horizon leaving only a soft orange glow. The darkness gathered. Lights had been lit in the fort and the homes outside the fort, and still the guards and the crowd waited for the Guru to return. An alarm was raised. Boats were sent out with professional divers to look for the Guru. But it was of no use, his body was never found by his tormentors.

Guru Arjan Dev had been the head of the Sikhs for twenty-five years. During this time he continued with the work that the Gurus before him had started. All the five Gurus had tried to combine the best features of Hinduism and Islam into Sikhism. They respected all religions and tried to build up an understanding among them. They were all peace-loving and spent their lives in prayers, meditation, and the service of others. They preached that the focus of a good life was one of love for God and service to humanity. They set up new centres of worship and new townships and collected money for projects that would benefit the whole community. They were all great poets; Guru Arjan too gave the Sikhs many hymns, including Sukhmani or the song of peace, which is one of the most popular hymns in the Punjab.

Two of Guru Arjan Dev's greatest achievements were the building of the Harmandir Sahib and the compiling of the Guru Granth Sahib. Both of these gave the Sikhs a distinct identity. The Muslims had their Mecca; the Hindus their Haridwar; and now the Sikhs had their Harmandir Sahib in Amritsar. The Muslims looked for an answer to all their problems in the Quran, the Hindus had their own holy books. For the Sikhs the Guru Granth Sahib now contained all the lessons that they needed to learn; all the answers to their question.

But it is with his death and the manner of his dying, that Guru Arjan Dev gave a new and important lesson to his followers. His followers learnt from their Guru that they must resist evil even if they had to give up their lives to do so. They must fight evil and injustice with all the force at their command.

The last message that he sent to his son was to arm himself and to prepare himself for the struggle ahead – a struggle against the cruelty and oppression of the Mughal rule. Through his martyrdom, Guru Arjan Dev provided the strength which was to keep the Sikh religion alive in the difficult years ahead.

Sikhs all over the world remember Guru Arjan Dev's intense pain and suffering. His death anniversary is commemorated at the hottest time of the year. On this day, Sikhs put up stalls along all roads. They beseech the passengers of all buses and cars, riders of scooters and bicycles, and all pedestrians to have the chilled sherbet they serve. By quenching the thirst of thousands of travellers, the Sikhs hope to quench a little of the memory of the terrible thirst their Guru must have felt as he sat stoically on that hot iron plate four-hundred years ago.

Chapter 10

Guru Hargobind
(1595–1644)

There was always a period of time between the evening prayers and the evening meal when Guru Arjan Dev and Mata Ganga, his wife, would be alone together. This was considered a very special time by both of them. Ganga looked forward to this time as her very own. She had the Guru to herself and could share all her thoughts and her feelings with him; and during this time he was not only her Guru but also her husband. There was always happiness and warmth in being together. But one evening, when the Guru was thirty-one years old, the Guru sensed unease in his wife's manner. 'What is troubling you Ganga?' he asked coming straight to the point.

The couple had been childless, and this was what was troubling Mata Ganga.

'It is the will of God. We must accept His will and live with it,' The Guru said.

'But in this matter the blessings of holy men are also important. Many women who were childless have been blessed by holy men and have received the gift of children,' Said Mata Ganga.

'Who can be more holy than you? Why do you not give me your blessings?' Mata Ganga said and started weeping. The Guru put his hand on her head.

'I am not holy. I am just a servant of God and of my people, and I try to serve them to the best of my ability. That is all. Besides, even if I were holy, it would not be right for me to bless myself or my own family,' said the Guru with all humility.

Mata Ganga began to weep again.

'Do not weep. There is a holy man who can give you the blessings you seek. Bhai Budha is a man of God. Go to him and seek his blessings. They will bear fruit,' said the Guru.

Mata Ganga saw the sense of this. Bhai Budha was indeed a man of God who was greatly respected for his piety. Surely his blessings would bear fruit. She wiped the tears from her eyes, smiled at the Guru, then hurried into the house to supervise the evening meal.

The next day Mata Ganga went to visit the saint. She had woken up early and was dressed in her best attire. She took with her baskets of food and sweets and many rich presents. She rode in a horse-drawn carriage and was escorted by a troop of servants.

Bhai Budha, at that time, lived in a little forest just outside Amritsar. He heard the approach of horses and came out of his hut to see who was coming. He saw the group of people and then the carriage. Before the leading rider could announce Mata Ganga's arrival, Bhai Budha asked, 'What is this commotion in the Guru's household?'

'Mata Ganga has come to seek your blessings,' said the servant.

'Tell her I will not see her,' Bhai Budha said. He turned abruptly and went back into his hut. The rider went up to the carriage and repeated what Bhai Budha had said. Mata Ganga was hurt and upset and ordered her party to return.

That evening, when they were alone together, she would not look at the Guru at all.

'What is the matter? I heard you went to Bhai Budha's house today. Did he not give you his blessings?' the Guru asked. Mata Ganga could not control herself and broke down.

She said, 'He would not see me. He just locked himself in his hut and would not see me.'

Mata Ganga then told him the details of all the preparations she had made. As he listened, he smiled and said, 'You made a big mistake. You must go to him in humility. You are seeking a favour from him and you must appear before him as a humble supplicant, and not as the wife of the Guru.'

The next day Mata Ganga set out to see the saint again. This time she was dressed in very simple clothes made of homespun cotton, wore no jewellery. She took no presents or rich food. On a simple brass thali she took four *bajra rotis* and some onions. The thali was covered with a simple cotton cloth. She had no attendants or maid-servants, and carried the thali herself. She did not ride in a carriage but walked barefoot to the saint's hut.

It took longer for her to reach and she was afraid that he might already have eaten his food. But when she reached the hut she found him sitting outside. 'Come, come little mother. I have been waiting for my food and 1 am hungry,' said Bhai Budha. He took the tray from her and she bowed in greeting. She sat on the ground at his feet. He drew the cover off the thali. Then he squashed the onion with his fist.

'You will have a son,' he said as he began to eat. 'He will be a very handsome man. He will also be a brave man, a very brave man, and will crush his enemies the way I have crushed this onion,' he added.

Mata Ganga was sure now that with the saint's blessing, her wish would at last be fulfilled. She waited till the saint had finished eating. Then she bowed to him and picking up the thali, hurried home.

That evening, the Guru saw his wife in a different mood. When they were alone together, he said, 'You look very happy. I can see that the saint has given you his blessings.'

'Yes. The saint has given me his blessings. He said that we

will have a son who will be both handsome and brave,' said Mata Ganga.

Nine months later a son was born to her and they named him Hargobind. As soon as the child learnt to walk, he was put in the charge of special teachers who taught him riding, fencing, wrestling, and boxing. The Guru himself would supervise this. Bhai Budha and Bhai Gurdas were confused by this. They did not understand why there was a need to learn the martial arts.

'What is this strange education that you are giving your son? You were not given such an education by your father and your grandfather,' Bhai Budha asked the Guru.

'It is not strange education. He is being taught the scriptures and everything that he needs to know. But we are living in troubled times and things are going to become very difficult for the Sikhs. So it is important that every Sikh must know how to defend himself. This he can do only if he is strong, and learns all the skills that a soldier needs to learn,' the Guru explained. He knew that the education he imparted to his son would become the model for the education of all Sikh children, especially the boys.

By the time Hargobind was ten years old, he was well on his way to mastering all the skills that his father wanted him to learn. He was a very handsome young boy, tall and well-built and wherever he went, people turned to look at him. He was sure of himself and had the confidence of a grown-up man.

A year later when Guru Arjan Dev was arrested and led away to prison in Lahore, he sent a message to Bhai Budha that, in an eventuality, Hargobind should be anointed as the next Guru. The last message that his father sent him was that he must fight evil with all the strength at his command. The son took this message to heart and it was the message that he taught all his followers.

At his anointing, Bhai Budha brought the *seli* or the sacred headgear which had been worn by all the Gurus from Guru Nanak onwards. This headgear was a symbol of renunciation. The Gurus continued to live in the world of men but by wearing this headgear they showed that they had no attachment to material things. Guru Hargobind pushed the seli away and would not wear it. Instead he wore a *kalgi,* an aigrette (the head-plumes of the egret bird) on his turban. On his waist-band he wore two swords – one representing the *miri* or temporal powers and the other representing *piri* or spiritual powers.

The Guru had established a regular routine for himself. This routine was a mixture of the way of life of the previous Gurus, and a new way of life that Guru Hargobind felt was the need of the hour. He would wake up long before dawn and bathe in the holy tank. Then he would join his followers in prayer and meditation. The rest of the day would be spent in military activity. He had raised an army, and would watch the soldiers as they trained. He engaged experienced generals to teach his soldiers the principles of battle. These manoeuvres were practised over and over again till they had been perfected. The Guru himself took an active part in these exercises. He also spent a lot of time in hunting and encouraged his disciples to do likewise. This taught the Sikhs to ride fast over difficult terrains. Many brave disciples proved their strength and fearlessness and were appointed as commanders by the Guru. Among these the most prominent were Bidhi Chand, Pairana, Piara, and Lehngi.

The Mughals had hoped that by subjecting Guru Arjan Dev to horrible torture they would frighten people to such an extent the no one would want to become a follower of the Guru and the Sikhs would be crushed. However, Guru Arjan Dev's martyrdom had just the opposite effect. The Guru's great courage motivated more and more people to turn to Sikhism. The Sikhs were now ready to lay down their lives to protect their religion. From being a purely spiritual head, the fifth Guru had now adopted the lifestyle of a ruler. He held court, listened to complaints, and also settled disputes. He received agents and ambassadors from rulers and princes and exchanged presents with them.

Bhai Budha was upset by the amount of time the Guru spent in physical activity. He had been with five Gurus and so he felt it was his duty to point this out to Guru Hargobind. The Guru reassured him, 'You must understand that never before has a Guru had to face circumstances like the ones that I am facing. I want to make sure that never again will they be able to do what they did to Guru Arjan Dev. Besides, you had prophesized that I would crush my enemies the way you crushed the onion that my mother brought for you? How can I do this if I am not strong?' Guru Hargobind asked.

emperor Jahangir had ordered that Guru Arjan Dev's children should also be arrested along with him. He had also ordered that all the Guru's properties should be confiscated. But the Governor of Lahore, Murtaza Khan felt that Guru Arjan Dev's death was such a terrible death that the Sikhs would be crushed and did not feel there was need to do anything more. He felt the sixth Guru was only a boy and there was little that he could do.

As a result, he did not notice that the young Guru had completely changed the nature of the Sikh organization. But as reports of the growing strength of the Sikhs and of the Guru's army were brought to him, he realized that he had underestimated the young boy and was greatly alarmed. He sent an urgent message to Jahangir requesting him to take action. Jahangir knew that he must act firmly and decisively against the Guru, but he needed an excuse to do this but he did not have one. It was the Empress Nur Jahan who came to his rescue. 'Did you not ask this Guru's father to pay a fine for helping Khusrau?' The emperor nodded. 'And did he not refuse to pay the fine?' she asked her husband.

'Yes, that is why he was tortured and killed,' replied the emperor.

'Well then, you really have no problem. Legally, as his father's successor, the Guru is liable to pay his father's fine. Ask him to pay it. He will refuse, like his father did before him and you will then have an excuse to punish him. You can keep him in a prison far away from Punjab. Without the Guru's presence, this movement will soon die out,' she suggested.

A messenger was sent to Guru Hargobind's court asking him to pay the fine. As was expected, the Guru refused to pay.

Jahangir issued orders to the Governor of Lahore for the Guru's arrest and the Guru was arrested and brought to Gwalior, where he was imprisoned in the fort. There were some other political prisoners, including some princes who were also imprisoned in this fort. In a very short time the Guru, with his cheerful, helpful ways, had won the hearts of all these princes. They were also impressed by his knowledge and understanding of religious and spiritual matters.

Groups of Sikhs came to Gwalior to have *darshan* of their beloved Guru. They would wait near the walls of the fort for hours on end, and when he appeared on the ramparts for a moment, they would bow to him and shout their greetings. This became a daily ritual and as the days went by the number of 'pilgrims' increased tremendously.

The governor of the fort was a kind man, who was very impressed by the Guru and admired him greatly. But he was afraid of the ever increasing number of Sikhs who came to the fort every day. He stopped the Guru from coming on the ramparts and showing himself to his followers. Again this move backfired. Despite the Guru's absence from the ramparts, the number of Sikhs visiting Gwalior kept increasing. They would go around the fort exactly in the way they made a *parikrama* or perambulation of their temple. They would then stop at a particular spot which was thought to be closest to where their Guru was imprisoned, silently bow to the ground, ask for the Guru's blessings, and then return home.

The governor of the fort became alarmed. He sent a detailed report to the emperor and once again the emperor turned to Nur Jahan for advice.

'The only way to stop this is to release this Guru from prison. At the same time, you cannot let him return to Amritsar because once in Amritsar, he will again become a threat to you. Release him from Gwalior and invite him to come and be your guest here in Delhi. He will not be able to refuse your invitation. Once he is here in Delhi, you can hold him hostage indefinitely,' suggested the empress.

It is said that the Guru refused his freedom unless the other prisoners were freed along with him. This was done, and to mark this event, there is a Gurdwara called Bandi Chhor in the Gwalior Fort. This occasion is still celebrated as *Bandi Chhor Divas* or 'Release the Prisoners' Day on every Diwali at the Golden Temple. The Guru was released after he had been in prison for a little more than a year. He was asked to come to the emperor's palace in Delhi, where he was treated like a royal guest and accompanied the emperor everywhere. Nur Jahan's ploy seemed to have been very effective in controlling both the Guru and the Sikhs.

'I have heard that you are very fond of sports. I am going out on a tiger hunt and wish you to accompany me,' Jahangir said to the Guru one day.

'That I will do gladly,' the Guru replied.

The royal party waited on a piece of high ground at the forest, which was shielded from all sides by tall trees and bushes. The beaters had spread out on the other three sides to ensure that the tiger would be forced to move towards the spot where the royal party waited. The emperor and the Guru looked down at the spot below them because it was expected that the tiger would first appear there. Suddenly there was a sound behind them and the Guru saw the tiger leaping from a hillock just above them. The tiger landed on the emperor's back and pulled him off his horse. All the members of the party panicked and horses and elephants ran around in confusion. Some of the hunters tried to shoot at the tiger but missed. The Guru urged his horse forward and, riding towards the tiger plunged at the animal with his sword. Threatened by this new adversary, the tiger turned away from the emperor and focused its attention on the Guru.

A single-handed battle between the tiger and the Guru ensued and finally the tiger was killed. The Guru had risked his life to save Jahangir, and the hearts of both the emperor and his queen were filled with gratitude, and all hostility and suspicion were replaced by the warm glow of friendliness.

As an expression of her gratitude, Nur Jahan came often to visit the young Guru and during these interactions she was not only charmed by his personality but also learnt that the Sikh religion was an extremely tolerant religion and that the Guru Granth Sahib, the holy book of the Sikhs contained the teachings not only of the Sikh Gurus, but also of many Hindu and Muslim saints. She was convinced that such a man and such a religion could pose no threat to her husband or to Islam; and she persuaded Jahangir to let the Guru return to Amritsar.

With the Guru's return to the holy city, it was generally felt that the conflict with the Mughals was over and there would now be only peace and cordial relations between the Guru and the emperor. The Guru, however, was sure that this lull in hostilities was only a temporary phase and so very discreetly and unobtrusively, he began to build up his army again. He selected the strongest and bravest among his followers to become his soldiers. He also hired mercenaries, mainly Pathans, the most famous of whom was Painda Khan.

He heard rumours that the Governor of Lahore was sending reports of his activities to Delhi and feared that this would soon lead to trouble for him. He did not wish to come into open conflict with the Mughal emperor and decided that one way of avoiding this conflict, was to fulfill his long cherished wish of visiting his followers in the different centres and of setting up new centres. One of his disciples, Almast, who looked after the temple of Nanakmata near Pilibhit, wrote to the Guru to say that a band of yogis was troubling him and were trying to take over control of the temple. The Guru decided to go to his disciple's aid. He travelled to Pilibhit and restored the temple to Almast, stopping at many places on the way and spreading the message of the Gurus. He also visited Nankana Sahib and other places that were sacred to the memory of Guru Nanak.

During this time, in 1613, a son was born to his wife, Damodri. The boy was named Gurditta. It is said that Gurditta looked exactly like Guru Nanak. In 1617, a second son Suraj Mal was born to the Guru's second wife Mahadevi. The Guru's third wife Nanki, bore him three sons, Ani Rai in 1618, Atal Rai in 1620, and Tegh Bahadur in 1622.

Guru Hargobind then went to Kashmir and met his followers there and also visited the Hindu holy shrines in Garhwal. Everywhere the Guru went, he built temples and appointed missionaries to go out to preach the teachings of the Gurus. They also explained why the peaceful ways of Guru Nanak had been changed to a military mission by Guru Hargobind. On his way back to Amritsar, he met the raja of Bilaspur. The raja was very impressed by the Guru and gave him the gift of a large plot of land at the foothills of the Himalayas on the banks of the Sutlej, where the Guru built a small retreat called Kiratpur.

For more than fifteen years, there was peace between the

Guru and the Mughals. This was partly because he had won the goodwill of Jahangir and Nur Jahan; and partly because he was very discreet and did not openly engage in activities that might annoy the Mughals.

In his heart, the Guru had always known that this period of peace was a temporary phase. Jahangir and Nur Jahan had, for various reasons, been tolerant of the Sikhs. But during the short period that he had spent at Jahangir's court, the Guru knew that none of Jahangir's sons would be as tolerant. This is why the Guru made every effort to prepare for what was to come.

Jahangir died in 1627 and was succeeded by his son Shah Jahan. Shah Jahan was to earn a name for himself as one of the greatest Mughal emperors. He built many buildings which, even today, are considered among the most beautiful in the world. But though he showed so much feeling for beauty in lifeless structures made of brick and stone, he showed no feeling in his relationship with human beings. He was a very intolerant king – especially as far as religion was concerned. The moment he came to the throne, he ordered that no new Hindu and Sikh temples were to be built. Even the temples that were half complete were not to be completed, and no repairs of temples were permitted. Wherever he could lay claim to places that were sacred to other religions, he did so. For example, he claimed the baoli built by Guru Arjan Dev in Lahore, filled it up, and built a mosque over it. He also passed an order considering all marriages between Muslim women and non-Muslim men were illegal. Over the years, many Muslim women had married into Hindu and Sikh families. Now they were separated from their husbands and children, and returned to their parents. He passed an order that no Muslims were to be allowed to convert to any other religion. This was considered to be a direct attack on the Guru and on the Sikhs because many Muslims came to Amritsar and, being influenced by the teachings of the Guru, converted to Sikhism.

Naturally all these imperial orders created tension and fear in the minds of non-Muslims. This fear became so great that it was only a matter of time before there was an open conflict between the Muslims and non-Muslims, especially the Sikhs. It only required a small excuse to blow up the whole situation.

This excuse was provided in 1628. Both Shah Jahan and the Guru were hunting in the same forest outside Amritsar. Both their hawks attacked the same duck. The Guru's followers captured the emperor's hawk and refused to give it back. Hot words were exchanged and the emperor's soldiers were beaten up. After a few days, Shah Jahan ordered his general Mukhlis Khan to attack the Guru's camp. At this time preparations were being made for the wedding of the Guru's daughter. When news came of the advancing army, the women and children were quickly evacuated from the camp to a place of greater safety.

The Guru marshalled his soldiers and took up position in the fort of Lohgarh, which he had built outside Amritsar. The forces of the Mughal emperor reached Amritsar in the middle of the night, and a fierce battle took place between the two armies. The battle raged for many days and many brave and famous warriors were killed on both sides and yet the result remained inconclusive. In order to spare further loss of life, it was decided that the Guru and Mukhlis Khan, commander of the Mughal forces, would engage in single combat. The result of this duel would decide the outcome of the battle.

The Guru galloped into the field and asked Mukhlis Khan to strike first. He said this was part of the code of conduct of the Sikhs: They did not seek war. Nor did they strike the first blow, but when a blow was struck against them, they faced it with courage. Mukhlis Khan was a much older and more experienced soldier than the Guru, and was also thought to be more skilled. He took great care and aimed a blow with his sword at the Guru which the Guru received on his sword and pushed aside. The Guru's skill with the sword was a surprise to Mukhlis Khan but he was still sure of success. He raised his sword and tried to strike a second blow which the Guru received on his shield.

'You have had two turns. It is my turn now,' said the Guru. He swung his sword down and, even before Mukhlis Khan realized that the blow had been delivered, the sword had slashed across his neck and his head fell to the ground. A loud cheer from the Sikh forces greeted the success of the Guru and a shocked silence fell over the Mughal forces: A saint had defeated a skilled and experienced soldier. According to the rules of battle, they accepted defeat and left the field. There is a shrine called Sangrana Sahib in Tarn Taran in memory of the Guru's first great victory against the Mughal army.

Shah Jahan wanted to send in another army to avenge this defeat at the hands of Guru Hargobind, but one of the Guru's admirers, Wazir Khan, convinced him against doing this. Wazir Khan pointed out that the Guru was a man of peace who did not seek to capture any territory and only wished to be left alone. He was a saint, a man of God, and wished only to pursue matters of religion and matters concerned with the welfare of his followers. Shah Jahan followed Wazir Khan's advice and decided to leave the Guru alone. The Guru took advantage of this period of peace and consolidated his position further. The people now began to suggest that the Guru was more powerful than the Mughal emperor. Stories of his great courage were repeated again and again. These stories inspired brave young men to come forward to join his army, which consequently became large and strong. Those who could not themselves join the army, sent to the Guru gifts of horses, weapons, and gold. The people who were tired of the cruelty and tyranny of the Mughal rulers began to build hope in the Guru began to feel that he could free them from their suffering.

The Guru retreated from Amritsar to Kartarpur and then to Hargobindpur, a small town which his father had built.

There was not enough accommodation available to lodge the Guru and his large number of followers and, as a result, the town had to be expanded. The building activity once again attracted the attention of the Mughals, who felt that the Guru was again building up his strength and could be a threat to them. Hence there was a growing conviction that he should be crushed before he became too strong.

Abdullah Khan, the *subedar* of Jalandhar, decided that this was a good chance to win the emperor's favour. He collected all his forces and marched towards Hargobindpur. He sent a message to the Guru that he should leave the town so that bloodshed could be avoided – a message which the Guru ignored.

He addressed a number of meetings of his followers and explained his position clearly to them. He said that he had no desire to go to war against the Mughals but since the battle was being forced upon them, they had to take a stand and face the enemy. According to their code of conduct, they would not fire the first shot, but once the enemy fired upon them they would go all out to annihilate them. He reminded them that it was against the tenets of their religion to harm a soldier who had surrendered, or one who was retreating from the battle field. Also, on no account were they to harm women and children or indulge in looting civilian properties. The Sikhs were fighting for the right to live in honour and peace, and not for gain of any kind.

Abdullah Khan's soldiers swooped upon the Guru's forces. The Mughal forces were far greater in number than the Guru's army, but the Guru's soldiers fought with greater courage. Finally the Guru's warriors won the day. In 1630, two years after the first battle, the Guru won another major battle against the Mughals.

After winning the battle he completed the expansion of Hargobindpur. To everyone's surprise and wonder, one of the greatest buildings in Hargobindpur was a mosque which the

Guru built. Many of his soldiers and workers were Muslims and he wanted to make sure that they had a place where they could worship. So even while he was fighting against the Mughal army and its great Muslim generals, he showed respect and tolerance for their religion.

It was during this time that Bhai Budha, who had served six Gurus with complete devotion, passed away. Bhai Budha had lived a full life and seen the Sikh religion through all its stages of growth.

'My Guru, my only regret is that I am going at such a difficult time. You, of all the Gurus, have had to face the most difficult time. I would have liked to go with the knowledge that you have crushed your enemies,' were Bhai Budha's last words.

The Guru put his hand on the saint's shoulder. 'You gave me this blessing before I was born. I will crush my enemies. It may take time but I will overcome them. Do not worry about me. You have served me, as you have served all the Gurus, with complete devotion. You have been fearless and strong and you have not hesitated to speak your mind when you have had doubts about my conduct. God will reward you for this, so go in peace. Go with the knowledge that all your work has borne fruit. Your son Bhai Bhana, who is one of my favourite disciples, will take your place, and continue all the good work that you have done.' Bhai Budha was reassured, and folding his hands in farewell to his Guru, he left this world.

Guru Hargobind built a new town at Kiratpur in Ropar district. The work of building this town was taken up by his son Gurditta, who planned the buildings and organized the construction. Gurditta did a wonderful job in the building of the new township and everyone who came to see the new town admired its beauty.

In 1629, another great follower of the Guru, Bhai Gurdas, passed away. Bhai Gurdas had been the scribe who had transcribed the Guru Granth Sahib. He had been one of the great disciples of Guru Ram Das and Guru Arjan Dev; and Guru Hargobind had always regarded him with great respect. But differences had come up between Bhai Gurdas and the Guru, because Bhai Gurdas could not understand the way of life adopted by the Guru. He could not understand why the Guru had taken to a military way of life. In his poems he had compared the way of life of the sixth Guru with the way of life of the earlier Gurus, and expressed his unhappiness with the change. But when he saw the two battles fought against the Mughals, he understood why the Guru had adopted the change in his way of life and came to terms with the change. He died with the knowledge that the Guru had forgiven him for harbouring doubts.

Horses were the immediate cause of the third battle between the Guru and the Mughal forces. The Sikhs of Afghanistan sent many presents for the Guru, including two wonderful horses, Dilbagh and Gulbagh. It was said that they ran so fast that their hooves did not appear to touch the ground. Their fame had spread far and wide, and when they passed through Lahore, an official captured them and gave them as a gift to the governor.

The Sikhs were incensed by this and wanted to use force to regain the horses. The Guru was against precipitating another war. Bhai Bidhi Chand disguised himself and went to the governor's stables, where he met Sondha Khan, the keeper of the governor's stables, and gained employment there. He proved to be so good with the animals, that he was soon given charge of the two prized horses. When he was sure that he had won the confidence of the Mughal officials, Bidhi Chand made his move. He plied the guards and stable-hands with wine, and when they were drunk he escaped with the two horses. The Mughal army led by one Lai Beg was sent to recover the horses. The Guru, on the advice of a disciple, Rai Jodh, had retired into the wild countryside near Bhatinda, as this would be a more favourable battleground for him. In 1631, a fierce battle, which lasted eighteen hours, was fought between the Mughals and the Sikhs. All the important Mughal warriors were killed and the Guru's side counted twelve hundred casualties and many more that were wounded. Bidhi Chand and Rai Jodh were both amongst the wounded. This is called the battle of Nathana Tank. What remained of the Mughal army, fled from the battle-field. This was the third decisive victory for the Guru and his Sikhs. After this battle the Guru returned to Kartarpur.

At this point, however, the Guru Hargobind fell out with his famous general, Painde Khan. The relationship deteriorated to such an extent that Painde Khan and his son-in-law, Asman Khan, were both dismissed from the Guru's service.

Painde Khan went to the Mughal court and offered his services against the Guru.

'I have been with the Guru for many years. I know all his strengths and all his weaknesses. If you send a strong army with me, I am sure I can defeat the Guru,' claimed Painde Khan.

The Mughals decided to take advantage of this offer. So in 1634, a large force under Kale Khan (the brother of Mukhlis Khan) along with Painde Khan and Asman Khan was sent out against the Guru. It is said that on the eve of the battle, Dhirmal, Guru Hargobind's grandson, wrote a secret letter to Painde Khan promising to help the invading forces with information about the Guru's army.

The Guru had taken up position in Kartarpur and the Mughal forces surrounded him from all sides. The defence of the town was divided among his generals Bidhi Chand, Jati Mai, Lakhi, and Rai Jodh. The Mughal army attacked the town and a fierce and bloody battle followed.

The Guru's sons, Tegh Bahadur and Gurditta, fought with great skill and courage. In fact Tegh Bahadur wielded his sword so well that he caused great harm to the Mughal army and it seemed that the battle would go in favour of the Guru's forces. Some of the remaining Mughal generals now called upon Painde Khan. 'Where is your knowledge of the Guru's forces?' If you really have such knowledge you must use it now,' they said. Painde Khan had no choice but to lead a fresh attack against the Guru. He came face to face with the Guru and tried to strike him, but he only managed to cut the Guru's stirrup. A single blow from the Guru and Painde Khan fell to the ground, mortally wounded. The Guru dismounted from his horse and held Painde Khan's head in his lap. 'I have always regarded you as my child. You came to me as an orphan and I gave you all my love and built you into a great warrior. I find no joy in your defeat. Your time is near. Recite the *kalma* so that you can be at peace with God,' said the Guru with great sadness. Painde Khan moved his lips in silent prayer and then breathed his last.

In another part of the field, an arrow from Bhai Gurditta's bow had killed Asman Khan. Like the Guru, Bhai Gurditta too gained no joy in this victory. Asman Khan and he had grown up together and had been playmates, and now the Pathan had died at his hands. He turned to his father and surrendered his arms. 'Let me go home. I want no more part in this bloodshed,' saying this he left the battlefield.

The battle still raged on. Kale Khan and Qutab Khan, great Mughal generals, were among the many Mughal soldiers who were killed. The losses on the Sikh side had been heavy too:

The Guru had lost seven hundred brave generals and soldiers. Finally the Mughal forces were left without any leader and abandoned the battle. So in 1634 the Guru inflicted the fourth successive defeat on the imperial forces.

In these four battles, Guru Hargobind had suffered great losses. He knew that he needed time to recruit more soldiers and to regroup his army, before he could face the Mughals again in an open battle. So he withdrew to his mountain retreat in Kiratpur, where there could be no open battle, only skirmishes. Even if the Mughals attacked, the terrain was such that his smaller army could face them. But after four major defeats, the Mughals decided to leave him alone.

The Guru's fame spread far and wide and people called him '*Miri Piri da Malik*', i.e. 'Master of both temporal and spiritual powers'. He had shown that he carried the torch of Guru Nanak. He had travelled over large areas teaching people and bringing the word of the Gurus to them and he had also worked hard for the welfare of his people, and thus proved that he was a great spiritual leader. By defeating the Mughals he had shown that he was also a great military leader who had the strength to defend his followers even against the might of the Mughal Empire. In spite of the draconian laws passed by Shah Jahan, people embraced Sikhism by the thousands. Mohsin Fani, a Muslim historian, who lived at the time, has written: 'From this time the disciples of the Guru increased considerably and in this mountainous country, as far as the frontiers of Tibet and Kahota, the name of the Musalman was not heard of.'

Gradually, as the danger of another Mughal attack receded, Guru Hargobind reduced the strength of his army. He now had only a personal bodyguard of three-hundred horsemen and sixty artillery soldiers.

The Guru's last years in Kiratpur were marked by great personal tragedy. In the course of a few years, he lost five members of his family in quick succession. These included three of his sons. The saddest of these losses was that of his son Gurditta in 1638. Gurditta had earned a name for himself not only as a brave and intelligent young man, but also as a great follower of the Gurus' teachings. Added to this was the burden of his grandson, Dhirmal, turning against him.

In Punjab, when a man dies, one of the ceremonies performed at the funeral relates to the tying of the turban and is called the *rasam pagri*. In this ceremony, the eldest son of the deceased is recognized as his successor. On Gurditta's death, the Guru sent for Dhirmal to come for the turban ceremony. In this way Dhirmal would be recognized as the legal heir to Gurditta. He would at least inherit Gurditta's personal property. Dhirmal refused to come to Kiratpur. He knew that he had betrayed both the Guru and his own father through his actions and was afraid that the Sikhs would object to his being recognized as Gurditta's successor. So the turban ceremony was performed by his younger brother Har Rai.

The Guru kept his grandson Har Rai always with him and came to love him dearly. He gave him all the instructions – both spiritual and secular – that he had given Gurditta. Har Rai was also trained in the use of arms. The Guru spent the last ten years of his life in Kiratpur in prayer and meditation. It was a peaceful later life in contrast to all the years of war and bloodshed that he had been through in the earlier phase of his life.

As his end drew near, he was not sure as to who should succeed him. He watched his two surviving sons and grandson closely. Suraj Mal, his eldest surviving son, showed no interest at all in religious affairs. His other surviving son, Tegh Bahadur, had withdrawn into himself and detached himself from the world.

The Sikh community was growing rapidly. There was need for a Guru who would be actively involved in the affairs of the community and would show a keen interest in the welfare of its members. Guru Hargobind decided in favour of his grandson Har Rai. In March 1644, Har Rai, who was then fourteen years old, was consecrated as the seventh Guru of the Sikhs. Guru Hargobind had invited all his friends and relatives and a very large gathering was held. Prayers were recited and hymns were sung. Then Har Rai was led by the Guru to Guru Nanak's seat and Bhai Bhana, Bhai Budha's son, applied the saffron tilak. Guru Hargobind bowed before the seventh Guru and offered him five copper coins, a coconut and flowers. All those present, bowed before the new Guru and made their offerings.

A few days later, Guru Hargobind passed away. Before his end, he advised his son Tegh Bahadur to go and settle in the village of Bakala in Amritsar district. He also gave instructions that there should be no formal mourning on his death. There should only be the recitation of hymns from the Granth Sahib.

It is easy to understand how Guru Hargobind inspired devotion in his followers. He was tall and handsome. He had a very good sense of humour and had a very pleasing manner of speech. He showed concern and regard for everyone and always worked for the welfare of his followers. His father's torture had strengthened his will. He was a young boy at the time, but he was determined that he would make his followers strong enough to stand up against the strength of the Mughals. Before him, the Gurus had all been pacifists. Guru Hargobind was a very practical man and understood that the times had changed. He believed in peace, but he also emphasized that the Sikhs had the right to defend their faith. If they were threatened, they would take up arms and fight to protect themselves and their right to practice their faith..

By the time the Guru died, the Sikhs had been transformed. They were still a peace-loving people; and did not seek to take what belonged to others, and had no desire to extend their land holdings by any illegal means. But at the same time they were ready to defend what was rightfully theirs. They would fight to protect their faith and their property to the point of death. The Guru had set an example and shown the way: A true Sikh was now not only a saint but also a warrior.

Chapter 11

GURU HAR RAI
(1630–1661)

The child Har Rai was a great favourite with everyone in Kiratpur. He was a handsome, intelligent child, and very friendly with everyone. If he was aware of his importance as the Guru's grandson, he never showed it. Even as a child, he cared deeply for the pain and suffering of others. Both his grandfather and grandmother loved him dearly and this love became even stronger when he lost his father Gurditta. The Guru kept him always by his side, and the boy's grandmother made him the centre of her life.

The Guru made sure that his grandson got the best training in riding, swordsmanship, and archery. By the time he was in his teens, Har Rai had become an excellent rider and a skilled swordsman. Har Rai observed his grandfather closely and learnt a great deal about his religion and its special ways. He soon knew most of the Sikh prayers and hymns by heart. He would also go hunting with his grandfather, but unlike his grandfather, he did not kill animals. Instead, he captured animals and brought them back to the little zoo he had built in Kiratpur.

In March 1644, a few days before Guru Hargobind's death, Har Rai was ordained as the seventh Guru of the Sikhs. Within a year of becoming the Guru, Guru Har Rai had to face the first crisis of his stewardship. Kiratpur was situated within the territory of the raja of Bilaspur. The raja was facing trouble brought on by the Mughal rulers and it seemed that there would be war between the two. If the Guru stayed on in Kiratpur, he would have to take sides with the raja, and the Sikh soldiers would have to fight alongside the raja's army. The Guru considered his position very carefully and decided against being drawn into a battle. He realized that he was too young and inexperienced to lead his soldiers into battle. He also realized that the Sikh community had yet to recover fully from the effects of the four battles that his grandfather had fought. Even though the Sikhs had won all four battles, they had suffered heavy losses and could not afford more losses at this stage. In addition, there was the problem posed by the Guru's elder brother Dhirmal, who in his antagonism towards the Guru had already formed an alliance with the Guru's enemies. If the Guru came into open conflict with the Mughals, it would mean being in conflict with his own brother. But above everything else, the Guru was not convinced of the justness of the raja's cause, the raja himself was to blame for the position he was in. As such, he decided against taking part in the impending war and decided to move out of Kiratpur and go further into the hills. So, with his family, servants, and 3,200 armed men, the Guru moved to Taksaal, a small village in Sirmour state in Himachal Pradesh. Here he was able to live a life of peace and prayer, and avoid conflict both with the Mughals as well as his brother Dhirmal.

Days turned into months and months into years. Reports from the various centres came to the Guru and he was worried by what he heard. Without a Guru at Amritsar to look up to, the administration in the centres had begun to weaken. Without the physical presence of the Guru to give them spiritual strength, some of the Sikhs had begun to turn to the other claimants to the Guruship. People like Dhirmal had gained strength because the Guru was absent from Amritsar. The masands now did not report to the Guru and had stopped coming to Amritsar. Some of them kept the donations that they collected from the Sikhs for themselves, and were becoming rich and powerful.

Guru Har Rai decided that he would not return permanently to Kiratpur or Amritsar. The factors that had made him move out of Kiratpur still existed. At the same time, he had to take steps to counteract what was happening in his organization. He decided to travel from Taksaal and visit all his centres turn by turn. He spent some time in each centre and examined the working of his missionaries. Both the disciples and the missionaries came into personal contact with their Guru, and received his blessings, and in the process the faith thus regained its lost strength. The Guru's rivals found that their followers had begun to leave them and return to the Guru's fold. In the past the Sikhs used to go to their Guru, now their Guru had come to them. As a result many who would otherwise not have gone to Amritsar and been influenced by the Guru's teachings, now found themselves being drawn to him and the number of people converting to Sikhism, once again, began to increase. Many prominent families in various places in Punjab like Patiala, Nabha, Jind, Kaithal, and Bagrian had been impressed by Guru Hargobind. Now the heads of these families met Guru Har Rai and listened to his teachings and converted to Sikhism.

At the end of 1658, Guru Har Rai decided to return to Kiratpur. Once again Kiratpur became the important centre of the Sikh religion that it had been during Guru Hargobind's time.

Guru Har Rai was a man of peace who lived a life of prayer and meditation. His life was a great deal like the life of Guru Nanak. Every morning he would get up early, bathe, and listen to the Gurbani together with his followers. Then he would explain the teachings of the Gurus to his followers. The day would be spent in tasks that were connected with the welfare of his people. In the evening too there would be a prayer meeting and the singing of hymns. He travelled from centre to centre and remained very close to his people. He would stop at the huts of the poor and eat with them. This would give them great happiness and it also gave them a chance to share their problems and difficulties with the Guru.

Guru Har Rai worked very hard to remove the differences of caste. He often came out openly in favour of people of low-caste and encouraged inter-caste marriages.

The Guru did everything possible to avoid conflicts. But when he was attacked, he did not hesitate to strike back. Once, while he was returning to Kiratpur, the women of the Guru's household lagged a little behind the main body. A Mughal force, headed by the grandson of Mukhlis Khan, was travelling from Lahore to Delhi. Seeing the unattended ladies, he felt it was his chance to take revenge for his grandfather's death, and attacked the party. The Guru and his soldiers heard the noise, rode back and attacked the Mughal soldiers. There was fierce fighting and the Mughal force fled before the courage and strength of the Guru and his soldiers.

There was, at this time, tension between Shah Jahan's sons because each of them wanted to be the emperor after their father's death. Dara Shikoh had no interest in wordly matters. But he was the eldest son and was also his father's favourite. So it was obvious that he would be the next emperor.

Dara Shikoh suddenly fell ill. It was a mysterious illness and none of the vaids and hakims in the emperor's court could diagnose it. There were persistent but unsubstantiated rumours that he had been poisoned by his brother Aurangzeb. All medical treatments proved ineffective and it was feared that Dara Shikoh would die. Shah Jahan had special prayers said for his son's recovery and sent his messengers to all the holy men in his kingdom to ask them to offer special prayers for him. One of the messengers came to Guru Har Rai. In spite of all the hostility that had existed between Guru Hargobind and Shah Jahan, Guru Har Rai treated the messenger with courtesy and listened patiently to what he had to say.

Guru Har Rai was a practical man. He knew that life and death were in the hands of God. He also knew that God often acted through men. So he sent for his own hakim, who had built up a reputation of being extremely skilled in his profession.

When the messenger had finished giving details of the prince's illness, the hakim said at last, 'The prince has been poisoned. I think I know the poison that has been used. If I am right, I know the herb that will cure him.'

So the Guru sent this herb back to Shah Jahan. The hakim's diagnosis was correct and Dara Shikoh was cured of his illness.

Much later, one of Guru Har Rai's disciples asked him, 'Guruji, the emperor Shah Jahan caused so much trouble for Guru Hargobind and for the Sikhs. Yet when his son was ill, you sent a herb to cure him. I find this inexplicable.'

The Guru smiled and said, 'When the axe cuts the sandal tree, the sandal tree perfumes its blade. When you pluck a flower, the flower perfumes your hand. We must learn a lesson from this. We must return good for evil.'

Shah Jahan was grateful to the Guru for saving his son's life. For some time there were friendly relations between the Sikhs and the Mughals. But then Aurangzeb – impatient to become the emperor – rebelled against his father, captured him, and made him a prisoner. He then turned towards his brother Dara Shikoh. When his brother's soldiers came to look for him, Dara Shikoh fled to Punjab. He came to Guru Har Rai for help and was given asylum.

There was no clash between the Mughal army and the Guru's soldiers, but the Guru did help Dara Shikoh to escape to safety. Finally Dara Shikoh was captured and brought back to Delhi, convicted by the qazi, and beheaded. Aurangzeb was angry with the Guru for having helped Dara Shikoh and he sent a message to the Guru asking him to come to Delhi.

When this message was received, the Guru called an assembly of his Sikhs to decide what should be done.

'No Guruji, you should not go to Delhi. The emperor put his own father in prison and beheaded his own brother. How can such a man be trusted?' one of the senior disciples said.

'There is no harm in going. After all, the message is in the form of an invitation. For many years now, we have had a good relationship with the Mughals and they have left us alone. Now if we refuse the invitation we will invite their anger and this relationship will be affected,' said another.

'No, no Guruji. We cannot let you put your life in danger. We know that Aurangzeb does not like non-Muslims and looks for every chance either to destroy them or to convert them to Islam. He has destroyed many Hindu temples in Mathura, Ajmer, and Varanasi. No good can come from this meeting,' said yet another.

The debate went on, and the Guru saw that there was a lot of truth on both sides. At this point, Guru Har Rai's son Ram Rai spoke up and said, 'This is the first move by the new emperor towards us. He has held out the hand of friendship and we should not turn this hand away. Instead we should also reach out to him with friendship. Through this meeting, we can make him see that we only wish to follow our religion and to live in peace. Since there is every reason to fear for the safety of the Guru, let me go in the Guru's place. I will be his envoy.'

Ram Rai was only eleven years old at that time and everyone was amazed at the wisdom of his words. He had suggested a simple and practical way out of what was a very difficult situation. A small group of senior disciples, known for their wisdom, were selected to accompany Ram Rai. They would remain with him throughout the trip and advise him on what he would say or do. Before he left, there was one last meeting with his father.

'Remember, my son. Our Granth Sahib is our holy and sacred book and we are not permitted to adapt or change even one word that is written in the Granth. In your discussion with the emperor, you must be sure that you quote the Granth exactly as it is,' the Guru said.

'Do not worry Guruji. I respect the Guru Granth Sahib more than I respect anything else in the world,' said Ram Rai and left to meet Aurangzeb.

Aurangzeb greeted the Guru's party with great respect and they were treated as very special guests. Ram Rai was singled out for special attention. The emperor spent a lot of time with the boy and asked many questions about the Sikh religion. A cordial relationship was established between the two and the Sikhs began to feel that it had been wise to accept the emperor's invitation.

One day, the emperor spoke to Ram Rai. 'There is one line in your Granth that I do not understand. Everywhere else your Gurus have spoken about other religions with respect. But in this one line they have criticized the Muslims, and this has hurt the Muslims very much.'

The line the emperor was referring to was: 'The Musalman's body, when reduced to dust, is used by the potter to make pots. When these pots are put in the kiln, the dust cries out as it burns.' This is part of one of Guru Nanak's hymns. The context is that the end is the same for everybody. A Hindu's body, when he dies, is cremated. The Muslim's body is buried. But this too finally goes into the fire. So it is not our religious practices which make us different from each other, but our actions.

Ram Rai had shown great confidence when he had suggested that the emperor's invitation should be accepted. He knew large parts of the Guru Granth Sahib by heart, but he was not old enough or learned enough yet to discuss the finer points. The emperor's question left him confused and he did not know what to say. Prakash, one of his admirers, suggested that they should give a simple, easy answer and not get involved in any discussion or arguments. In this way, not only would they save their skin, but they would protect the friendly relations that seemed to have been built up with the emperor. Probably on the disciple's prompting, Ram Rai prepared his answer. 'There was a mistake made by the scribe while writing down that line. The original word is *beiman,* faithless, and not Musalman,' said Ram Rai.

The report of Ram Rai's explanation was brought to the Guru. He had feared this might happen and had so warned Ram Rai against this danger, and yet Ram Rai had fallen into the trap. He was aware that Ram Rai was only a young boy. He was also aware that Ram Rai had probably only repeated what one of his advisors had told him to say. But his mind was turned against his son. 'The milk of the tigress is only kept in a cup of gold. The Guruship is like this milk. Ram Rai has shown, by his action, that he is not made of pure gold and so he is not a fit vessel for holding the Guruship. Ram Rai shall never see my face again. My younger son Har Krishan will be the next Guru,' said the Guru.

Ram Rai tried to make up with his father. He sent many messages, offered many apologies. He requested again and again that he should be allowed to meet the Guru in order to explain his position. But the Guru turned a deaf ear to his pleas. Even though it had hurt him greatly to do so, he had turned completely away from his son and never saw him again.

Guru Har Rai passed away in 1661 at the age of thirty. It is probable that he died because of some fatal illness and that the end came suddenly and unexpectedly. But before he died, his younger son Har Krishan, then only five years old, was ordained as the next Guru. Once again Bhai Bhana applied the saffron tilak. Guru Har Rai put five copper coins and a coconut at the young boy's feet and went around him four times and Guru Har Krishan became the eighth Guru of the Sikhs.

Guru Har Rai had been the Guru of the Sikhs for seventeen years. He gave the Sikhs seventeen years of much needed peace, during which they were able to rebuild their strength. He travelled from centre to centre and made sure that these centres became as strong as Amritsar and Kiratpur. He came very close to his people and worked for their welfare. He protected the sanctity of the Guru Granth Sahib, even when he had to disown his own son. Guru Arjan Dev had compiled the Granth to ensure that the teachings of the Gurus remain in their original form. If anyone changed even one word in the Granth Sahib, he would be tampering with the teachings of the Gurus. Guru Har Rai made sure that no one would ever make such a change, by disowning his own son for changing just one word in the text.

Guru Har Rai was a simple man of God who lived a simple life. He was kind and compassionate. His message to the world was: 'When a temple or a mosque is damaged you can repair it. When a temple or a mosque is broken you can rebuild it. But you can never repair or rebuild a broken heart.'

Guru Nanak (1469–1539)

Guru Angad Dev (1504–1552)

Guru Amar Das (1479–1574)

Guru Ram Das (1534–1581)

Guru Arjan Dev (1563–1606)

Guru Har Gobind (1595–1644)

Guru Har Rai (1630–1661)

Guru Har Krishan (1656–1664)

Guru Tegh Bahadur (1621–1665)

Guru Gobind Singh (1666–1708)

Chapter 12

Guru Har Krishan
(1656–1664)

Ram Rai must have been hurt and upset by what his father had done. But he respected and loved his father. By himself, he would have accepted his father's wishes and would not have claimed the succession. But a group of very senior and powerful masands, who wanted a puppet Guru, persuaded Ram Rai to send a petition to the emperor, claiming that he had been deprived of his birthright.

The petition asked the emperor to use his influence to settle the matter and ensure that the Guruship was restored to Ram Rai as he was the Guru's elder son.

Aurangzeb decided to send a message to Kiratpur, asking Guru Har Krishan to come to Delhi so that he could decide about this matter.

Raja Jai Singh was a very important officer in Aurangzeb's court. He was an admirer of the Gurus and their teachings and was not happy at the sequence of events that was taking place. He was afraid that Guru Har Krishan would refuse to come to Delhi and this would give Aurangzeb the excuse to attack the Sikhs. Raja Jai Singh requested permission to take the message to Kiratpur personally and escort the Guru back to Delhi, a request which the emperor granted to the officer.

Raja Jai Singh arrived on the outskirts of Kiratpur in the late evening. It was a beautiful place. As a background to the prayers, there was the sound of the river and the sound of the wind in the trees. The prayers themselves were so beautiful that Raja Jai Singh sat on for many hours listening to them.

The prayers finished, and the sangat was at last aware of the strangers in their midst. The raja was escorted up to the platform where the Guru sat. He greeted the Guru, the Guru's mother, Mata Krishan Kaur, and other Sikh elders. The Sikhs had heard good things about the raja, but they were suspicious of his sudden arrival in their midst. Despite the suspicion, the raja was greeted warmly and made comfortable.

The discussion took place the next day after the morning prayers.

'As you are aware Guruji, your brother Ram Rai has presented a petition to the emperor. Before he takes any decision, he would like to hear your side of the case and has asked me to escort you to Delhi,' said the officer The Guru did not say anything, only looked straight into the raja's eyes.

'As far as we are concerned, there is no case, there are no sides,' Mata Krishan Kaur said. The Guru looked quickly, once at his mother, as she began to speak, and then back again at their visitor.

'Guru Har Rai anointed Guru Har Krishan as his successor; for the Sikhs that is final. There can be no argument, no conflict, no doubt in this matter; he is the inheritor of Guru Nanak's light. There is no need for him to go to Delhi to settle this.' she clarified.

There was a pause and Raja Jai Singh realized how difficult his task was going to be.

'I agree with you mother. This fact is beyond doubt. But if he does not go to Delhi, there are those who will think that he is afraid because he is not sure of his position, and this will strengthen the lies that Ram Rai's admirers are spreading,' said Jai Singh.

Still the young Guru did not say anything. His eyes were fixed on the raja's face. After a pause, Mata Krishan Kaur spoke again. 'We do not trust the Mughals. Nothing good has ever come for the Sikhs from him. We cannot even be sure of the Guru's safety while he is in Delhi,' she said.

'I will take personal responsibility of that, Mother. The Guru will be my guest. You know the Rajput code of conduct with regard to guests: I will give my life before I allow a hair of his head to be touched. 1 will be by his side always,' said Jai Singh.

He further added, 'This will be a chance for the Sikhs to meet their Guru. All the way to Delhi and in Delhi itself, hundred and thousands of Sikhs will get a chance to have darshan of their Guru. Many of these Sikhs will never be able to come to Kiratpur, and this is something they will talk about for years. "We saw the Guru," they will tell their children and their grandchildren and the Guru's blessings and their memory of these blessings will make their lives richer. Would you deprive them of this?'

Mata Krishan Kaur turned to the other senior masands sitting behind her. They had a short discussion in low voices and then she lowered her head and spoke to the Guru. The Guru listened to her words and nodded his head. Then he turned back to the raja and said. 'My mother and my masands advise me that I should go to Delhi.' His voice was strong and unafraid. He added, 'I bow to their advice. I will go to Delhi with you, but I will not see the emperor.'

There was a gasp of surprise from the people around, and the raja knew that this was a decision the Guru had made on his own. Again there was a discussion between the Guru's mother and his advisers. Again she whispered to him. Again he shook his head, but this time in the negative.

'My mind is made up. My father, my Guru, made me promise that I would never see the emperor's face. I gave him this promise. I will not break this promise,' he said.

The raja recognized the steeliness in the Guru's voice and knew that there was nothing that would change his mind. He realized that he was in a difficult position. Guru Har Krishan's refusal to appear before the emperor would enrage him. At the same time, if he did not accept the Guru's decision, the Guru would refuse to go to Delhi.

'I promise you that you will not have to see the face of the emperor. I myself will act as your ambassador. I will see the emperor on your behalf and tell him whatever you wish to say to him,' Jai Singh said at last. There was silence for a while. Doubts and suspicions and misgivings seemed to have all been laid to rest.

The raja had been right. As they moved towards Delhi, word of their coming had reached before them. Large crowds had gathered even before dawn, and when the Guru arrived, there were hundreds and thousands of people jostling for a glimpse of their beloved Guru.

All through the journey, the Guru conducted himself with such confidence and dignity that looking at him Raja Jai Singh marvelled at the fact that he was only five years old. It was as if it was Guru Har Rai who walked amongst his people, as if Guru Hargobind walked amongst his people.

In Delhi, the Guru and his party were escorted to Raja Jai Singh's house in the village of Raisina. He was treated with great respect by the raja's household and given every comfort. A beautiful Gurdwara, Bangla Sahib, now stands at this site.

Word of the Guru's arrival spread quickly. Ever-increasing crowds gathered each day at Raja Jai Singh's house. The emperor did not seem to be in a hurry to take a decision. Raja Jai Singh, sensing the conflict in the emperor's mind, spoke on behalf of the Guru.

'Do not decide in favour of Ram Rai, Your Majesty,' he advised the emperor at one of their private meetings. 'You have seen what a large following the Guru has here in Delhi. I have seen the people who came to meet him all along the way. I can assure you that his following is far, far greater in the Punjab. If you support Ram Rai, you will earn the enmity of all the Sikhs. There will be unrest among them, which might lead to an open revolt,' he further added.

This was a strong argument because Aurangzeb could not afford unrest so soon after he had become the king.

'Besides, think of the insult if the Sikhs do not respect your decision. They have already made their decision. You have seen for yourself the hundreds and thousands of people who have accepted him as their Guru. Do you think you can force them to change this?' Jai Singh pointed out.

The raja was, of course, right and Aurangzeb understood this. He sent his son to meet the Guru to express his support. At the same time, he gave Ram Rai a large piece of land in the Doon Valley to set up his dera. By doing this, he indicated that Ram Rai would not be going back to Kiratpur. Ram Rai founded his own gaddi in Dehradun, which continues to this day. In fact Dehradun got its name from Ram Rai's dera.

At this time, smallpox broke out in Delhi and within a few days, thousands of people had died of the dread disease. Many of the Guru's followers were of the view that the Guru should not risk his life by staying on in Delhi, and should return at once to Kiratpur. Others said that even if he did not return to Kiratpur, he should remain quarantined in his apartment and not meet anyone. If he continued to meet his disciples, there was the risk of his contracting the disease. The Guru ignored both these groups: Perhaps he felt it would be cowardly to turn his back on danger; that he could not turn away from his people when they needed him the most. He continued to meet all his devotees and tried to help those who were sick.

What his admirers feared did come to pass eventually. The Guru was struck by smallpox, and soon it was clear that their Guru was close to his end. Before he died, his mother and his masands collected around him. They put five copper coins and a coconut on a thali and asked the Guru to name his successor.

With Ram Rai and Dhirmal both claiming the Guruship, it was important that the dying Guru settle the issue of succession before he breathed his last. The words he spoke came slowly, one at a time. But they were spoken clearly and everyone present heard them and understood them. 'Baba Bakala,' he said, and having performed his final duty as the Guru, Guru Har Krishan found eternal peace.

Guru Har Krishan was about eight years old when he died and he had been the Guru for nearly three years. He was a friendly, cheerful boy who won the hearts of all he met. He respected the age and wisdom of his mother and the masands, and listened to their advice. But he was quite capable of taking his own decisions and of sticking by them. He was sensitive to the world around him and was a keen observer of men. He showed great concern for his people and was aware of his duties as their Guru, and did not let anything come in the way of performing these duties. He showed flashes of great maturity and wisdom, most notably in the choice of his successor.

Chapter 13

GURU TEGH BAHADUR
(1621–1675)

'Baba Bakala'. These were the two words by which Guru Har Krishan indicated who would be the next Guru. But these two words were enough to indicate to his trusted followers: Diwan Dargah Mal, Mati Das, Sati Das, Guruditta, and Dyal Das, who the Guru had chosen as his successor. When Guru Har Krishan used the term Baba, he meant somebody who had the relationship of a grandfather to him. The only living person who bore such a relationship to the Guru was his granduncle, Tegh Bahadur, who lived in Bakala.

Tegh Bahadur, the youngest and the sixth child of Guru Hargobind, was born at Guru Mahal in Amritsar in 1621. His mother was Nanki, daughter of Hari Chand Khatri, a prosperous trader from the village of Bakala. It is said that at his birth he was given the name of Tyagmal.

In addition to reading, writing, arithmetic, religion, and music, Tegh Bahadur also learnt to ride, hunt, shoot, and use the sword. Guru Hargobind took an active interest in his children's education and he would often be present during their lessons. He always had an encouraging word for them and would praise them if they did well. In order to win this praise, Tegh Bahadur would work even harder. As a result of this intense physical training, Tegh Bahadur grew into a strong boy.

When Tyagmal was eleven years old, Lai Chand Khatri, one of the prominent citizens of Kartarpur, offered his daughter Gujri's hand in marriage to him. Guru Hargobind was very fond of Lai Chand and Mata Nanki had taken a strong liking to the little girl, Gujri. So, they readily accepted the proposal.

Shortly after the wedding, Guru Hargobind's troubles with the Mughal forces began. From 1633 onwards a series of battles were fought between the Mughal forces and the Guru's army. When the first of these battles was fought, Tyagmal was just twelve years old.

The Guru kept Tyagmal at his side during the battle and from the reports that came from the battlefield, and the discussions that followed, the boy learnt a great deal about the strategies and manoeuvres of battle.

In 1638, during the battle of Kartarpur, the Guru knew that Tyagmal was, at last, ready to go into battle himself and sent for his son.

It was a fierce battle. At the end of the battle, Tyagmal came to report to the Guru. He was tired and his face and clothes were covered with dust and stained with blood and smoke from musket fire. The Guru listened to him carefully.

'You talk of the courage and bravery of others, my son. You do not say anything of your own deeds,' said the Guru.

'I only did what I had to do,' Tyagmal said. 'If there was anything worthy of note that I did, it was because your light shone in me during the battle. I cannot take credit for it,' he added. The Guru was pleased by this humility.

'You have fought so bravely, shown so much courage with the sword and the gun that from now on you will be known as Tegh Bahadur, lord of the sword,' said the Guru.

Tegh Bahadur, as he was now called, was greatly respected by the Sikh community. Stories of his great courage were told and retold and he became a hero. But like his brother, Gurditta, Tegh Bahadur could not put the bloodshed and the horrors of the battlefield out of his mind. He had seen hundreds of soldiers lying dead and wounded on the battlefield and, as he went around the dera, he saw hundreds of devastated faces of women who had been widowed, and children who had been orphaned.

As the years went by, he became more and more withdrawn and he turned to religion and to prayers for comfort.

The Guru saw the change in his son and was saddened by the signs that his youngest son showed of becoming an ascetic. But the Guru also understood what was troubling the young man's mind and left him alone to work it out for himself.

Then occurred in quick succession the deaths of Tegh Bahadur's three brothers: Gurditta, Atal Rai, and Ani Rai. These deaths filled him with grief and he was sure that life was meaningless. He turned away completely from the world of men and spent all his time in reading the holy book. He withdrew to Bakala and, in deference to his wishes, the Guru and his followers left him alone.

Shortly before his death, Guru Hargobind decided that his grandson Har Rai would be the next Guru. He decided against Tegh Bahadur because Tegh Bahadur had cut himself off entirely from the world of men, and was for all practical purposes, an ascetic. Tegh Bahadur understood and respected his father's decision and felt no bitterness and came to the ceremony at Kiratpur when his nephew Har Rai was made the seventh Guru. He sat by his father's deathbed; serving him in every way he could.

'You have been a good son. And you are a good man. Take your mother and go back to Bakala and stay there. There is some land in Hargobindpur registered in your name and the revenue from this will be enough to support your mother and you,' said the Guru.

Tegh Bahadur did not want anything. His needs were few and his grandparents were only too happy to take care of these. He stayed long enough in Kiratpur to attend to all the funeral ceremonies and then, taking his leave from the new Guru, and accompanied by his mother, went back to Bakala.

At Bakala, Tegh Bahadur followed a set routine. He had a basement built in his house. Here he would meditate for hours on end. His fame as a sage and a man of wisdom, spread far and wide, and even though he did not like to meet people, yet people came to him in droves for help and for advice. For twenty-six years he lived the life of a saint. The Sikhs remembered him as a brave young soldier but they also knew him as the sadhu who gave help and comfort to people in need. This was the man whom Guru Har Krishan had nominated as the ninth Guru.

The five Sikh elders escorted Guru Har Krishan's mother to Kiratpur in 1664. They stayed there for a few months to help her to come to terms with her grief and to settle her affairs. Then, carrying the thali with the five copper coins and the coconut which Guru Har Krishan had blessed, they went to Bakala.

News of Guru Har Krishan's last words had spread far and wide. It is said that by this time twenty members of the Sodhi families of Kiratpur, Kartarpur, and other places had come to Bakala and had all set up their deras. They were all related in some way to the Guru and they all claimed that they were the one Guru Har Krishan had referred to in his last words.

The most serious claimant was Dhirmal, Guru Har Rai's elder brother. He claimed that the father's elder brother is also often referred to as Baba. He also said that since he had the original copy of the Guru Granth Sahib, he had the strongest claim to the Guruship.

The five Sikh elders came at last to Bakala in August 1644, went straight to Mata Nanki's house, and told her everything that had happened. Then they called a meeting of all the prominent citizens of Bakala, both Sikhs and non-Sikhs, and repeated what they had told Mata Nanki. Bhai Gurditta turned to Tegh Bahadur. He placed the thali with the sacred articles at Tegh Bahadur's feet and bowed to him.

Tegh Bahadur accepted the charge that had been given to him and became the ninth Guru of the Sikhs.

Guru Tegh Bahadur's succession to the Guruship was not accepted by Dhirmal. He made one last effort to gain the Guruship. He incited his faithful masand, Sihan, to make a physical attack on the Guru. But Sihan only succeeded in wounding the Guru. The Guru recovered from his injuries, Sihan confessed to his misdeeds, and Dhirmal stood discredited. He returned to Delhi.

The Guru now decided to move to Amritsar. He bathed in the holy waters of the tank. Then he took a round of the holy tank as all pilgrims do. When he reached the door leading to the bridge it was banged shut on his face and locked from inside, he found that he could not have darshan of the temple. His followers, who had come with him, were very angry and wanted to break the door down but he held them back and set up his camp a little way from the temple.

When Guru Hargobind had moved out of Amritsar, the control of the Golden Temple had passed completely into the hands of Prithi Chand's grandson, Harji, who was afraid that if Guru Tegh Bahadur came and lived in Amritsar, he would lose control of the Golden Temple. This is why he had shut the door in Guru Tegh Bahadur's face.

One of the Guru's disciples, a lady by the name of Hariyan, was most upset by the Guru's exclusion from the Harmandir Sahib. She organized the other ladies of Amritsar and they decided to take action. They led the Guru back to the Golden Temple in a big procession and Harji was shamed into opening the doors and letting the Guru in.

The Guru did not want to create a conflict. So he stayed in Amritsar only long enough to have darshan of the Harmandir Sahib. Then he moved on to Khadur. He stayed for a few days in Khadur and then went on to Kiratpur. Here, too, he only stayed long enough to have darshan of the shrine and to meet all his disciples.

Guru Tegh Bahadur knew when he became the Guru that he must do what all the other Gurus had done before him. He must build his own centre. But he could not decide where to build it.

Once he stopped to rest at a place about eight kilometres from Kiratpur. This place was at the foot of the Shivalik Hills. Further away, he saw the Dhauladhar range covered with snow. At his feet was the river Sutlej. He felt a complete stillness in his heart and knew that he had found the place he was looking for.

The Guru bought the land from the Raja of Kahlur (in Bilaspur). The place was named Nanki Chak to honour the Guru's mother and the Guru asked Dewan Dargah Mal to take charge of the planning and the building of their centre. The Dewan consulted many master-builders and drew up a plan for a small township. The three most important buildings would be the temple, the rest-house and the Guru Mahal; and these three buildings would be built first. The foundation for the new centre was laid in June 1665 by Bhai Gurditta. Most of the important Sikhs built houses here so that they could be close to their Guru. As more and more people began to live here, traders and shopkeepers also came and settled here.

While construction was still in an early stage, the Guru decided to visit his followers outside Punjab. The Guru left Dewan Dargah Mal and Bhai Gurditta in charge of the construction, and towards the end of the year, set out on his travels to the East. He was accompanied by his mother, his wife, Dyal Das, Mati Das, Sati Das, and some other devoted followers.

The Guru travelled through the South-East of Punjab and came to an area called Bagar, now in Haryana. Here he was horrified to see the sad economic condition of the people. They were very poor and many of them had taken to a life of crime and sin. He spent a lot of time in this region and helped to improve the condition of the people and taught them how to lead useful lives. By the time he left this place and moved on towards Delhi, he had brought great changes to this area and signs of development could be seen all around.

The Guru came to the outskirts of Delhi and set up his camp and thousands of Sikhs came to have darshan. Ram Rai, who was in Delhi, heard reports of the Guru's large following and this aroused his jealousy. The emperor was not in Delhi at the time, so he went to the Kotwali and complained to the *darogah* that the Guru and his followers were creating a disturbance by forcing people to give them money and other presents and by speaking ill of Islam. The darogah, fearing that there might be a riot, arrested the Guru.

All this happened so suddenly that the Guru's followers did not know what to do and they decided to turn to Raja Jai Singh, who had always been a great admirer of the Gurus, for help. Raja Jai Singh was at this time away in the Deccan, actively involved in the war against Shivaji. Raja Ram Singh, Raja Jai Singh's son, took up the Guru's cause. He stood surety for the Guru and the Guru was released from prison. He also argued the Guru's case most eloquently and convinced the authorities that the charges against him were wrong. Before moving on, the Guru gave Raja Ram Singh his blessings and told him that if ever there was anything that the Sikhs or their Guru could do for him, it would be done.

The party moved through Agra, Allahabad, Banaras, and Gaya. From Gaya, the Guru's party was taken to Patna by Bhai Jaita, one of Guru Hargobind's favourite Sikhs. Mata Gujri was now expecting a child, and it was not safe for her to travel in this condition. So the Guru made all arrangements for her in Patna and left her in the care of his mother and brother-in-law, Kirpal Chand, and travelled on towards Assam.

Many Sikh sangats had been set up by Guru Nanak when he had made his journey to the east and these sangats had increased during the tenure of the other Gurus, especially during the time of the sixth Guru. Masands had been appointed to look after the day-to-day needs of the Sikhs and this had made the sangats better organized and stronger. But none of these sangats had been visited by any Guru since Guru Nanak had come this way 150 years ago. In the face of this fact Guru Tegh Bahadur's visit assumed great significance.

The other reason he travelled eastwards was to fulfill his promise to Raja Ram Singh. When Aurangzeb had imprisoned Shivaji and his son, Sambhaji, he had placed them under Raja Ram Singh's charge. The prisoners had escaped and Aurangzeb felt that Raja Ram Singh had failed in his charge. The raja was divested of his official position as punishment, and was also ordered to lead an army against the King of Ahom in Assam. The last Mughal general who had been sent into Assam, Mir Jumla, had died in the attempt. Raja Ram Singh felt that he was being sent to certain death and was reluctant to go. At the same time he was afraid of the emperor's anger if he refused to obey his orders. He visited Guru Tegh Bahadur while the Guru was at Gaya and sought his help and advice. The Guru remembered what the raja had done for him in Delhi and felt a deep obligation to help the raja.

'Do not worry. When you are on the right side God is with you, you must not be afraid of what the Mughal can do to you. I will come with you to Assam,' Said Guru Tegh Bahadur to Raja Ram Singh.

The Guru and the raja crossed river Brahmaputra. The Guru visited the Sikh centres at Sylhet, Chittagong, Sondip and Dhaka, all now in Bangladesh. And it gave him great satisfaction to see flourishing sangats in each of these towns. On 26 December 1666, a son, Gobind Rai, was born to Guru Tegh Bahadur. This happy news reached the Guru while he was in Dhaka.

Some new biographies of the Gurus put the year of Gobind Rai's birth as 1661, instead of 1666. Kartar Singh Duggal, in his *Sikh Gurus: Their Views and Teachings* (1993) supports the new date, which is 1661, as the tenth Guru's year of birth.

At Dhaka, Raja Ram Singh's personal bodyguard of 4,000 horsemen was joined by the army of 18,000 horsemen and 30,000 foot-soldiers left behind by Mir Jumla. He also recruited 15,000 local archers. With this army the Guru and the raja moved into Assam. They camped at Dhuhari, where Guru Nanak had stayed. The Guru having taken stock of the situation, advised Raja Ram Singh not to attack, but to come to a settlement with the king of Assam. While the negotiations were going on, he himself toured Assam, and through his teachings and his good work for the people, won a great deal of respect. The king too was favourably inclined towards the Guru and one of the princes came to the Guru for his blessings and became his follower.

The talks between Raja Ram Singh and the Ahom king went on and on but there did not seem to be any chance of a treaty being signed. In the meantime, a few of the tribes started showing signs of revolting against the king. The king was in an unhappy position: On the one hand, he had a large foreign army at his doorstep, and on the other, some of his own people were turning against him. He came to the Guru for help and advice.

'Make peace with Raja Ram Singh. Sign a treaty with him. He will then take his army back to Delhi and you will be free to settle your own affairs,' the Guru advised the king.

'You know the raja well,' the king said. 'Help me, O holy one, to make a treaty that will not bring me shame or dishonour.'

The Guru protected the interests of both sides and was able to work out a treaty which was accepted by both the king and Raja Ram Singh. In this way, war and bloodshed were avoided. Raja Ram Singh made an offering of a large sum of money to the Guru and the raja of Assam also gave him many presents. The Guru had come to Assam for two reasons: to help his friend Ram Singh and to visit the Sikh sangats in the North-East. Both these tasks had now been accomplished and he decided to return to Patna to rejoin his family.

For the next three years, the Guru's greatest pleasure was to be with his little son Gobind Rai. Gobind was a very handsome boy who showed signs of great intelligence. But the Guru did not stay for very long in Patna. He received the disturbing news from Punjab of the forcible conversion of Hindus and Sikhs to Islam. The Guru decided to go back to Punjab to be with his people in their hour of need.

The Guru reached Nanki Chak, later known as Anandpur in 1672. What had been a cluster of a few buildings, when he had left, had now become a town. He was pleased at the way the town had grown. The Guru's family joined him in Anandpur a few months later.

The Guru made sure that Gobind got the best instructors for each subject that he was studying. He kept a close eye on his son's progress and found pleasure in seeing how well he was doing. He would talk to his son preparing him for the difficult times ahead. He would talk to him about the Gurus' teachings and tell him stories from their lives. It was here that Guru Tegh Bahadur composed many of his beautiful hymns which mark him out as a poet of great sensitivity. 115 of these poems were later included in the Guru Granth Sahib by Guru Gobind Singh.

Special orders were given against the Sikhs. Kafi Khan, the Mughal historian writes, 'Aurangzeb ordered the temples of the Sikhs also to be destroyed and the Guru's masands to be expelled from the cities for collecting the tributes and donations of the faithful.'

The local officials, in order to win favour with the emperor, began to use very harsh measures to convert non-Muslims. People were tortured and killed without mercy and hundreds were thrown into prison. This filled the people with fear and hopelessness.

Guru Tegh Bahadur knew that something must be done to help the people and to give the non-Muslims encouragement and strength so that they could face Aurangzeb's cruelty with firm and unfaltering courage. He decided to go from village to village to instill confidence in them.

There had been some earlier attempts to make a stand against the Mughals. In 1669, the Jats of Agra and Mathura had rebelled against the emperor, but the Mughal Army had crushed them. Thousands of Jats were killed in battle and thousands more were captured and tortured. The Jat houses were plundered and the Jat women were raped. Seeing this, around 1,000 Jats embraced Islam. In 1672 the Satnamis, a Hindu sect of farmers and traders who carried arms, rebelled against the emperor. They fought very bravely and won a few battles. But finally they were defeated and most of them were killed. The few who survived were forced to become Muslims.

Now it seemed that people had accepted the inevitability of the Mughal rule with all its attendant cruelty and tyranny. This is why Guru Tegh Bahadur wanted to go from village to village to give them hope and courage. He chose, first of all, the land between the rivers Ghaggar and Sutlej, the area that is called Malwa. There had been no rain in this region and there were no irrigation facilities and the land had become a desert. The people were cowed down not only by the Muslim officials but also by their poverty. The Guru used the money he had brought from Assam to help the people to improve their lives. He dug wells so that they could get water both for drinking and for their fields, and he built tanks so that rainwater could be collected and stored. He bought cows and buffaloes and gave them to the poor. He also had many kinds of trees planted so that the whole area would become rich and green.

Reports of the work that the Guru was doing travelled far and wide. The Hindus and Sikhs came to the area to see the development that had been carried out. It was a time when everything seemed dark and bleak because of Aurangzeb's cruelty, but now, through the Guru's work, they felt there was hope: Here was a Guru who could give them new life.

Aurangzeb's orders to convert all non-Muslims to Islam were being carried out with the greatest zeal against the Kashmiri Pundits. The Brahmins are the highest caste among the Hindus and the Kashmiri Brahmins were considered to be the most learned and intelligent of all Brahmins. So if the Kashmiri Brahmins were converted to Islam, it would be easier to convert all the other non-Muslims.

The emperor Aurangzeb had said that he did not want to see a single tilak or janeu, the sacred thread, in Kashmir. Iftikar Khan, the Governor of Kashmir, was determined to carry out the emperor's wishes in totality. In the first few months, he forced a large number of Kashmiri Pundits to become Muslims. Those who refused to convert to Islam were killed. Soon the Pundits who could afford to start a new life began to flee from Kashmir because they saw in this the only way they could both escape death and keep their faith. All the crucial administrative posts in Kashmir were held by Kashmiri Pundits, many of whom fled from Kashmir. Iftikhar Khan realized that if this trend continued, he would soon have no one to run the administration for him. He called a halt to the forcible conversions and sent for all the prominent Pundits in the state. He explained to them that there was no escape from the emperor's orders. He tried to convince them that it was in their interest to embrace Islam of their own accord. He offered them all kinds of inducements and temptations to persuade them to convert. If they did not accept, he would be forced to adopt his old policy of forcible conversion and they would not get anything out of it. Pundit Kirpa Ram of Mattan, who was the spokesman of the delegation, asked Iftikhar Khan for six months' grace period so that they could convince their congregation that it was best to accept Islam. The Governor acceded to this request.

It was the season of the annual pilgrimage to the holy cave at Amarnath and Kirpa Ram and his friends set out on this pilgrimage. Perhaps God would provide a solution to their problem. In spite of the large scale conversions and the restrictions placed on the Hindus, there was still a very large number of Hindus who Kirpa Ram and his colleagues met while they were on the way to the holy shrine. While interacting with them, Kirpa Ram felt a deep sadness in his heart. Would this be the last time that the pilgrims would be going for darshan of the shrine? Next year, at this time, would there be no one making the pilgrimage? No, it couldn't be. For hundreds of years, their hearts bursting with faith, thousands and thousands of pilgrims had come from the four corners of the country to this holy shrine. Surely their faith, their prayers would keep this pilgrimage alive. The sadness left Kirpa Ram's heart. He knew that God would give them an answer.

But even after he had completed his pilgrimage to the sacred cave and returned to Pahalgam, there was still no answer. He was stronger, stronger to face the end, but the end was inevitable: It would come when the six months period of grace was over.

Then, on that last night at Pahalgam, a fresh group of pilgrims came in to share their room. Immediately there was an exchange of greetings, a rush of introductions. Kirpa Ram's group moved closer to make place for the new group. The new group cooked a simple meal and invited Kirpa Ram and his companions to join them, an invitation that was declined because they had already eaten. Kirpa Ram watched them in the flickering light of the cooking fire, in the dim light of the oil lamps. They were simple people, simple rustic people. But there was something special about them. It took him some time to realize what it was – it was the absence of fear in their eyes. Later, after the group members had eaten and they sat exchanging news, Kirpa Ram understood why there was an absence of fear, this was because of their Guru, with the strange name of Tegh Bahadur.

The pilgrims talked of his coming to their village and of all that he had done for them. They talked of how he had given a new lease of life to them. Just as Kirpa Ram drifted off to sleep, his thoughts turned again to the Guru with the strange name. Strange how one man could affect the lives of so many people! The sleep left him, he was wide awake and his heart beat with wild excitement. He thought that if the Guru could bring hope to others, he could certainly bring hope to the Kashmiri Pundits too. God had after all given them an answer. They would go and meet this Guru and seek his advice.

Kirpa Ram discussed his proposal with the other Kashmiri Brahmins the next morning and they all agreed that they should go to the Guru for help.

So from Pahalgam, the sixteen Pundits went down to Anandpur as quickly as they could. Still it was almost a month before they reached Anandpur. The Guru was away with his son Gobind, walking the high grounds and an attendant was sent to inform the Guru of the arrival of the Kashmiris. The attendant found the Guru and his son sitting side by side under a tree, lost in conversation. The Guru looked up and saw the attendant coming towards them. He stopped in mid-sentence. His heart told him that this was the end of the perfect period of his life. He waited for the attendant to catch his breath and to speak:

'Guruji, there is a group of Pundits from Kashmir who have come to see you. They said it was urgent,' the attendant said.

'Attend to their needs. I will come soon,' the Guru said. But even after the attendant had gone, the Guru made no move to return to Anandpur. He sensed that this was the last time he would be alone with his son, the last time he would know such peace and he was reluctant to let it go. Gobind sensed this reluctance.

'The pundits are waiting,' he reminded his father. Together father and son walked back to Anandpur.

The pundits met the Guru after the evening meal. Kirpa Ram told the Guru of their problem and of the six months' period of grace that they had been given.

'We have come to you for advice, Guruji,' he said.

The situation seemed hopeless and there was no help or advice that the Guru could give them at the moment. 'You must be tired after your long journey. 'Leave your problem with me and go and rest. I will think upon it. Perhaps God will help me to find an answer for you,' the Guru said. The pundits went to rest while the Guru sat on in the gathering darkness.

The Guru told his son of the pundits' problem. 'I am sure that there is only one solution to their problem: If a holy man can give his life, the pundits can still be saved.'

'Who can be holier than you, father?' the boy said without a moment's hesitation. The Guru smiled at his son. He too had been considering that it was he who should make the sacrifice. His son's words confirmed him in this thinking. He drew Gobind into an embrace.

'You are right, my son. It is your father who must make the sacrifice,' said the Guru to his son. The next morning, the Guru sent for the Kashmiri Pundits.

'You must go back to your Governor and tell him that you are all ready to become Muslims, each and everyone of you, but on one condition. The condition is that Tegh Bahadur must become a Muslim. If this condition is fulfilled, all the Kashmiri Brahmins will become Muslims too,' he said.

The Kashmiri Pundits found reassurance in the Guru's proposal. The Guru would refuse to be converted and the pundits would be spared both their lives and their right to remain Hindus. Kirpa Ram alone understood that what the Guru was suggesting was prompted by a willingness to make the extreme sacrifice in order to protect the right of the Hindus to practice their faith. All through the rest of the meeting, he could not take his eyes of the Guru's face; so overcome was he both by wonder and amazement.

The next morning, long before the rest of the group as awake, Kirpa Ram stole out of bed, and made his way to where he was told he could find the Guru. He threw himself at the Guru's feet and wept as if his weeping would never end. The Guru let him be for a while and then drew him up into an embrace and sat him down besides him.

'What is it Punditji? What is it that troubles you?' asked Guru Tegh Bahadur.

'I am not troubled, Guruji. In fact I have not been more at ease with myself for as long as I can remember. My tears are tears of awe and reverence. I am, blessed, truly blessed to have been in the presence of a man of your stature. All my life I have practised piety, and lived by all that is sacred and true and I have prided himself on having evolved to a high state of spiritual attainment. I find now that in your presence, I am but a shadow,' Kirpa Ram said.

'Your humility becomes you, my friend. But do not underestimate your spiritual achievements. We all do the work that has been allotted to us by God, to the best of our abilities: Nothing more and nothing less,' said the Guru.

Kirpa Ram and the other pundits reached Srinagar long before the period of grace was over and asked to meet the Governor.

When they were brought into the presence of the Governor, Kirpa Ram said, 'The Kashmiri Pundits have all decided to become Muslims. But we have great respect for

Guru Tegh Bahadur, the Guru of the Sikhs, and he must give us the lead. If he becomes a Musalman we will all become Musalmans.'

Iftikhar Khan was more than satisfied by this outcome. It would be easy to convert the so-called Guru of the Sikhs and with this one conversion, the knotty problem of the Kashmiri Pundits would be solved once and for all.

Aurangzeb was still camped at Hassan Abdal, close to the borders of Kashmir, and Iftikhar Khan brought the message of the Kashmir Pundits to him. The emperor too, felt that an easy solution to the problem of the Kashmiri Pundits had been provided to them.

The emperor sent a strong force to Anandpur to arrest the Guru and bring him to Delhi so that his conversion could be effected. The Guru along with Bhai Jaita, Bhai Dyal Das, Bhai Sati Das, and Bhai Mati Das and a few other faithful followers had already left for Delhi to give himself up to the emperor. The Mughal force set out from Anandpur and caught up with the Guru's party at a place near Ropar. The Guru advised his followers not to offer any resistance. The Guru and his four senior disciples were arrested. The Guru was locked up in an iron cage and the cage was put on a high cart so that the Sikhs could see how their once great Guru had been humbled. The four disciples were bound in shackles and chained to the sides of the cart. All his followers who stood along the way to see him pass, were shocked to see him locked up in a cage like an animal. They knew they were seeing the Guru for the last time. Some of them just looked on, too dazed to do or say anything; others began to weep. There were still others who raised angry slogans against the Mughal soldiers. At a few places it seemed that the Sikhs were going to take the law into their own hands and attack the party and free their Guru.

But always the Guru smiled and counselled his Sikhs. 'You must have patience, and courage. Do not do anything rash.

Though I am locked up in a cage, I go to Delhi of my own free will,' he told the followers.

His words stilled the anger of the Sikhs but they could not take away the sadness from their hearts.

'What will become of us?' they asked.

'God will take care of you, as He has always done. Bow to His will – accept whatever He does to me; secure in the knowledge that He will only do what is best for me and for you,' the Guru said.

The party moved on and came at last to Delhi. The Guru and his disciples were brought to the *kotwali* in Chandni Chowk.

The next day, Khwaja Abdullah, the darogah of the kotwali, came to see the Guru in his cell. He offered all kinds of inducements to the Guru to tempt him to become a Muslim. When this failed, he tried to emotionally blackmail the Guru by saying that his young son would be left without a father, his wife and his old mother would be left without support.

The Guru smiled. 'You do not know what you say darogah. God will be a father to my son and will also look after my mother and my wife. He will give strength to my followers and lead them along the right path as He has always done. Do not waste your time and your breath, do what you have to do,' the Guru said. The darogah turned and left the cell. The Guru was once again lost in prayer.

The darogah had failed to convert the Guru to Islam. He now decided that he would make the punishment to the Guru and his followers so severe that it would be a lesson to everyone else, and would deter people from becoming followers of the new religion.

The morning of 11 November 1675 saw bright and clear skies. There was a cold, sharp wind to remind everyone that winter had come. But there was not a trace of cloud in the sky and the sun, when it came up, was bright and warm. It brought relief to the thousands of people who had formed up in row upon row around the square, in the early hours of the morning. They had been shivering in the cold. Now the warmth of the sun brought them some comfort. In the brightening light, they saw three objects arranged close to each other. There were two poles driven into the ground about three feet apart. Next to them, on a stool, they saw ropes and a saw. A few yards away, in an open fire-place, a large quantity of wood and coal were burning and over the fire was a huge cauldron, three quarters full of boiling water. Close by, there was a third pole that had been driven into the ground. Next to it were bundles of cotton and ropes and a container with tar in it. They also saw a raised platform at one end of the square.

Everywhere, there were armed soldiers and policemen. The Guru and his four followers, escorted by armed soldiers, were brought to the square and the Guru was led onto the platform. The Guru sat down cross-legged and almost at once, began to pray. A soldier removed Bhai Jaita's chains and a broom was handed to him.

'Go, Tegh Bahadur's Sikh. Go and sweep the courtyard. Let the people see that this is all that a Sikh is fit to do,' the darogah said. Bhai Jaita bowed to his Guru. Then he took the broom in his hand and began to sweep the courtyard. A few of the spectators laughed and jeered, but most of them just watched in silence.

The qazi, in flowing black robes, walked into the square and the crowd fell silent.

'You, who call yourself Mati Das, step forward,' the darogah ordered. Bhai Mati Das stepped forward.

'Mati Das, you have been ordered by the emperor to become a Muslim,' the darogah spoke loud and clear.

'I am a Sikh,' Bhai Mati Das said in an equally loud, clear voice. 'And I will always remain a Sikh,' he added.

The qazi stepped forward and said, 'You are guilty of treason. For this I sentence you to death.'

A soldier removed the chains on Bhai Mati Das' hands and legs. Bhai Mati Das bowed to his Guru, and the Guru held up his hand in blessing. Bhai Mati Das hands and feet were tied to the poles so that his body was stretched between them. Jalaluddin, the executioner, picked up the saw and stood on the stool. A gasp went up from the crowd as they realized what was about to happen. They looked closely at Mati Das' face. He too had realized what was going to be done to him, but he only smiled. Jalaluddin placed the saw in the centre of Mati Das' head. With slow deliberate movements he began to saw. Mati Das did not cry or protest. Jalaluddin sawed through the body till the body was in two parts. The ground was covered with blood. All eyes turned to look at the Guru. He had watched the execution of his beloved disciple without blinking his eyes and without any expression on his face. His lips moved always in silent prayer.

'You have seen what has happened to one of your faithful Sikhs,' the darogah said when the executioner had finished. 'Do you want your other followers to suffer the same fate? You can save them. All you have to do is to become a Muslim,' he added. The Guru said nothing in response.

Bhai Dyala and Bhai Sati Das were called forward, turn by turn. They refused to become Muslims and the qazi condemned them to death as well. Bhai Dyala was thrown into the boiling water, whereas Bhai Sati Das was wrapped in cotton, smeared with coal tar, and set alight. The Guru did not turn away from the suffering of his followers. He watched it all from where he sat, with a calm and serene expression on his face; his lips always moving in silent prayer.

By now the crowd was still; shocked into silence by this set of cruel deeds. There was not a sound, save the rustling of the leaves on the trees. At last the darogah turned to the Guru. Two soldiers stepped forward to help the Guru to his feet. He ignored their help and rose on his own. The darogah and the qazi stepped onto the platform.

The crowd watched, unable to believe what had happened, or what was going to happen. The darogah addressed the Guru and repeated the question he had asked three times already.

'Do you refuse to become a Muslim?' the darogah asked.

'I do,' said the Guru in a calm clear voice.

The darogah then turned towards the qazi and the qazi read out his fatwa, 'You, Tegh Bahadur, the Guru of the Sikhs, have refused to obey the orders of the emperor. You are guilty of treason. For this you are condemned to death.'

The the Guru's chains were removed. Jalaluddin, the executioner, sharpened his sword. The moment seemed to stretch on endlessly. At last he tested his blade against his thumb – it was sharp enough.

'Do you have a last wish?'

'Yes. Give me five minutes to make my peace with God,' the Guru said. The Guru sat down again, his head bowed, his eyes closed, his lips moving in prayer. But this time it was not a silent prayer. The prayers flowed loud and clear and beautiful and filled the square with their music. They sounded on the ears of the crowd and stilled all pain and anger and sorrow. The hush remained. But it was a hush of acceptance, of peace, and of strength. The Guru was lost in his prayers. He was already one with his God. Exactly five minutes later Jalaluddin lifted his sword high in the air. The sound of the sword, as it swished through the air, was drowned in the sound of prayer. The prayer stopped, cut off in mid-sentence. The severed head lay on the ground. The Guru still sat cross-legged, blood gushing from the neck.

At last Abdullah was sure that all those who were present had learnt a lesson. He made a sign and the soldiers hurried the crowd away.

The square was left to the bodies, the guards, and the wind. All through the morning and into late afternoon, the bodies lay in the sun and swarms of flies buzzed around attracted by the blood. Vultures began to collect on the trees. Groups of people formed on the rooftops and at street corners and looked at the bodies. They would have liked to go and claim them but everywhere there were soldiers.

Then, in the late afternoon the sky began to darken. There were no clouds, but the sky was covered with a blanket of red. The red turned to brown, and the brown became darker still, till it was black. It was the coming of a sandstorm, a phenomenon unheard of during winters. The wind became stronger and lashed at the faces of all who were still in the square. It clawed at their clothes and blew sand into their eyes and their mouths.

Everyone hurried inside. The soldiers drew the end of their turbans across their faces but this was no real protection. It became so dark that they could not see their hands when they held them in front of their eyes. So they hurried to the shelter of the kotwali, secure in the knowledge that no one would come to steal the bodies in this blinding sandstorm.

The square was deserted. The streets leading to the square were deserted. The wind blew strong and sand piled up against the walls. There was not a soul around. Not a soul except Bhai Jaita. All through the afternoon, he had stood there, still as a statue. The crowd and the guards, in the face of the terrible things that had happened, had forgotten him. Now he was sure, no one would see him, that there was no one to stop him for what he had to do.

He moved as quickly as the blinding storm would allow and collected the bodies of the three disciples. The Yamuna flowed close by and, as quickly as he could, he cast the bodies into the water. Then he claimed the Guru's head. He hid it under his robe and, under the cover of the darkness and the storm he stole away with his precious possession.

Another person waited in the shadows near the square. He was Bhai Lakhi Shah, a low caste potter and was a big devotee of the Sikh Gurus and their teachings. He too, took advantage of the storm and the dark. He hid the Guru's body in his cart and drove quickly to his straw-thatched hut.

He drove the cart into his hut, untied the bullocks and led them to safety. Then he set fire to his hut so that the Guru's body could be cremated and spared any further indignity at the hands of the Mughals.

After two hours, when the storm at last abated, the guards stumbled back into the square. They saw that the bodies had disappeared and reported the matter to the darogah. The darogah was furious. He would have liked the bodies to rot in the sun and for the vultures and the dogs to feed on them. This would be a lesson to all those who refused to obey the emperor's orders to embrace Islam. Now the bodies had disappeared. The darogah made inquiries everywhere and sent out search parties but to no avail.

To mark the spot where Guru Tegh Bahadur was executed, now stands a beautiful Gurdwara called Gurudwara Sisganj. Another beautiful Gurdwara, called Gurudwara Rakabganj, marks the place where his body was cremated. A Gurdwara, also called Gurudwara Sisganj, in Anandpur, marks the place where his head was cremated.

It is said that while Guru Tegh Bahadur was a prisoner in Delhi, he was questioned by the officers of Aurangzeb's court. In answer to one of these questions he had replied, 'Hinduism is not my religion. I do not believe in many things that the Hindus believe. I do not believe in caste system, in idol-worship, in pilgrimages. Yet I would fight for the right of all Hindus to live according to their religion. 1 would fight for this right even if I had to give up my life in this fight.'

We must remember how Guru Nanak had refused to wear the sacred thread, the janeu. In the light of this fact it seems ironic that Guru Tegh Bahadur should have given up his life to protect the Hindus' right to wear the sacred thread.

Through this sacrifice, Guru Tegh Bahadur saved the Brahmins of Kashmir and saved the country from a flood of forced conversions to Islam. By so doing, he earned, in full measure, the name *Hind-di-Chadder* – The Protector of Hindustan.

Part III

GURU GOBIND SINGH
(1666–1708)

Chapter 14

The Early Years

Bhai Jaita, one of Guru Tegh Bahadur's disciples had carefully and successfully brought back the Guru's severed head to Anandpur, where the latter's family was staying.

'I come from Delhi and I bring a special message for the Guru', Bhai Jaita said to the gatekeeper.

It is not strange that Bhai Jaita was not recognized. He had a flowing beard; his robe was in tatters and hung loosely on his body, which was now little more than skin and bones.

The Guru, who was only nine years old, was in conference with his mother and his senior disciples and the traveller was escorted into the Guru's presence. A hush fell upon the gathering at the appearance of this stranger.

'Yes,' the Guru said, not recognizing the traveller immediately. 'They say you have a special message for me,' he added.

The traveller nodded his head. He bowed again to the Guru, then he put his bundle on his head and, stepping forward, placed it on the empty seat next to the Guru.

Very carefully, he untied his bundle and let the folds of the cloth fall away. There was a loud gasp. There, on the seat, lay the head of Guru Tegh Bahadur. Those who were sitting sprang to their feet and some in the congregation began to weep.

'Who are you?' the Guru asked. The traveller had got down on his knees and with the corner of the piece of cloth, he was wiping the sand from Guru Tegh Bahadur's face and from his hair. 'I am Jaita Rangretta,' he said quietly. His work finished, he lowered his head. The Guru went down to him and drew him to his feet.

'Rangretta, Guru *ka beta*,' the Guru said and embraced the traveller. Then he turned and looked at his father's head. He looked at each of those beloved features so still in death and his child's heart filled with grief. He felt that if he did not weep, he would choke to death, his heart would break.

His father had said during one of their last walks together. 'In all things you are the Guru. Everything that you say, everything that you do, is a model for your people.' This memory came back clearly now and Guru Gobind knew that he could not cry. Even if his heart broke, even if he choked on his grief, he could not cry, for if he cried all his followers would cry. With that one decision, the Guru left his childhood firmly behind and stepped into his life as an adult. He knelt before his father's head and touched the ground with his forehead. Then he sat down at the foot of the seat.

'Tell me, if you know, Jaita, the manner of my father's death,' asked Guru Gobind Singh.

'I was there Guruji,' Jaita said and went on to relate the manner of Guru Tegh Bahadur's death.

The pyre of sandalwood was set on Guru Tegh Bahadur's favourite spot on the high ground. Everyone in Anandpur had collected to watch the funeral. The crowd was large. But there was pin-drop silence because of the deep sense of shock. It had all been so sudden; the sangat had not had a chance to react. In the silence, Guru Gobind Rai walked up to the pyre, carrying his father's head on of his own head. The sand had been washed from the face, the hair had been washed and oiled and a turban had been wrapped around the head. The young Guru carried his father's head and placed it on the funeral pyre. Then he knelt before the head and bowing low, touched his forehead to the ground. Everyone followed his example. Then he got to his feet and recited the Japji Sahib and set the pyre aflame.

Nanak's light had indeed passed from Tegh Bahadur to Gobind. The Sohila Sahib, the last of the Sikh's five daily prayers, was then read and prasad was distributed to all present.

Young as he was, Guru Gobind realized that the Sikhs must remain strong in the face of this terrible tragedy.

The popularity and following of Sikhism increased manifold in North India. The story of Guru Tegh Bahadur's martyrdom, his great courage in sacrificing his life for the Kashmiri Pundits, spread far and wide. People wanted to know what had inspired this saint to do what he had done. They came to Anandpur to learn more about the Guru's teachings and about the Sikh religion. The Sikhs themselves had a new Guru and, as was the custom, each Sikh felt that he must come personally to pay homage to him. As a result there were thousands of pilgrims who now came to Anandpur to meet Guru Gobind Singh. The Guru was very happy to meet his followers, to mingle with them and to listen to their problems. His followers brought all kinds of gifts for the Guru. The Guru, like Guru Hargobind before him, indicated that the most welcome gifts would be weapons and horses and money with which he could raise a strong army.

The growing popularity of the Guru and the growing strength of the Sikhs aroused the suspicion of some of the kings of the neighbouring regions of Anandpur, a suspicion which was further strengthened by the activities of the Guru. Guru Gobind had ordered the making of a huge drum which was named Ranjit Nagara and whenever the Guru wanted his followers together, the drum would be beaten. On hearing the sound of the drum, all the Sikhs of this area would collect at Anandpur. But a drum is normally beaten during battle and when the local rajas heard of this, they felt that the Guru was giving signal for battle and this aroused their fears.

The raja who was most hostile towards and most suspicious of the Guru was Raja Bhim Chand of Bilaspur, from whom the land for Anandpur had been bought. He began to approach the other rajas, seeking their help against the Guru.

The Guru's masands learnt of what Raja Bhim Chand was doing. They knew that the Guru was not yet ready for battle and they advised the Guru to invite Bhim Chand to visit Anandpur. Once Bhim Chand came to Anandpur he would see that the Guru was interested only in religious and spiritual matters and had no intention of extending his territory. This would convince the raja that the Guru was a man of peace and posed no threat to him.

The Guru's invitation was accepted by the raja. He was looked after well when he came to Anandpur and made most comfortable. It seemed that all Raja Bhim Chand's suspicions and misgivings had been laid aside and that he had been won over to the idea that the Guru only meant well by him because shortly before leaving Anandpur, he embraced the Guru in a warm, friendly embrace and exchanged expensive presents with him.

No one could see that behind the smiles of friendship, the raja had a jealous heart. He knew that the Guru was not a threat to him because he was sure the Guru did not seek to extend his territorial holdings. But at the same time he had seen the thousands of people who came to visit the Guru. He had seen that the love and respect that the Guru commanded was far greater than what he received from his subjects. He carried this jealousy in his heart and it became stronger with each passing day and made him more and more determined to destroy the Guru and the Guru's popularity. He had seen that the Guru did not yet have a large or strong army. If he could provoke the Guru to battle, he would be able to destroy him. But to do this he needed an excuse.

This excuse he found soon enough. His son was due to be engaged and he invited the Guru to attend the festivities.

He also asked for the loan of the wonderful canopy and the elephant that had been gifted to Guru Gobind Singh to add colour to the festivities, a request that he knew would be refused, and the refusal would provide him with the excuse that he needed to attack the Guru.

The Guru was not attached to worldly possessions. He would have been happy to give away the canopy and the elephant and would not have felt the loss. But he knew that these two things were symbols. The canopy was a symbol of the love and affection of his many followers in Kabul, and the elephant was a symbol of the faith that Raja Ram's widow and countless other people like her, had in the Guru. If he gave away these two symbols he would be striking against this love and this faith. Besides he knew that the matter would not end there.

'It is not a question of the canopy and the elephant,' Mata Gujri said. 'It is a question of accepting the raja's authority. If we give him these two things, we will accept his right to exact tribute from us, the way stronger kings demand tribute from weaker kings. We have to decide whether we are willing to reduce ourselves to this position of subjugation,' she added.

There were loud murmurs of protest. It was obvious that, when looked at in this way, none of the masands were willing to give up the canopy and the elephant, none of them was willing to recognize the raja's right to exact tribute from the Sikhs.

After considerable thought, it was decided to accept the raja's invitation to the engagement. At the same time a polite refusal would be made to his request for the canopy and the elephant.

Bhim Chand's messenger returned to his court at Bilaspur with the Guru's messages and the raja now had the excuse he sought. The raja called a meeting of his generals and gave orders to prepare for a battle against the Sikhs.

The kings of the hilly regions were all jealous and suspicious of each other. The cleverer ones had their secret spies posted in the courts of the other rajas, who would give them information about everything that happened. The raja of Sirmour had his spies in Raja Bhim Chand's court who sent information back to Nahan and gave details of all the preparations that Bhim Chand was making for his war against the Sikhs.

The raja of Sirmour, Medini Prakash, was a devotee of the Gurus. Ever since Guru Tegh Bahadur's martyrdom, he had felt himself drawn even closer to the Sikhs. When his spies sent him the news of the impending war between Bhim Chand and the Guru, he was anxious and worried. It was true that Guru Gobind was a very brave and sensible boy. But it was also true that he was very young and inexperienced. He was not yet mature enough to lead his Sikhs into battle and the Sikhs themselves were not prepared for war. If Bhim Chand did declare war, the raja of Sirmour knew that neither the Guru nor the Sikhs would turn their backs. They would make a stand and fight, but in their present condition there was little chance of their success.

This thought troubled him greatly. He had to help the Guru and the Sikhs but he did not know what he could do. At last he found the answer. He sent a message to the Guru and requested him to come and spend some time with him. Nahan, the capital of Sirmour, had a cool climate and the raja suggested that the Guru would escape the intense heat of the plains. There were thick forests with plenty of game around Nahan and the Guru would be able to indulge in his favourite pastime of hunting.

The Guru understood the real reason for the raja's invitation. Once again he called a meeting of his senior masands. Once again he invited his mother to preside and once again different views were expressed. The Guru himself felt that he would be running away from battle if he was to leave Anandpur now.

'But no battle has been officially declared,' Mata Gujri

pointed out. 'So no one can accuse you of running away. You are young and inexperienced, you have no organized army. If you are going away now, it is only a strategic retreat, it is only to give yourself time to prepare, to prepare so well that when you do finally come face to face with the enemy, there will be no doubt about your success,' she added. She paused for breath and realized that her son was not completely convinced. So, she continued, 'Remember what Guru Har Rai did. He was older than you. Yet he knew that he was not old enough, not organized enough, to go into battle. He went further into the hills where he got a chance to prepare himself. You too must take this chance. Accept this invitation – it will give you a chance to prepare yourself and your Sikhs for the battle that you know you will have to fight.'

The Guru bowed to his mother's advice and wisdom. He accepted the raja of Sirmour's invitation and, a few days later, the Guru's party left Anandpur for Nahan. Now with the Guru's absence from Anandpur, the tension between Bhim Chand and him was diffused, for the moment, and the battle was averted.

Chapter 15

Paonta Sahib:
A Centre for Literary and Cultural Activities

Before leaving Anandpur, the Guru called a meeting of all his senior disciples. He told them that even though he would be away from Anandpur, the town must not be abandoned. Then in the summer of 1686, accompanied by his family and five hundred Sikhs, the Guru left Anandpur.

When they met, the raja was impressed with the Guru's bearing and his fearlessness. Even though he took an active interest in matters of the world, in the day-to-day problems of his followers and of his own family, there was an air of detachment to everything he did, and on his face there was a glow of saintliness. He offered the Guru land to build a fort for himself. The Guru replied that he would say a yes only after consulting his mother and his advisers.

The Guru's advisers and his mother unanimously decided to accept the raja's generous offer. What now remained to be done was to choose the site for the Guru's centre. One day while the Guru and the raja were out hunting, they came to a beautiful spot on the banks of the river Yamuna. It was high ground with thick forest all around. Building plans were drawn up of a small fort and work started almost at once. When the Sikhs heard of this, they came out in large numbers to help with the construction. The raja's men also worked side by side with the Sikhs and in, a very short time the fort was completed. It was called Paonta, which means footstool. Unlike a chair or a bed, the footstool is used to sit upon only for a short time. So the Guru and his followers, whenever they used the expression, would know that they were only resting here – this was not their home. The Guru created a smaller Anandpur at Paonta and was absorbed once again in pursuing his education. He was determined that not one of his followers should remain illiterate. He engaged many tutors, not only to teach all the children and young men and women of his sangat, but also all the grown-ups who did not know how to read and write.

He also realized that mere book learning was not enough. Like most of the Gurus before him he firmly believed that a healthy body was as essential to a human being as a healthy mind. So he insisted that all his followers should involve themselves in physical activity, which would give strength to their bodies. Regular sports activities and athletic competitions were conducted in the Guru's camp at Paonta. As in Guru Angad's time, there were prizes and honours for all the winners. The young men amongst his sangat, learnt skills in martial arts and in riding and hunting and the use of arms like swords, bows and arrows, the spear and the discuss.

By now, there were strong well-organized Sikh communities from Kabul down to Ceylon, Sri Lanka and from Karachi all the way to Assam. There were Sikh communities even outside India at places as far away as Central Asia. All these followers regarded the Guru as the source, the fountainhead of all their spiritual strength.

Guru Gobind realized, quite early, that his greatest strength lay in the large number of his followers, and he must organize them and give them a sense of unity so that they would be able to rise up as one against their enemies. He asked all the able-bodied amongst his followers, to offer their services to the Sikh community by coming to Paonta and joining the Sikh army.

All those who joined his army, had to undergo rigorous training, which made them competent in riding, swordsmanship, and shooting. They took part in mock battles and then in discussions about the mistakes that had been made during these battles. With each of these exercises, the Guru's army came closer to being well-prepared for a real battle.

Like the Gurus before him, Guru Gobind too was deeply interested in music. Music had always formed an important part of the Sikh religious ceremonies and no prayers could be complete without the singing of hymns.

Guru Gobind himself was very fond of playing the rabab, and played the instrument both in solo performances as well as an accompaniment to the singers. This encouraged the other members of the sangat to learn music. When Aurangzeb banned music from his court, all the famous musicians and singers who had served the Mughals for generations, sought the patronage of other kings and princes. Many of them heard about the Guru's interest in music and came to Paonta to seek employment with him. The Guru welcomed them with open arms and Paonta soon became the home of many famous musicians.

The Guru had made a deep study of classical literature and of mythology. This classical education and the beauty of his new surroundings brought out the poet in Guru Gobind and he began to write poetry in Hindi, Sanskrit, Persian as well as Punjabi. When Aurangzeb banned poetry too from his court, some of the court poets too sought employment at Paonta. The Guru invited them to come and live in Paonta and work on their poetry. He would hold *kavi darbars* and *sammelans* on the banks of the Yamuna. Finally, fifty-two poets from the Mughal court came to live in Paonta.

Inspired by all this literary activity, the Guru too wrote beautiful poetry. He took stories from Hindu mythology and rewrote them in the form of poems. His favourite themes were connected with the deeds of the Goddess Chandi. He wrote poems about the beauty of his surroundings, about the flowers and trees of the forest, about the mountains and about the beautiful rivers. His writings marked a clear break with the tradition of poetry set by the earlier Gurus. His poems were full of stories of warriors and of war. Their purpose was clear. It was to teach the Sikhs that a glorious death in battle, in fighting for a cause that you believed in, was far better than a life that was lived in fear.

Paonta became the centre for literary and artistic activity in North India and the fame of the Guru and of the poets and musicians spread far and wide. The Guru gained many new disciples amongst the visitors who came to Paonta primarily to listen to the great poets and musicians.

Ram Rai, Guru Har Rai's elder son, had by this time established himself in Dehradun. He had given up all claims of being the Guru of the Sikhs and had become famous as a pious and saintly man and had gained many followers. Dehradun was less than a day's ride from Paonta and when Ram Rai heard that his uncle Guru Gobind was in Paonta, he felt an overwhelming desire to meet him. At first, the memory of the difficulties he had caused for Guru Tegh Bahadur acted as a restraint. But then he sent a message to the Guru, expressing his desire for a meeting and when he received a positive answer he rode out to meet Guru Gobind. The uncle and nephew met on the banks of the Yamuna. There was no trace of bitterness and hostility and when, after many hours, the two parted, it was with mutual affection and respect.

Raja Fateh Shah of Garhwal was, at this time, having problems with some of the other kings, especially with Raja Medini of Nahan. His advisers advised Fateh Shah to go to Paonta to seek the Guru's help and advice. Fateh Shah obtained a promise of safe conduct from the raja of Nahan and arrived at Paonta with many declarations of devotion and friendship. The Guru gave Fateh Shah a patient hearing and then invited King Medini Prakash to come to meet him at Paonta.

He told the raja of Nahan, 'Fateh Shah and Bhim Chand will soon be related through marriage. If you have war with one, you will have war with the other. You will have enemy soldiers on both your borders and they can easily move into your kingdom and force you out. It is far more sensible to talk to your enemy, to sort out your differences and to negotiate a peace.'

The raja of Nahan listened to the Guru and marvelled at the way the young Guru had matured in a few years. He had been little more than a boy when he had first come to Nahan, but now he spoke with all the wisdom and knowledge of a grown-up leader of men. Of course, the Guru was right. He could not afford to have enemy soldiers on two of his borders.

'In poem after poem you tell of courage on the battle-field and praise the use of the sword in heroic acts. Would you now advise me to sheath my sword and seek a solution through a cowardly act of negotiation?' the raja asked.

'Using a sword is not always a heroic act; and not wishing to fight is not always a cowardly act. I have in my poetry praised acts of valour. But I have also said that the sword should be drawn when all other means of resolving a problem have failed.'

'I will do what you advice, Guruji,' the raja said.

Long negotiations followed between the two rajas. In the end, the rajas embraced each other warmly and friendly relations were established between them.

In Sadhaura, a place close to Paonta, lived a Muslim saint, Sayyad Badruddin. Sayyad Badruddin was also known as Budhu Shah and was greatly respected by people of all religions. Budhu Shah and Guru Gobind had grown to respect and love each other. At this time, Aurangzeb disbanded a troop of five hundred Pathan soldiers on a charge of treachery. Amongst these soldiers were great warriors like Hyat Khan and Amir

Khan. This troop of Pathan soldiers came to Sadhaura to seek the saint's help. They pleaded their innocence and asked the saint to help them find employment. The saint was convinced that the charge against the soldiers was untrue and he gave them a letter of recommendation to the Guru. On the basis of this recommendation, the Guru recruited the Pathan soldiers into his army.

One morning, just after the prayers, a messenger arrived from Dehradun. He had ridden through the major part of the night and had then crossed over to Paonta, a few miles upstream, in the early hours of the morning. The Guru knew that he had come from the dera of his nephew Ram Rai.

The news was that saint Ram Rai was dead and his mother, Mata Punjab Kaur, needed help from Guru Gobind.

'Mata Punjab Kaur is afraid that some of the more powerful masands might try to set themselves up as the Guru. She asks you to help her secure the succession for her son,' said the messenger.

'I will help her,' the Guru said.

The Guru rode out at the head of a small group of armed soldiers to Dehradun. There he defeated all opposition to Ram Rai's son, banished the troublesome masands and paid his respects to Mata Punjab Kaur.

While on his solitary walks along the river, his mind turned to other more serious matters as well. He began to consider, with concern, the state of the country and he pondered over his own role as the Guru and what he could do to improve the conditions that existed around him. All through the period of his education, he had read and re-read stories relating to the lives of the nine Gurus before him. He had learnt much from these stories. He had learnt how powerful the path of peace could be. Guru Nanak and his four successors had always followed a peaceful path and under them the new religion had grown from strength to strength. He had read of the martyrdom of Guru Arjan Dev and how Guru Hargobind had taught his followers that they should learn to defend their faith with the sword. Guru Hargobind himself had fought many successful battles against the might of the Mughals. In his young mind, the image of his father's martyrdom was fresh and clear and, like Guru Hargobind, he too was training his followers for battle. Was he right in doing so? The path of the first five Gurus and the path that Guru Hargobind had followed seemed to be in conflict. But by pondering over it again and again, the young Guru Gobind was able to see the unbroken thread and continuity of mission which ran through all that he had read, and everything he had heard of the lives and teachings of the Gurus.

The Guru believed that hatred and the desire for revenge brought out the worst in men; while love and forgiveness bring out the best in us. We must try always to follow the path of love. But once we are attacked and we know that the enemy means to destroy us and our beliefs, we must resist him with all the strength that we can command. The battle is then a battle for the survival, not only of our lives but also our beliefs. It is a battle for righteousness, a *dharmayuddh*.

Guru Gobind, before he left Paonta to return to Anandpur, had worked out his future role as the Guru of the Sikhs, as a leader of his community. He would wage the battle of righteousness; he would uphold right and destroy sin and evil. This is a role he performed to the very end of his life.

Chapter 16

THE BATTLES OF BHANGANI AND NADAUN

The Guru's peaceful days in Paonta came to an abrupt end. Once the fort of Paonta had been built, the Guru attracted Bhim Chand's attention again. Once again the raja of Bilaspur's jealousy was aroused. He was considered the most powerful of the hill rajas and, according to tradition, all the other rajas would come to him to seek his help in settling all their disputes and quarrels. Now the Guru had taken over this role.

The raja sent a carefully worded message to various kings in the neighbouring regions. Why does the Guru need to build up a strong army, he asked the other kings. He went on to say that the answer was obvious; the Guru was going to use it to defeat the rajas, one by one, and take over their kingdoms. Unless they all united to throw him out, the Guru would soon get rid of them. This struck a chord in the rajas' hearts because it echoed their own fears and suspicions of the growing influence of the Guru and the growing strength of the Sikhs.

One of the main reasons why the rajas wanted to throw the Guru out of the area was his influence on the poorer sections of their people. For centuries they had treated the people of the lower castes as their slaves. But now the Guru had taught them that caste was created by man in order to exploit other men. In the eyes of God there was no caste and all men were born equal. He taught those amongst his followers who had been born in the lower castes to stand up for their rights and to be afraid of no one, but God.

The rajas saw in this an undermining of their authority and a reduction in their strength and power, and were quick to respond to Bhim Chand's overtures. They all pledged their support, except Fateh Shah and Medini Prakash, who were both great admirers of the Guru.

Bhim Chand blackmailed Fateh Shah to get his support against the Guru by threatening to break off his son's engagement to his daughter. Fateh Shah had no option but to pledge his support, even though it meant fighting against the Guru, whom he admired above all other men.

Having secured Fateh Shah on his side, Bhim Chand made one final effort to isolate the Guru completely. He sent a secret message to Medini Prakash. In this message he said he knew that the raja of Sirmour could not draw his sword against the Guru as the Guru was his guest. At the same time, Medini Prakash should realize that the hill rajas, including Fateh Shah, were now all on one side. If Medini Prakash fought against them on the Guru's side, he would become their enemy for life; and his children would be the enemies of their children. Medini Prakash knew that this was not an empty threat, because Rajputs never forgave an enemy. Sometimes revenge was taken a hundred years after a wrong had committed. Slowly, King Medini Prakash began to avoid the Guru. Many of the Guru's messages to him went unanswered.

The Guru understood the reason for the cooling off of both of Fateh Shah's affection and Medini Prakash's friendship. He would have wished for them to have had more courage, but he did not blame them.

He knew that when the crisis came, he could not expect help from anyone. So he began to make all the preparations that he could. He had among his followers, one Ram Singh from Banaras, who was a skilled artisan in brass casting. With his help, the Guru designed a canon, which Ram Singh cast for him and before the battle, the Guru was able to train a few of his soldiers in the use of this canon, so that they could fire the canon with a fair degree of accuracy.

Bhim Chand heard of the Guru's preparations and knew that he had to strike at once. A council of the rajas was called, and after much deliberation, a message was sent to the Guru at Paonta asking him to leave the hills and promising him a safe passage if he did so. The Guru replied that he was a guest of the raja of Sirmour. Only Raja Medini Prakash could ask him to leave Sirmour. When he did leave Paonta, it would be to return to his home in Anandpur. His father had bought the land on which Anandpur was built. As such no one had the moral or legal right to ask him to leave Anandpur. If the rajas felt they could evict him by force, they were most welcome to try and do so.

Having sent off the message the Guru knew that there were only a few days left at his disposal. He had made a detailed study of the craft of battle and of different strategies and battle formations. He had practised all that he had studied and knew what movements would be suitable to his men and to the geographical area around Paonta. He knew that the occupation of a strategic position was of prime importance. Quickly and carefully, the Guru made his choice of the battle-ground. He moved his men out of Paonta and positioned them in the area between the Yamuna and the river Giri.

On the day of the battle, when the sun rose, the Guru's men saw the vast army of the rajas that was drawn up against them and some of them felt fear grip their hearts. The first group that gave in to this fear was the Udasis, who had come from Anandpur as the Guru's escort. All of them, except their leader Mahant Kirpal Das, fled from the field even before the battle began.

The second group to desert the Guru was that of the Pathans. They had been offered rich rewards of land and money if they deserted the Guru's army and came over to the side of the rajas. Now, seeing the vast army arrayed against them, the Pathans, forgetting all their promises of devotion and allegiance, gave in to the temptation of this offer and went over to the enemy's side.

He smiled when he heard the news of this desertion. He moved amongst his men, encouraging them, modifying his battle plans and rearranging his positions according to the changing needs.

The Guru's disciple, Syed Budhu Shah who had heard about the impending battle, gathered all the able-bodied men of his dera and armed them with whatever weapons he could lay his hands on. With seven hundred armed men, including his own sons, he rode out to the Guru's assistance as fast as he could. They reached the battlefield well in time to help the Guru. Quickly the saint's soldiers moved to the positions the Guru assigned them. When the Guru's men heard of the new arrivals, they felt a revival of their strength and morale. The news of the Pathans' desertion had travelled back to Paonta and, as the first light broke in the sky, every able-bodied man in Paonta, who could ride or walk, gathered whatever weapons he could lay his hands on and came out to join his Guru. Shortly after the sun rose, the Guru gave the orders for his men to charge towards the much bigger army of the rajas.

It was a short but fiercely fought battle, which the Guru's army won. Guru Gobind has described this engagement in *Bachitar Natak*, a part of the Dasam Granth:

> Angered by the battle, Hari Chand shot his arrows at me. One of them hit my horse. He shot another arrow. God protected me and the arrow only grazed my ear. Then Hari Chand fired his third arrow. This went through the buckle of my waistband. God Himself protected me and though this arrow touched my body, it did not harm me. I was angered by this. I picked up my bow. I began to

rain arrows on the enemy. The enemy fled before this. I took aim and hit Hari Chand. As he collapsed, my brave soldiers rushed forward and destroyed them completely. Those who escaped my soldiers, fled in terror. It was the mercy of God Almighty that gave us victory. I rewarded the deserving soldiers generously. There was rejoicing all around.

The Guru realized that it was now time for him to return to Anandpur. He had left Anandpur because it was felt that he was not yet ready to face an open conflict with Raja Bhim Chand. The victory at Bhangani proved that this situation no longer existed. He had successfully defeated the combined strength of the rajas. He also did not want to stay in Paonta any longer because his presence there had now become an embarrassment for his host. Medini Prakash had been very kind to him and given him help when he had most needed it. The least he could do, in return, was to spare him any awkwardness with his fellow rajas. So, shortly after the battle, the Guru sent an affectionate message to his host; thanking him for all that he had done for the Guru. And then the Guru made a quiet departure for Anandpur.

It was as if without the Guru, Anandpur had become a ghost of its former self. Now with the Guru's return, Anandpur came alive once again. All those who had left the town, now returned to live there again. News of the Guru's success at Bhangani had spread far and wide and more and more people returned to take up residence in Anandpur.

The Guru's victory won him the admiration of Raja Bhim Chand of Bilaspur as well. The raja had to admit that the Guru was a military genius. The Guru's army had been very much smaller than the army of the hill rajas and yet, with his skill in planning battles and his ability to inspire his followers, the Guru had won a resounding victory. The raja admired him for this. He felt that it would be more sensible and practical to have the Guru as his friend rather than as his enemy.

A few months after the Battle of Bhangani, Aurangzeb, who was still in the Deccan sent an urgent message to Mian Khan, the Governor of Jammu, asking him to collect tribute from the hill rajas.

As long as Aurangzeb was in Delhi, the hill rajas had sent their tribute regularly to his court. Now that he had been away in the Deccan for many years, the threat of being attacked by the Mughal army had receded into the background, and no longer appeared real. So many of the kings, including the hill rajas, had stopped paying tribute and, by so doing, had asserted their independence.

Aurangzeb realized that the refusal to pay tribute weakened his position and felt that action needed to be taken to reassert his supremacy. He himself could not come away from the Deccan. Nor could he spare his army. So he wrote to the most powerful Governor in each region asking him to collect the tribute on behalf of the emperor. The implication of the message was clear: those who refused to pay the tribute must be destroyed.

Mian Khan sent messengers to each of the hill rajas asking them to send their tribute to him in Jammu.

Bhim Chand had savoured the freedom from Mughal supremacy and had no desire to return to the state of being a vassal of the emperor, a feeling that was shared by most of the other hill rajas. He also realized that on their own, they did not have the skill to organize their armies into an effective fighting force, a fact that the disastrous battle of Bhangani had proved only too clearly. The only person in the region who could help the rajas was Guru Gobind. He alone could bring their armies together and and knit them into a strong, cohesive fighting force. If he agreed to lead their army, Bhim Chand knew that they could defeat Mian Khan. It was important that the Guru should be won over as quickly as possible. His wazirs agreed that it was more urgent to secure the raja's position as an independent king than to avenge their defeat at Bhangani. It was decided to send an envoy to Guru Gobind asking for his help.

The Guru put all past differences aside and responded at once to the rajas' request because he believed that their cause was just. The hill rajas had been ruling their little kingdoms for centuries and they had a right to rule without interference from the Mughal emperor. He invited Raja Bhim Chand and his queen to visit Anandpur and at the end of the visit, he pledged support to the raja. With the promise of the Guru's support, the rajas all united under one flag and refused to pay tribute to the emperor.

Once again, after careful consideration, the Guru chose the battlefield. The place was Nadaun, twenty miles southeast of Kangra, on the left bank of the Beas. This chosen site would give the allies the greatest advantage in battle.

In the opening moments of the battle, the Mughal army appeared to be extremely strong, almost invincible. Hussain Khan, the Mughal commander, fought with such great courage that it seemed that he would win, and Bhim Chand began to have doubts, and wished to sue for peace.

Then the Guru himself rode into battle. The battle raged on and the Mughal soldiers began to fall back under the fierce attack of the allied soldiers. The next morning, when the allied army took up their position again, they found there was no enemy to oppose them. Great was the joy in the allied army at this splendid victory.

In spite of this great victory, the rajas could not overcome their fear of the Mughals. As part of the victory celebration, they held a council to decide what course of action they should adopt in the future. Many of the rajas felt that their victory would not buy them peace for long because the moment Aurangzeb heard of this defeat, he would send a much bigger and much stronger army against them, an army against which they could not hope to make a stand, and Raja Bhim Chand, who had so vociferously demanded that the rajas should take a stand against the Mughals and thus give them a resounding slap in the face, now rescinded from this stand. He advocated that the rajas should make their peace with the Mughals by paying the tribute that Alif Khan demanded. So the tribute was collected from all the rajas, and one of Bhim Chand's senior ministers was appointed as ambassador to deliver this to Alif Khan in Jammu.

The Guru was disgusted by the Rajas' lack of courage and did not want to have anything more to do with them. He withdrew from the court and from the victory celebrations and returned home to Anandpur.

Chapter 17

THE BIRTH OF THE KHALSA

Aurangzeb was angered both by the kings' initial refusal to pay tribute and by the defeat of the Mughal forces in battle. He was not satisfied by the settlement that had been reached and wanted the defeat avenged, and the kings punished. This was the only way to reassert the authority and supremacy of the Mughals. His son Muazzim, who later became emperor Bahadur Shah I, headed the campaign against the kings. The prince was assisted by General Mirza Beg, a very experienced and able soldier.

Though the prince fought a series of battles against the kings, he left the Guru alone. He realized that when he became emperor, it would be useful to have the support of the ever-increasing number of the Guru's followers, and this support he could easily get by keeping peace with the Guru.

The Guru welcomed this period of peace, but was also aware that the situation was extremely fluid and could change at any time. So he used these intervening years to strengthen his position. He bought the land around Anandpur and built a chain of four strong forts: Anandpur, Keshgarh, Lohgarh, and Fatehgarh. These fortresses safeguarded Anandpur and also gave the Guru control over most of the area between the Sutlej and the Yamuna. The Guru prepared for war in many other ways too. Every evening the Sikhs gathered and listened to inspirational songs which praised the brave acts of soldiers and warriors, who had fought against tyranny and oppression and had given their lives fighting for a right cause. Anandpur took on the ambience of a military cantonment.

During this period of peace, the Guru also continued the spiritual and literary activity that he had started at Paonta. His fifty-two poets wrote beautiful poetry. Some of this great poetry has come down to us. Among the better known works of this period are:

Gur Sobha by Saina Pat which gives details of the Guru's life and stewardship; *Bhagat Ratnavali* by Bhai Mani Singh, who was later executed in Lahore in 1738; and of course the beautiful poems of Bhai Nand Lal, who had once been one of the chief poets at Aurangzeb's court. The poets also translated the Upanishads and other great works of classical literature.

The writings of the Gurus were full of references to the Hindu religious texts and to Hindu mythology and this required an understanding of the Hindu religious texts. For this they required teachers who could teach Sanskrit and the finer points of the Hindu religion. The Guru sent some of his disciples to Pundit Raghu Nath for this purpose, but the pundit refused to accept these Sikhs as his students because they belonged to the low castes.

The Guru realized that he would have to create a group of Sanskrit scholars within the Sikhs and, with this in mind he sent five of his disciples to Banaras. They were Karam Singh, Ganda Singh, Vir Singh, Saina Singh, and Ram Singh. As was the custom among students at that time, they gave up all worldly pleasures and worldly attachments and spent all their time studying Sanskrit literature. On the completion of their studies, when they returned to Anandpur, the Guru gave them the title of 'Nirmala' i.e. the pure ones. They founded a sect which exists even today. Their followers are called Nirmalas, and they do not marry, wear white clothes, and are strict vegetarians. They begin their studies with Sanskrit and the Vedas and then use their knowledge to help people to understand the teachings of the Sikh Gurus.

Harjas, a Khatri from Lahore, who was a very devout follower of the Gurus, came every year to visit the Guru. When the Guru was eleven years old, Harjas approached Mata Gujri and offered his daughter Jeeto's hand, in marriage, to the Guru. Mata Gujri was impressed by Harjas' faith and his humility and accepted the offer. The Guru bowed to his mother's wishes and in 1677, Guru Gobind and Bibi Jeeto were married. Jeeto made an ideal wife for the Guru. But as the years went by, Bibi Jeeto's face sometimes took on a look of sadness and the Guru knew that this was because God had not blessed them with a child. When seven years had gone by, Mata Gujri was sure that Jeeto would never bear a child, and felt that the Guru should marry again. She thought of Sundari, daughter of Ram Saran from Lahore, as a suitable bride. But the Guru initially refused.

Mata Gujri however longed for a grandchild. She knew that no purpose would be served by any further discussion at this point and she held her peace.

That evening, when the Guru returned to his home, it was a strange Jeeto who came to him. She was dressed in very simple clothes and came into his presence with her head bowed. She stood in the doorway, as if waiting for his instructions. 'What is this Jeeto? Why do you behave so strangely?', he asked.

'Tell me, what it is you want. You know you only have to ask and, if it is in my power, it will be yours,' he added.

'It is in your power, my Guru. Give me your promise that you will accept Mata Gujri's proposal,' said Jeeto.

The Guru was stunned and could not find words to express his surprise.

'So be it,' he said. Thus, the Guru got married a second time. Sundari came to Anandpur with all her innocence and her simple child-like heart. From the beginning she turned to Jeeto for everything that troubled her, and the two shared a good relationship. In the same year, Ramu from Rohtas, another devout follower of the Guru, came to see him with a very special request. Ramu had a daughter named Sahib Devan who was deeply religious and led a simple and pious life. She was a follower of the Guru and spent her time in singing his hymns and bringing his teachings to people who had not read or heard of them. She had pledged herself as a bride to Guru Gobind and swore that she would marry no one else. Faced with this problem, Ramu came to see the Guru and begged of him to accept his daughter's hand in marriage. The Guru was polite but firm. He explained that he already had two wives, both of whom he loved dearly, and had no wish to marry again. By doing this he would be doing a great injustice not only to his wives, but also to the girl Sahib Devan, as he could not possibly give her the love and attention that a husband should give to a wife. Ramu said that Sahib Devan would be content even with this; all she wished for was to remain in the Guru's household, and would lay no claim to any conjugal rights.

The Guru did not accept this suggestion. But Ramu and Sahib Devan approached first Mata Gujri, and then Bibi Jeeto and Sundari in turn. To each they repeated their strange request. The ladies were impressed and moved by the girl's great devotion to the Guru and they used their influence and persuaded the Guru to accept Sahib Devan into the household. He agreed on the condition that she would not make any conjugal claims on him.

So Sahib Devan became the Guru's third 'wife'. But she was his wife only in name. She remained a virgin all her life and the marriage is described by historians as the *kuara dola* (literally meaning virgin's palanquin). She was quite happy with this as she wanted only to serve the Guru and his sangat, to be near the Guru and to bring help to those in pain and need.

A year after her marriage, a son was born to Sundari in 1687 and was named Ajit. When Ajit was four years old,

God finally gave Jeeto her first child, in 1691, a boy whom she named Jujhar. Two more sons were born to her: Zorawar in 1696 (or 1697), and Fateh in 1699. But till her death in 1701, Ajit remained her favourite child.

All through his stay in Paonta, and then during these years in Anandpur, the Guru had studied the growth and development of the Sikh religion. He studied not only the teachings of the Gurus but also the entire history of the movement. He compared the Sikh movement as it was when Guru Nanak had started it, with what it had become in his own time. He felt that a great deal of disunity had arisen among the followers, and there was also a decline in the purity and strength of his followers, and in their attitude towards their religion. He thought about this a great deal and finally realized that there were two main reasons for this. One was the functioning of the masands and the other was the disputes that often arose when a new Guru was appointed.

The masands had first been appointed to help the Guru in the task of administration. The Gurus' following had grown so large that administration could no longer be carried out from just one centre by the Guru alone and the masands worked honestly and looked after the welfare of all the Sikhs in their area and helped the poor and the needy. They collected all the offerings that people made to the Guru and brought them to the centre. But over the years, many of the masands became corrupt and began to function independently. They kept a large part of the offerings for themselves and became rich landlords. Some of them even had small private armies.

The death of a Guru had often led to a division among the Sikhs because claimants to the gaddi who did not succeed often set up their own deras and gathered large followings.

Guru Gobind Singh had, before him, the examples of Datu, Prithi Chand, Dhirmal, Meharban (the elder brother of Guru Arjan Dev), and Ram Rai. While at Anandpur, the Guru tried solving these two problems.

He sent out a *hukamnama* and invited all the masands to come to Anandpur. Once they were all there, he announced that the order was being abolished once and for all. He had collected charges against various masands. These charges were read out and the masands were given a chance to explain their actions. Those who were found guilty of corruption and misuse of power were dealt with very severely. In this way the sangat was finally freed from the cruel and tyrannical power of the masands and the people were now directly linked with Anandpur and to their Guru.

The Guru's followers came to him for two reasons. One was to seek help and guidance in questions about religion and about spiritual matters. The other was to seek his advice regarding their day-to-day problems. It had been well established that the Granth contained all the religious and spiritual advice that any Sikh might need and it was only a matter of studying the sacred text carefully and the answer would be found. In their day-to-day lives, the Punjabis had for many generations been taking their problems to the Panchayat. The Guru felt that if the Panchayat could be modified a little it would be able to help his followers the way the Guru had been able to help his followers. So between the Granth and the elected representatives of the community, the panth, the function of the Guru could continue to be performed even in the absence of a living Guru. The Granth would perform the spiritual function, and as such would be the spiritual Guru, while the panth would perform the day-to-day functions and would be the secular Guru. So the Guru decided to end the line of personal Gurus and invest the Guruship in the Granth Sahib. In this way the Guruship would rest in something permanent, something which was sacred and above all dispute. He waited for a suitable moment to announce this decision to his followers.

Guru Gobind realized that Baisakhi would be an ideal day on which he could give new life to the faith. For the festival in 1699 he sent out a hukamnama to his followers very early in the year, asking them to make every effort to be present in Anandpur on Baisakhi day. As Baisakhi drew near, the visitors started pouring in: everyone knew that there was something very special about this Baisakhi. So in addition to the normal excitement and joy, there was also a feeling of expectancy.

On the morning of the main day of the fair, March 30 1699, Guru Gobind rose early as usual. After his prayers and meditation, he returned to his room. When he came again before the huge sangat of more than eighty thousand, he came wearing the clothes he wore when he rode into battle, he came fully armed. He was greeted with great joy and reverence by all his followers. Then they all sat quietly waiting for him to begin his discourse. Instead he got to his feet and drew his sword and the steel flashed in the light of the morning sun.

'This is the moment of truth. You are all my devoted followers. Which of my followers is ready to give up his life for me? I need a head that I can offer in sacrifice,' the Guru asked. The Sikhs were stunned. Never before had a Guru asked his followers to make such a sacrifice.

Finally, Daya Ram, a Khatri from Lahore, responded to the call.

The Guru led him to a tent which had been erected nearby. The sangat sat in silence. They heard the swish of the Guru's sword as it flashed through the air and then the thud of a head falling to the ground. The Guru returned; his sword covered with blood and his eyes flashing with a strange excitement.

'I need another head,' he said in the same thundering voice. This time, Dharam Das, a Jat from Hastinapur came forward.

Once more the Guru led his Sikh into the tent. Once more the sangat heard the swish of the sword. Some people were so frightened that they fled. Some went to Mata Gujri and begged her to stop her son in this seeming madness.

Three more times the Guru repeated his call and three more times brave and faithful Sikhs rose to answer the call. They were Mohkam Chand of Dwarka, Himmat of Jagannath, and Sahib Chand of Bidar. With each sacrifice, more and more of the congregation fled. They had come to celebrate the festival of Baisakhi and now their Guru was 'butchering' them in the most cruel and blood-thirsty manner. It was best to leave Anandpur and return to their homes before any harm came to them.

A few minutes after the fifth sacrifice, the Guru returned from the tent with the five Sikhs behind him, now dressed in beautiful new robes. For a moment the sangat could not understand what had happened. The Guru had been testing his disciples. Each time they had seen the fresh blood on the Guru's sword, it had been the blood of a sacrificial goat. Each time they had heard the sound of a falling head, it had been the head of a goat falling to the ground.

The Guru introduced his five faithful followers as 'Panj Pyare' or the Five Beloved Ones. He said that by offering themselves up for sacrifice, the five had passed the final test. He said that these five would form the heart of the Khalsa – the new order that he was going to start.

The Guru now took a bowl of steel in which he put pure clean water and stirred the water with his double-edged dagger. By a fortunate coincidence, at this precise moment, Mata Sahib Devan came to the Guru with a container of *batashas* or sugar crystals, as an offering.

Sahib Devan put the batashas into the bowl, and the Guru stirred the water with his dagger till they were dissolved. While he was doing this, the Guru recited hymns both from the Granth Sahib and of his own composition. Then he baptized the five Sikhs by pouring the holy water or amrit onto their palms. After this, he asked them to drink in turn from a common bowl to emphasize that there was no distinction of caste between them.

By drinking the amrit, the Guru explained, the five had experienced a rebirth. They had left behind their previous family ties and now belonged to the family of the Guru. They had also left behind their previous professions which had given them their place in society. They were now all soldiers of the Guru – equal in rank, status, and occupation. They had left behind their earlier beliefs and rituals. Their father was Guru Gobind and their mother Sahib Devan and their birth-place was Anandpur. They had made a complete break with the past and made a new beginning.

The choice of the number five has a special significance. It is the same number as the number of members of the Panchayat and the Guru himself has said:

'Where there are five, there am I; Where the five meet, they are the holiest of the holy.'

The five were given the same powers as the Guru and by through this, the Guru had taken the first step in abolishing the tradition of a living Guru.

The five Guru-Sikhs were to wear five symbols of purity. These became the symbols of the Khalsa. They were *kesh* – uncut hair and untrimmed beards; *kara* – a steel bracelet; *kangha* – a small comb; *kachha* – short, breeches-like underwear; and *kirpan* – a sword. The Guru at the time of the birth of the Khalsa explained the importance of the five symbols. But there is no complete record of this speech and this has led to many different interpretations as to the meaning of these symbols. When we try to explain these symbols, we must remember that the Guru's idea of a true Khalsa was of one who was both a saint and a soldier. Long hair in India has always been associated with saintliness. It can safely be assumed that all the Gurus from Nanak onwards wore long hair and all of them (with the obvious exception of Guru Har Krishan) had untrimmed beards. Many of the Guru's followers must also have let their hair grow long, so when Guru Gobind asked his followers to keep long hair and beards, they at once understood the significance of this. By keeping long hair and beards, they were promising that they would lead good and virtuous lives. The kangha or the comb was to make sure that the long hair was kept neat and clean. This was to emphasize the difference between the Khalsa and the Jatta Sadhus. The Jatta Sadhus kept long hair but they never combed it – they allowed it to grow thick and matted as a symbol of their renunciation of the world. The Khalsa would keep long hair but keep it neatly combed to emphasize that, though they were pledged to lead saintly lives, they had not renounced the world.

The kara and the kirpan both emphasized the martial nature of the Khalsa. The Khalsa was a soldier who would raise his sword to fight for right and defend the weak and the helpless. The kara was a thick steel bangle worn on the right wrist which gave strength to the wrist while flourishing a sword and protection against the enemy's weapon. The steel itself was a symbol of strength. The kachha was a symbol of cleanliness and hygiene, and also a symbol of restraint in sex.

The Guru then introduced a new greeting '*Waheguru ji da Khalsa, Waheguru ji di-fateh* – The Khalsa are the chosen ones of God, victory be to our God'.

The Guru now stood before the Khalsa with folded hands and asked them to give him amrit the way he had given them the amrit. The Khalsa and the sangat were stunned by this request. 'You are our Guru, our guide. How can we give amrit to you?' they asked.

'In my new order there is no high and no low,' the Guru said. 'There is complete equality among men, even among the Guru and his disciples.' On being given the amrit the Guru was also given the surname 'Singh' and he became Guru Gobind Singh.

After this, the Guru turned and spoke to the sangat. 'You must all follow one set of beliefs and get rid of all differences of religion. The four Hindu castes must forget all their differences and mix freely with each other. All men are equal and no man should think that he is superior or better than others. Let men of the four castes be baptized, eat from the same dishes and feel no contempt for each other.'

He told the sangat that the path of the Khalsa was not an easy one: it was a path of faith and sacrifice and strict self-discipline. He invited those of the sangat who were ready to follow this difficult path to come forward and be baptized and thousands of the Sikhs came forward and were baptized.

The news-writer of the Mughal court was present in Anandpur and he sent a detailed report to the emperor in which he says:

'He has abolished caste and custom, old rituals, beliefs and superstitions. He has brought his followers together in one brotherhood. All men will be equal and no one will be superior or inferior to another. Men of all castes have been made to eat from the same bowl. Some orthodox men said they would never accept a religion which was opposed to the teaching of the Vedas and the Shastras. They would not renounce, at the bidding of a boy, their ancient faith which had come to them from their ancestors. But twenty thousand men and women have taken the baptism on the first day. They promised to obey him because they had the fullest faith in his divine mission.'

Chapter 18

SPARROWS MEET HAWKS

The famous baptism ceremony in Anandpur had far-reaching effects. The twenty thousand people, who were baptized on that single day, went back to their villages and towns and told of the new energy that the Guru had brought to the Sikh religion; and those who heard these reports, were inspired to seek baptism as well.

The Guru had said at Anandpur that wherever five baptized Sikhs met, he would be present. So groups of five Sikhs went all over the north and baptized many thousands more. The Guru gained many new followers and the Sikh faith once more became vibrant and strong.

At one stage, the Guru had written to the kings from the hilly regions, inviting them to join the new order. He had hoped that through this, the people of North India would be united as one large family of brave and strong soldiers, who would then be able to put up a joint defence against their common enemy, the Mughals.

But the kings from the hills were jealous and suspicious not only of the Mughals, but of the Guru, and of each other as well. Even at this critical juncture, when the Mughals had reduced them to petty chieftains, they could not overcome their differences and come together for a common cause.

When the kings received the Guru's invitation, they sent back a message in which they said, 'Each Turk can eat a whole goat. How can we, who eat only rice, cope with such strong men? Can sparrows kill hawks?'

In this message the kings showed a lack of self-confidence and a lack of faith in the Guru's abilities to create a strong force. The Guru took up this challenge when he received the Rajas' reply. He replied that he would 'train the sparrow to hunt the hawks, and one man to fight an army.' And this is exactly what the Guru did.

There were thousands and thousands of turbaned, bearded soldiers, fully armed; each of them well-skilled in the use of arms, well-versed in the art of battle; each one of them ready to lay down his life at the Guru's command. Everywhere they went they showed a spirit of faith, confidence, and optimism. They believed wholeheartedly in the Guru's injunction that 'The Khalsa shall rule. Their enemies will be scattered, only they that seek refuge will be saved.'

Guru Gobind Singh had transformed the religious centre his father had built, into a strong military base. The Guru himself was not only a spiritual guide, but also a skilled military leader. The kings from the hills observed this change, first with wonder and then with fear.

This hostility on part of the kings was to lead to four battles with the Guru, in all of which the Guru was victorious.

The first of these battles was a minor engagement.

Two of the rajas, Alim Chand and Ballia Chand, attacked the Guru's camp while he was out hunting. Their strategy was to attack the Guru while he had the least number of soldiers with him, and when he was least expecting the attack. The manoeuvre was to be secret and swift and to be directed against the Guru's person. The combined forces of the two kings far out-numbered the Guru's men. Yet the Sikhs fought with great courage and determination. Balia Chand was killed by one of the Guru's arrows. There was fierce fighting, which lasted many hours, during which Alim Chand lost one arm and fled from the battle. Seeing this, his soldiers realized that they had lost the battle and fled from the battlefield.

This incident added further strength to the growing fears of the kings. The Sikhs had been far outnumbered, yet they had succeeded in defeating the combined forces of the two rajas. They were convinced that the Guru should be crushed once and for all and this conviction led to the second battle. The kings sent an appeal to the subedar of Delhi:

> Knowing that Guru Gobind was a successor of the holy Guru Nanak, we made no objection to his residence amongst us. When he obtained power, we tried to restrain him. He went to Nahan and formed an alliance with the raja. He then came into collision with Raja Fateh Shah of Srinagar, which led to the battle of Bhangani, where there was destruction of human life. After his return to Anandpur, the Guru established a new sect as distinct from the Hindus and Mohammedans, to which he has given the name of Khalsa. He has united the four castes into one and made many followers. He invited us to join him and promised if we converted then we would obtain an empire in this world, and salvation in the next. He suggested to us that if we rose in rebellion against the emperor, he would assist us with all his forces, because the emperor had killed his father and he desired to avenge his death. As we did not think proper to oppose the emperor, the Guru is displeased with us and now gives us every form of annoyance. We cannot restrain him and have accordingly come to crave the protection of this just government against him. If the government considers us its subject, we pray for its assistance to expel the Guru from Anandpur. Should you delay to punish or restrain him, his next expedition will be against the capital of your empire.*

---

*Max Arthur Macauliffe, The Sikh Religion, Clarendon Press, Oxford, UK, 1909.

When the Mughal soldiers reached Ropar, they found the kings and their armies waiting to meet them. Reports of the approaching army had reached the Guru well in time. A large number of Sikhs had collected in Anandpur and the Guru had time to organize them and to plan his strategy for the battle. He decided not to wait for the enemy to come to him in Anandpur.

The Guru's Panj Pyare, who had shown such great courage in being the first to be baptized, were the commanders of the five divisions of the Guru's army. The battle was joined. The Mughal Commanders had been sure of an early victory because they felt that their men were better trained and were more skilled than the Sikhs. The Sikhs, though fewer in number, fought with great courage and determination and, in the fierce battle that followed, the Mughal soldiers began to falter. When it was certain that the battle had turned against the Mughals, their general, Painda Khan, called for a temporary truce and rode out to parley with the Guru.

'Guru of the Sikhs, I have many brave and famous soldiers in my army just as you have many brave and famous soldiers in yours. It would be a pity that they should lose their lives when there is a simpler way to resolve our conflict. Let you and I meet in single combat. As Allah is witness, let the better man win and let our armies abide by the outcome of this encounter,' said Painda Khan.

The Guru smiled and said, 'So be it, let the better man win and let our armies abide by the outcome of this challenge.'

The generals retreated to the prescribed distance. Painda Khan took careful aim and shot his first arrow. It whizzed past the Guru's head, narrowly missing his turban. He drew his bow a second time and took aim even more carefully. This time too he missed.

The Guru had been looking at his enemy very carefully and had observed that Painda Khan was covered in steel armour from head to foot. The only part of his body that was left uncovered was his ear. So when Painda Khan's second arrow missed him, the Guru immediately picked up his bow and took careful aim. His arrow shot through the air and pierced Painda Khan's ear and, in the blinking of an eye, the great Mughal general fell dead from his horse. Breaking all the rules and customs of battle, the Mughal army refused to honour the outcome of the duel, and shouting loud war-cries and calling for vengeance, they charged at the Sikhs, under the command of Din Begh.

The anger of the Pathan soldiers was great and they fought with even greater courage than before. But the Sikhs stood their ground firmly and met them blow for blow.

The kings from the hills felt that in spite of the fierce battle that was still being fought, the tide seemed to be turning in favour of the Sikhs. They decided not to commit their armies to the battle, and suffer unnecessary losses, and calling them back, they left the battlefield. This desertion weakened the morale of the Mughal soldiers. Din Begh fought very bravely and tried to hold the Mughal soldiers together. Then he got seriously wounded and could not continue to fight any longer.

He gave the call for retreat and the Mughal soldiers fled from the battlefield. The Sikh soldiers wanted to chase the fleeing army but the Guru held them back.

'They are fugitives and are weak and helpless. It is not right to chase them any further. It is enough that you have all fought with great courage and been so firm in your stand. Let us pray and offer our gratitude to our Maker for giving us this splendid victory,' the Guru said.

There is a temple at Khizrabad (in Mohali), which recalls this great victory of the Guru's Sikhs. This great victory of the Guru however did not bring him lasting peace. The kings were now even more determined that the Guru should be pushed out from Anandpur as soon as possible. Once again a meeting was called, and this time almost all the kings from the hilly regions attended the meeting.

They now decided to make a direct appeal to the emperor and wanted to send Ajmer Chand on this mission to ensure that the emperor saw how important it was to destroy the Guru's power as quickly as possible. This suggestion was opposed by Raja Bhup Chand of Handur. He felt that they should not depend upon the Mughals any longer and should combine their strengths and make a determined all-out effort to defeat the Guru.

Bhup Chand spoke with such courage and conviction that his arguments won the day. This led to the third battle against the Guru. It was decided that they must mount another attack against Anandpur, and this attack must be made with the greatest speed possible. The Rajas of Jammu, Nurpur, Mandi, Kulu, Keonthal, Chamba, Srinagar, and Dadhwal moved their armies as quickly as possible to a place close to Anandpur where they were joined by the forces of the local rajas. The Raja of Bilaspur, Ajmer Chand, was given overall charge of the combined forces and he sent a message to the Guru.

The message by Ajmer Chand said, 'You have been in illegal occupation of land that belonged to our father, and now belongs to us. We have tolerated your presence as your father was a saint and you are a successor of Nanak. But now we cannot allow this state of affairs to continue. You are given two choices: You must abandon Anandpur and move out of our territory; or if you choose to live on in Anandpur, you must recognize our ownership of this land and pay us rent for its use. If you fail to follow either of these alternatives, we will have no choice but to use force to evict you.'

The Guru received the messenger with all due courtesy and sent back a polite but firm message. He said that the land in question was freehold and had been bought by his father against payment in cash. As such, it had become his father's property, and thus, by the laws of inheritance, his property. There could be no question of payment of rent – a man did not pay rent in order to live in his own house. If they tried to force any decision on him, he would meet them with force, and answer blow for blow. He desired only to live in peace, and if the rajas put aside their pride and came to him in peace, they could take from him whatever they wanted. The Guru's house was open to all.

The rajas had come with the intention of destroying the Guru and they were not prepared to acknowledge that what the Guru said was reasonable. Many of the Guru's Sikhs had, after the last battle, gone to visit their families. But as news of the impending battle spread, they hurried back. The Sikh army was also helped by the arrival in Anandpur, of five hundred soldiers from Majha. Sher Singh and Nahar Singh were put in charge of the fort of Lohgarh, while Ude Singh was entrusted with the defence of Fatehgarh. Ajit Singh, the Guru's eldest son, now fourteen years old, was given the command of a company.

The armies of the hill rajas formed a cordon around Anandpur and laid siege, which lasted many days. The Sikhs, in small groups, would ride out at night and and carry away the enemy camp's supplies. Ajit conducted many of these raids. His acts of courage and fearlessness soon became common topics of conversation amongst the inhabitants of Anandpur. From time to time, the rajas too attacked what they felt were weak points in the fortification. But they were always pushed back and they were not able to break through.

When months had passed with little success, some of the senior rajas advised that they should make their peace with the Guru. 'There is no dishonour in making your peace with the house of Nanak,' the Raja of Mandi advised. 'All things said and done, the Guru is a man of God, a holy man, and there is no shame in coming to terms with him. I am sure he will give us terms that do not bring us dishonour. Far better an honourable peace now than a disgraceful defeat later,' he added.

His advice was supported by a few of the other senior rajas who had begun to feel that they could not win against the Guru. But, by and large, the rajas listened to the Raja of Mandi in sullen silence and it was clear that in spite of the failure of their efforts, they were not willing to negotiate for peaceful resolution.

However, at last the hopelessness of their attempt began to stare the rajas in the face. But before they abandoned their attack, they made one desperate effort to batter down the great gate of the Lohgarh fort. They got hold of a huge elephant and covered him in thick steel. Then the elephant was fed a very heavy dose of intoxicant to ensure that he would feel no fear or pain. The elephant was set on a ramp leading to the great gate and the rajas' armies formed up behind him. Meeting little opposition, the elephant battered at the gate and, for a while, it seemed that this scheme might meet with success. Guru Gobind Singh sent one of his bravest Sikhs, Bachittar Singh, son of Bhai Mani Singh, to deal with the elephant. Bachittar thrust at the elephant with his spear, and with the very first thrust pierced the steel plate and injured it in the head. It was a deep injury and the poor animal felt the pain in spite of the large dose of intoxicant he had been given. It turned and fled. The soldiers, massed up behind it, ready to storm the fort once the gate had been broken down, did not have a chance to turn around and flee and many of them were trampled to death.

The Guru's army came out into the open and fell upon their enemy. Both sides suffered heavy losses. But the army of the rajas had lost many of its important leaders and generals. Among them were Raja Kesri Chand of Jamwal, Jagatullah the great leader of the Gujjar and Ranghar tribes, Raja Chamund Chand of Kangra and Raja Bhup Chand of Handur – who had played a very important part in the battle – were both seriously injured. Without these leaders to lead them, the allied army was crippled and at last the Rajas, accepting the bitter truth of their defeat, lifted the siege and fled from Anandpur to safety.

All the rajas, except the Raja of Bilaspur, were content to lie low in their own states and to lick their wounds. The Raja of Bilaspur, who had been the commander of the allied forces, took this setback as a personal insult and was determined to avenge this defeat. He tried to approach some of the other rajas individually and in secret. From a few of them he received taunts about his poor leadership, from the others, extremely lukewarm support. He realized that if he was to join issue with the Guru, he could not expect any help from his former allies, the hill rajas.

But he was not put off by this. He had made up his mind and was quite determined that he must make a fresh attack on the Guru as soon as possible. If the rajas were not willing to help him, he would turn to another source for help. He approached the Faujdars of Sirhind and Lahore, and was pleasantly surprised to receive positive replies from both of them.

The combined forces of the two Faujdars and the Raja of Bilaspur marched on Anandpur. This was to be the fourth battle against the Guru.

The Guru had learnt a very valuable lesson from the last siege. Anandpur was very well fortified but it could stand up to a siege only if they had been able to stock up a sufficient supply of food. In the last siege, they had been saved by the supplies that Ajit Singh and his band of brave soldiers had looted from the enemy camp. But this was not a very dependable source of supply. If the enemy had continued the siege for a longer period of time, the Sikhs could have been in serious trouble. Now, when the Guru heard of the fresh forces marching towards Anandpur, he realized that there had not been enough time to prepare for a fresh siege, and they did not have enough supplies to last them for more than a month or two. So the Guru, with his usual skill, decided not to meet the enemy at Anandpur. Instead he took up position at Nirmoh, a small village near Kiratpur. A quick fierce battle took place and both the armies fought with great courage. To begin with, it seemed the allies would win but the Guru's forces held their own, and finally broke through the cordon and the allies were thrown back. They made one last effort to hold the Guru by trying to throw a fresh cordon around his army. But this effort too was defeated. The Faujdars of Sirhind and Lahore called off the battle and beat a retreat.

The Guru now moved to Basali (in Ropar), and sought refuge with the raja, who was his friend and who had often invited him to come and visit him. The Guru now appeared at his gates, tired and weary after the series of battles and the raja was happy to give him refuge.

Even though all his earlier efforts had failed, the young Raja of Bilaspur was still not ready to accept defeat. He called his men and followed the Guru to Basali and made a desperate last-ditch effort by leading an attack against the Guru. The Guru led his tired soldiers out against Raja Ajmer Chand. Once they marched on to the battlefield, all their exhaustion and their injuries were forgotten. They fell upon the raja's men and inflicted heavy losses. The king's forces fled in the face of this fierce fighting.

The Guru returned to Anandpur and was blessed with a short period peace which gave him some breathing time to prepare for the second phase of his military struggle.

Chapter 19

VICHORA – THE SEPARATION

Raja Ajmer Chand now realized that he could not prevail against the Guru, and felt it was better to be on friendly terms with him rather than to have him as an enemy. He wrote to the Guru asking for peace and in order to establish cordial relations between them, and suggested that the Guru should accept his ambassador at Anandpur. Guru Gobind Singh did not trust Ajmer Chand, and was sure that the so-called ambassador would be a spy. Yet he accepted the raja's offer because he knew that, as the victor in the recent battle, it would be ungracious of him to refuse an offer of peace from the loser.

The other kings too followed Ajmer Chand's example and made overtures of friendship, to which the Guru readily responded.

Peace seemed to have returned to the area and the kings and the Guru appeared to be on friendly terms. But in his heart the Guru knew that this was a prelude to more trouble. He began to prepare for this even before the dust had settled on the battlefield after his last battle.

The first thing he did was to strengthen Anandpur. Till now Anandpur had used the steep hill terrain, on which it stood, as a natural fortification. Now the Guru built a strong wall around the town, and Anandpur became a fort in the real sense of the word. The forts of Keshgarh and Lohgarh were repaired and made stronger and stocked with food supplies and ammunition that could last many months. Smithies were set up and weapons of all kinds began to be manufactured by the hundreds.

He knew that the excitement that all these preparations generated would breed an eagerness for war and the desire to strike the first blow. So in all his sermons to his followers, he preached again and again the teachings of the Gurus from Guru Nanak down to Guru Tegh Bahadur. He explained to them that Sikhs were men of peace. Their task was to serve the sangat and to work for the uplift of the weak and the suffering. Fighting was not their primary occupation and so they must never seek war. All the battles that they had fought were battles that were not of their making, but had been forced upon them. They had fought these battles not to win lands or to bring fame to the Sikh community but in self-defence. They had fought to defend their right to live their lives according to their beliefs and be able to continue to serve humanity. If someone tried to take this right away from them they should be ready to fight again to the last drop of blood. Once they had gained victory, they must turn again to what was their real aim in life: to live a life of peace, doing useful deeds for their fellow men.

There used to be an annual fair at Rawalsar, near Mandi (now in Himachal Pradesh), which was very popular and which was attended by almost all the hill people. Most of the hill rajas, their queens, their families and courtiers also attended this fair. The Guru was invited to come to this fair by the rajas, and he felt that this would be the ideal chance to convince them that he did not wish to encroach on their land or to threaten their security. So he accepted this invitation and the Guru and his family and a band of faithful Sikhs reached Rawalsar, where they set up camp like the other rajas.

Many of the kings and queens were impressed by the Guru, and were convinced that he was a deeply religious man; and that he was honest and sincere when he said that they should all live in peace and friendship. Princess Padma, who belonged to the family of the Guru's old friend Medini Prakash of Nahan, who was an ardent devotee of the Guru, had come to the fair with the express purpose of warning him of a conspiracy that was being planned against him. She had overheard a private conversation between Raja Ajmer Chand, who had come on a surprise visit to Nahan, and the Raja of Nahan.

Now at the fair in Rawalsar, Padma sought on opportunity to warn the Guru of the rajas' perfidy.

Late one night, when everyone in the Sirmaur camp was asleep, Padma, disguised as a poor old woman, stole out of her camp, dodged the sentries and made her way to the Guru's camp, and was able to warn the Guru against the conspiracy. The Guru thanked her and made sure that she got safely back to her camp.

The Guru returned to Anandpur as quickly as possible to prepare for the battle which was being thrust upon him.

While the rajas waited for the Mughal army to reach Anandpur, they fought two battles with the Guru. In the first, they depended on the two Mughal generals, Sayyad Beg and Alif Khan to lead them to victory. Sayyad Beg was so impressed by all that he saw and heard of the Guru, that he became a disciple Guru and fought on the Guru's side. The combined forces of Alif Khan and the hill rajas were again defeated. In the second engagement, the hill rajas combined their armies and attacked the Guru at a time when the Guru had only eight hundred men with him. This time too the rajas' combined forces were defeated.

Sayyad Beg looked forward to pitting his wits against a worthy enemy. He had heard about the Guru, heard about the Sikhs. Now he cast his mind back and pieces of information that he had gathered over the years, came back to his mind and from these, he built up a picture of his opponent. All the reports he had heard had said that the Guru was very handsome, strongly built, with clear bright eyes. They talked of his famous blue horse which ran with the speed of the wind and of the white hawk he always carried on his wrist. Then there were reports of his love for hunting and the tigers he had killed in single combat, with his sword. It was the picture of a brave fearless man, skilled in the use of weapons, with an almost limitless stamina.

He had also heard reports of the Guru's kindness and compassion and of the help that he always gave to the weak and the oppressed. He had heard of his teaching and once he had even heard a beautiful hymn that the Sikhs sang and been moved by its beauty.

He had never heard of another man who was both a religious leader and a warrior. He was very keen to meet this man face to face, look into his eyes and try to understand how anyone could be both these things – a saint and a soldier – at once.

There was another reason why Sayyad Beg was looking forward to this expedition to the North. He had been away in the Deccan for so long that he had lost touch with all his family and friends. He missed them all but he missed most of all, his sister Nasiran. She was older than him and, as a child; he had got from her, not only the love and friendship of a sister, but also the care and protection of a mother. Then his sister had married the holy man Pir Badruddin, who was called Budhu Shah, and gone to live with him at Sadaura. They had met from time to time, but as the years went past, these meetings became rarer and rarer. Now, because of his involvement with the emperor's wars in the Deccan, it had been many years since he had met her. He had heard reports that she was now a widow; that she had lost her sons in war and his heart had longed to be with her, but he was helpless.

He planned his march in so that his army rode close to his sister's home. He gave his soldiers a much needed rest in the camp they had set up. Then handing over responsibility to his deputy Ramzan Khan, he went to visit his sister. He had hoped to give his sister a surprise but a large army like his, could not move in secret and news had already come to her of the Mughal army that was moving to Anandpur under the command of her brother Sayyad Beg. She was sure in her heart that he would find a way to come to see her before he marched into battle. This meeting was of the greatest importance to her. She had not met him for so many years and wanted to know everything that had happened to him during this time. She had missed her 'little brother', missed all the love that they had shared, and now she waited eagerly to be with him again. But this meeting was important to her for another reason. Like her late husband, the pir, Nasiran too had become a great admirer of the Guru and her life was filled with her love for the Guru and in following the Guru's teachings. She was proud that her husband and her sons had given their lives for the Guru and, if the need ever arose, she knew that she too would gladly give up her own life for him. And here was her brother, leading a mighty Mughal army against her Guru. She knew that her brother was a loyal and devoted soldier of the Mughal emperor, and believed that his duty was to fight against the Guru and to defeat him. For this he would give his life. Yet, Nasiran also knew that, futile as it seemed, she must try everything to persuade her brother from embarking on this venture.

Sayyad Beg found his sister waiting for him and for a long moment they stood silently, just looking at each other, the feelings between them so strong that they needed no words.

Later she said, 'I cannot give you either my prayers or my blessings. My prayers are with the Guru; and with every fibre of my body, every last particle of my soul, I pray for his success, it cannot be otherwise. If you love me, my brother, you will give up this venture. Tell your emperor that you cannot lead his army, he has generals enough and he will find someone else to lead his soldiers.'

'If I do this, I can only be one of two things, a coward who is afraid of the Guru's strength, or a traitor who will not obey his emperor's commands. What would you have me be? Sayyad Beg asked his sister.

'I don't know. All that I know is that every arrow you aim at the Guru or at his men will be an arrow aimed at my heart. Every time you raise your sword, it will be raised to strike off my head,' she replied. Then she got up quickly and went into her room, locking the door behind her. Then she unrolled her prayer-mat and prayed to the powers-that-be to step in and resolve the difficult situation that they had created.

Finally, the battle started. On one side was the combined army of the Mughals and the hill rajas and on the other side was the small Sikh army. 'Remember, in the end it is not your weapons or the number of your soldiers that will lead you to victory – it is what is in your hearts,' the Guru told his men.

The fighting raged furiously. Through the smoke and dust of battle Sayyad Khan at last saw the Guru. He was indeed a handsome figure. He rode on his famous blue horse (called the *neela ghoda* popularly) moving from group to group of his soldiers giving them courage and strength with his words. All around him there was a rain of arrows and musket shots and he rode through it all as if he did not notice it. Sayyad Beg's heart filled with adoration for this remarkable man. He was everything that he had heard him to be and more. Then he checked his thoughts. He was his enemy and it was not right that he should think such thoughts of his enemy; it would weaken him. He thought of his duty, he thought of what the emperor had said to him at their last meeting. He raised his bow and aimed an arrow at the Guru. But as he aimed, Nasiran's words came back to him. 'Everytime you aim an arrow at the Guru, you will aim it at my heart,' and when the arrow at last left the bow, it went wide off its mark. This troubled him. He could not remember when he had last missed his target. His fame as a marksman had spread far and wide, for in battle after battle he had never failed to hit his target. He was angry with his sister for making him so weak. He would show her that he was still a man, still a great marksman. He pulled out his musket and loading it, took careful aim at the Guru. He would get him now and the whole thing would be over and done with and he could return to his wife and children. But when he had steadied his musket and taken careful aim, he saw in the sights, not the Guru but his sister, Nasiran, and she smiled at him, almost as if she was mocking him. He fired and again his aim was wide off the mark and he knew, at last, that this was one battle he would not win.

The Guru rode out to him, and, when he was within ear-shot, he called out to him and said, 'You are a great and famous general and I have all respect for you. You have shot at me twice but for some strange reason your weapons have not found their mark. You are famous for your marksmanship. What made you miss your target? Was the distance too great? I am before you now. Pull out your sword and perhaps your sword will be able to do what your bow and your musket have not been able to do.'

Sayyad Beg looked closely at the Guru. He saw the Guru smiling gently at him and knew, at last, why his sister followed this great man. The Guru waited and, along with him, all the soldiers who had heard the Guru's challenge waited. But instead of drawing his sword, Sayyad dismounted from his horse, walked up to the Guru and put his cheek against the Guru's stirrup. The Guru too dismounted and, drawing Sayyad into an embrace, gave him his blessings. Sayyad remounted to his horse. Without a word, without a backward glance, he rode away from the battlefield. Seeing this, his soldiers lost heart and also retreated from the battlefield.

Sayyad Beg gave up his leadership of the Mughal army and retired into the hills to meditate. It is said that when the Guru went to the Deccan, Sayyad Beg was amongst the band of followers who went with him.

In a little while, the allied army had regrouped. This time it was led by Wazir Khan, the Governor of Sirhind. Wazir Khan had already been defeated by the Guru in battle and was seeking revenge. Since he had lived long in Sirhind, which is close to Anandpur, he knew of the strengths and weaknesses of the forts which the Guru had built. The Governor of Lahore had also come out to join him with a very large force.

In the winter of 1705, the large allied army marched towards Anandpur. The Guru's army came out to meet the advancing enemy and a heroic battle was fought, in which both sides suffered heavy losses. The Guru realized that the enemy's number was so great that the Sikhs, in spite of all their courage, could not defeat them in open battle.

So he gave orders that the Sikhs should withdraw into Anandpur. Keshgarh was placed in the charge of his son Ajit Singh and Lohgarh was given to Nahar Singh and Sher Singh to defend. Seeing that the Sikh forces had withdrawn into Anandpur, the allied forces laid siege to the town. Wazir Khan had learnt from his earlier defeat. He decided to put a cordon of soldiers around Anandpur and keep anyone from either entering or leaving the town. He made no effort to break through the walls. Slowly he tightened the siege. Following Wazir Khan's instructions, the hill rajas also realized that they should not think of an immediate victory. They should wait patiently. They must make sure that no entered or exited from Anandpur, and then victory would be theirs.

The days stretched into weeks and the weeks into months. The food stock ran so low that wheat began to be sold for one rupee per ser, and even this was not always available. At the beginning, bands of brave Sikh soldiers rode out at night and captured food and supplies from the enemy camp, which helped to ease the food shortage. Then the allied forces became more vigilant. Most of the Sikh soldiers who rode out were killed and the quantity of food they brought back was so small that it did not lessen the suffering of the people. The Guru decided to abandon these attempts.

The people of Anandpur suffered greatly, specially the children and the old people. The Guru was pained by this suffering but he knew it was a price that had to be paid if the Sikhs were to keep their freedom. People ate whatever they could get hold of – grass, the leaves of trees and even the bark of the trees after it had been ground into a powder. And yet the siege went on.

The allied soldiers began to get impatient. They had nothing to keep them occupied. They had come ready for battle and now they had been turned into little more than guards. It seemed to them that they would not be able to force the Guru out, even after years of waiting.

There was a small mountain stream, gurgling and singing as it made its way down the hills. This stream flowed through Anandpur bringing to the Sikhs, not only its very special music but also the life-giving force of its fresh, sweet water.

In fact, it was this mountain stream which was the main reason why Guru Tegh Bahadur had built his centre here. The people of Anandpur had got so used to its presence that they had come to take it for granted. Now, when the siege of Anandpur had lasted for many months, those inhabitants of the town who had been able to sleep that particular night, woke to a strange silence, the absence of a familiar sound. For a little while they could not say what it was. But their instinct told them that something was terribly wrong. At last they realized that they could no longer hear the music of their stream. The people poured out to the banks of the stream and what they saw, filled their hearts with dread. There was no longer any water in the stream, it had been diverted. And they knew, without asking, that this was a fresh blow struck by the enemy. It was in fact, the latest move that Wazir Khan had made in tightening his siege of the town.

The condition of the people became truly pitiable. First the animals began to die of hunger and thirst and the Guru lost his favourite horses and then the famous elephant Prasadi. Everywhere people lay sick or dying and yet the Guru refused to give up. Some of the Sikhs began openly to talk of giving up the fort and even went to Mata Gujri and begged her to plead with her son.

It was at this point in the siege that a messenger arrived at the gates of Anandpur. He carried the sign of peace and the Guru gave orders that he should be allowed to enter the fort. He was a special messenger from the emperor Aurangzeb, and had brought a message signed by the emperor himself. The emperor praised the Guru and the Sikhs for their great courage and bravery and went on to say that he knew of the difficulties being faced by the Sikhs of Anandpur. He knew that there must be great suffering inside the fort without food and water and invited the Guru to leave Anandpur. He gave a personal surety that the Guru, his family and his Sikhs would be given safe passage from the town. Some of the Sikh leaders felt that the emperor's offer should be accepted. But the Guru was not yet ready to give up his beloved Anandpur, and the siege continued.

However, forty Sikhs formed a group and asked the Guru for permission to leave the fort. 'You will have to give me in writing that you are giving up your Guru: that from hence forth you will have nothing more to do with me. Then you can go,' the Guru said. This was a difficult thing for the Sikhs to do. Neither could they bear the hardships of living in Anandpur, nor could they leave their Guru, whom they loved so much. Then they thought that if they wrote this disclaimer, the Guru would let them go, and, with their departure, he might reconsider his decision not to leave the fort. So they signed a disclaimer and the Guru permitted them to leave.

It made the Guru sad to see them go because it was the first sign of the weakening of the resolve of his people – but he was not one to hold them by force. When the Mughals saw the band of forty Sikhs riding out of the fort under the white flag of surrender, they recognized it as the beginning of the end. They knew that their long wait would soon be over. All doubts vanished and they renewed the siege with greater vigour.

For a little while longer, the brave band of people tried to hold on in the fort. But the misery of the people increased with every passing hour. People were maddened by their suffering and the number of the dead and dying increased tremendously. The Guru could not bear the scenes that he saw when he went out into the streets. At last, he gave in to the pleading of his mother and his advisers, and decided to leave Anandpur. Before he left, he destroyed and burnt what was left of the town so that the enemy would not be able to use it as a stronghold. Then, on the night of December 5 1705, the Guru left his beloved city. The first party was made up of his mother, his wives, his two young sons and all the women and children, the sick and the wounded. Before he mounted his horse to leave Anandpur for the last time, the Guru made one final visit to the little shrine that he had built in memory of his father. He stood there in silence, his eyes closed, and his lips moving in silent prayer. All the wonderful memories of his great father passed through his mind one by one He placed the shrine in the care of Gurbaksh, a member of the Udasi sect, and then rode out with the Panj Pyare, his two elder sons, and what remained of his forces.

As he rode away, the Guru reined in his horse and turned to look, one last time, at the town. He could see the tall towers looming as shadows against the sky. This town had been his home for thirty years and most of what he had achieved had been here in this town. He wondered if he would ever return, if that golden period would ever be given back to him and to his Sikhs. Then he turned and rode away, never to look back again.

The two groups of Sikhs joined up on the banks of the river Sarsa. While the Guru was thinking of the best way to cross the river, the Mughal forces broke their promise and attacked the retreating Sikhs from behind. Ude Chand, one of Panj Pyare, collected a brave band of soldiers and turned to hold the Mughal forces, to give a chance to the rest of the party to cross the river. There had been heavy winter rains up in the hills and the stream was swollen. The river waters roared in anger as they raged against the banks that contained them. On this winter night, the waters were cold. But the Guru and his group had no choice. The only other choice was to face the attacking army and certain death. So while Ude Chand held the enemy back, the Guru made an uncertain crossing. The mules carrying his precious books and manuscripts were all swept away by the strong current. The Guru's party too was broken up as they came out of the stream on the opposite bank. The Guru's wives, Mata Sundari and Mata Sahib Devan, found themselves separated from the Guru. There was great danger all around and they were persuaded by a faithful Sikh, to go to his house in Delhi, where they could live in safety till they were able to rejoin the Guru.

Mata Gujri and her two younger grandsons, Zorawar Singh, and Fateh Singh, were washed out of the waters further downstream and found themselves separated from the rest of the party. But Mata Gujri felt they had nothing to fear. They had with them some money hidden in Mata Gujri's saddle bag and even more important, they had with them Gangu, a Brahmin cook who had worked long years in the Guru's household. Gangu offered to take them to the safety of his village, an offer which they readily accepted.

The Guru, when he got across the river, found that he had only forty soldiers left with him. These included his two elder sons Ajit Singh and Jujhar Singh.

Though the survivors did not know of it at the time, many of the party had been swept away in the icy cold water. It was also much later that they learnt of Ude Singh's death. He had died fighting, given up his life so that others would have a chance to live.

The Guru decided to take a fresh stand. He and his brave band of forty soldiers galloped as fast as they could to the little fortress of Chamkaur, near Ropar. They took up positions inside the stockade and, in the little time that was given to them, did everything they could to strengthen the defences. The attack was not long in coming. A detachment of the Mughal army had come in hot pursuit and this was joined by fresh troops, which had been sent out from Delhi. This force was also joined by the local Ranghars and Gujjars, who were looking for a chance to avenge their earlier defeat.

Now began the story of what must surely be one of the greatest acts of courage and sacrifice in the annals of history. Those inside the fort could see the enemy all around them, like the waves of an angry sea. Yet they remained unafraid. Their Guru had decided to make a stand and they would gladly give their lives to carry out his wishes.

The Guru and a few other brave warriors rained arrows on the enemy. Since they were shooting from a vantage point they were able to keep the enemy soldiers at bay. In the meantime, the other soldiers rode out, one small band at a time, and engaged the enemy in close-quarter battles. Death was certain. But it was the only way that they could inflict the greatest number of losses on the enemy forces. The enemy realized that the defenders were very few in numbers and there was no hope of any reinforcements coming to their help and was content not to attack the little fort. When the second brave band of soldiers had been killed, Ajit Singh and Jujhar Singh, the Guru's elder sons, asked for permission to ride out and face the enemy. Ajit was seventeen years old at the time and Jujhar, only fourteen. The Guru gave his permission and blessed them both. With them was Alam Singh, who had made a name for himself as a brave warrior. From the upper storey of the fortress, the Guru watched his sons engage the enemy soldiers and fight with the skill of experienced soldiers, determined that their deeds should make their father proud of them. They killed many enemy soldiers before they themselves were killed. The Guru, who had remained so calm and strong when he heard of his father's death, remained calm and strong when he saw his sons being killed too. He said a short prayer for them, and then turned again to the defence of the fortress.

The Mughal soldiers now realized that they were paying a very heavy price in terms of loss of life and decided to storm the little fortress. One group of Mughal soldiers, led by Nahar Khan, tried to climb up the wall of the fort but he was shot down by an arrow and the others fell back.

The battle was waged through the day without any sign of letting up till the Guru's force was reduced to five. Among those who died were Mukham Singh and Himmat Singh, two of the Panj Pyare.

The five surviving Sikhs decided that the Guru's life must be saved at all costs. The panth was passing through a difficult phase, and only the Guru could give it the leadership that was needed for its survival. They passed a resolution, a *Gurmata*, to say that the Guru must leave Chamkaur and seek refuge in a place of safety. The Guru had, at the birth of the Khalsa, declared that the word of five faithful Sikhs was the word of the Guru. Thus, much against his will, the Guru had to bow to the resolution.

Two Sikhs, Sant Singh and Sangat Singh, rode out to fight the enemy. Sant Singh had dressed up in the Guru's clothes and even wore the Guru's kalgi in his turban. The enemy soldiers were taken in by this deception and all attention was focused on Sant Singh. Taking advantage of this situation, the Guru, accompanied by Man Singh and the two surviving members of the Panj Pyare – Daya Singh and Dharam Singh – slipped out of Chamkaur.

The Guru and his followers tried to cover as much distance as they could and get as far away from Chamkaur as possible. Finally, tired and footsore, they came to the forest of Machiwara between Ropar and Ludhiana. Here they rested for a while. It is said that it was here that the Guru composed one of the few poems that he wrote in Punjabi, the beautiful, hymn – *Mitar pyare noo haal muridan da kahna.*

One of the Guru's Sikhs saw a detachment of Mughal soldiers camped outside the forest and realized that it was not safe for the Guru to remain in the forest any longer. They found refuge in the house of a Sikh named Gulaba. By now the Mughal soldiers had realized their mistake and knew that Sant Singh, whom they had killed, was not the Guru. They also knew that the Guru had escaped, and began to search for him. Reports of this search were brought to Gulaba, but he felt that the Guru was quite safe in his house and no one would find him there. The Guru, however, did not want to stay in Gulaba's house any longer as he did not want to endanger Gulaba's life.

By a happy coincidence, the Guru was visited by the Pathans, Ghani Khan and Nabi Khan. They were both horse-traders, who had often brought horses for Guru Gobind Singh in Anandpur, and had learnt to respect him and love him. Now they had heard that the Mughal forces were chasing the Guru and he was hiding somewhere near the forest of Machiwara and they came to look for him and to offer him their services. The Guru was happy to see his old friends again and their arrival and their offer of help, in these trying conditions, must have brought him no small measure of comfort.

The two Pathans found Mughal soldiers everywhere. They realized that in spite of the great love that the local people had for the Guru and their intense desire to protect him; it was only a matter of time before his whereabouts were discovered by the enemy. It was imperative to move the Guru to a safer place as quickly as possible. But to do this they would have to break through the cordon of enemy soldiers, and the only way this could be done was to disguise the Guru. But when they sought to buy the means with which they could affect this disguise, they found that the Mughal soldiers checked each purchase that was made and questioned everything that aroused the slightest suspicion. If, while making their purchase, they aroused the soldiers' suspicion, their plan would fail even before they had begun to put it into operation. They would have to try and get what they needed from some of the Guru's well-wishers.

When they were returning to Gulaba's house, they glanced through the open door of the neighbour's house and saw a middle-aged woman sitting at a loom, weaving a piece of fine cotton cloth. The two Pathans looked at each other and smiled: They had found what they were looking for. They stopped at the door and greeted the woman and found out that she was a follower of the Guru. When they told her of the grave danger that the Guru was in, and how they could not find any means to disguise him and bring him out of the forest, she readily offered the cloth she was weaving for the disguise.'

Her devotion to her Guru, her awareness of the danger he was in, gave her mind a sharpness that she had never before possessed. She gave the Pathans some food to eat, as she wove her plans and, almost immediately after the meal, put them into action. The only dye that was available was a deep blue dye – the blue that is the honoured colour of most Muslim saints. So the dye was mixed in an earthen pot, the cloth was dyed, dried and then cut and stitched into a robe.

So it was that the Guru was dressed in the robes of a saint, put into a palanquin and carried by the palanquin bearers – his three faithful Sikhs, and Ghani Khan, out of Gulaba's village. The doors of the palanquin had been veiled by thick curtains to guard them against curious eyes. Whenever they were stopped and asked as to who was in the palanquin, the palanquin bearers would reply '*Uch da pir*' – or the holy man from Uch. Uch, thirty-eight miles from Bahawalpur, was famous for its many Muslim saints or pirs. The moment the Muslims heard the name, they fell on their knees and asked for the Pir's blessings.

The small group stopped for a few days in the village of Hehar. Kirpal Das, the head of the Udasis, who had fought so bravely for the Guru in the battle of Bhangani, lived here. He welcomed the Guru and his companions. The Guru said goodbye to his two Pathan friends, and in recognition of their courage and all the difficulties they had faced to help him, he gave them a certificate in which he praised them and thanked them for all that they had done for him even at the risk to their own lives. This certificate or hukamnama is still in the custody of the descendants of the Pathans. Sikhs, even today, visit the Pathans' descendants to get a glimpse of this hukamnama and express their gratitude to members of the family which helped their Guru when he needed help the most.

After a few days, the Guru noticed that Kirpal Das was behaving in a strange way. It did not take him long to understand what was on the mahant's mind. He realized that this was not the Kirpal Das he had once known. Now Kirpal Das was the head of a rich dera and was used to a luxurious life. He was worried about the repercussions if the Mughal authorities discovered that he had given shelter to their enemy. To spare the mahant any possible trouble, the Guru decided to move on. He came, at last, to Jatpura where he was received by Rai Kalha, the Muslim chief. Rai Kalha welcomed him to his home and treated him with great respect and affection. The Guru was tired after all the travelling, but his spirit was still strong and full of hope. This strength remained even after he heard the news of the terrible death that his two younger sons had suffered.

Mata Gujri and her two younger grandsons, Zorawar, aged nine, and Fateh Singh, aged seven, had been brought by the cook, Gangu, to his village in Sahar. To begin with, he looked after them well. Then he noticed that there were three things that Mata Gujri never let out of her sight, her two grandsons and her saddle bag. He was sure that the saddle bag contained something extremely valuable. One night, while Mata Gujri and her grandsons were asleep, Gangu came quietly into the room and stole the saddle bag. He was thrilled to see that the bag contained a large quantity of gold coins. In the morning Mata Gujri saw that her bag was missing. It contained all the money that she had and, with it gone, she would now have to depend on the charity of others.

She questioned Gangu about the missing saddle bag. On being questioned, Gangu left the room and went down the street shouting at the top of his voice.

'Look at these people from the Guru's household. I did everything in my power to help his mother and his two young sons and see what I get in return: I am accused of stealing their gold,' he said. In this way the villagers learnt that Gangu's guests were the Guru's mother and his two young sons and this news was carried to the village headman. The headman knew that he would get a generous reward if he brought this news to the officials. Mata Gujri and her two grandsons were apprehended and brought before Wazir Khan, the Governor of Sirhind, who locked them up in a tower in the fort of Sirhind. It is said that Nawaz Sher Mohammad Khan, the Nawab of Malerkotla, appealed to Wazir Khan to spare the young lives.

It seems that for a while, Wazir Khan was inclined to listen to the Nawab's advice. But then another nobleman intervened and said, 'Do not forget they are Gobind Singh's sons. When they grow up they will be like their father and will cause much trouble for us. It is far better to kill them now.'

Wazir Khan ordered that the two boys be brought before

him. When the messenger came to fetch them, Mata Gujri feared the worst. She held them close to her heart and would not let them go. Zorawar, the elder of the two, felt his grandmother's frail thin body trembling with fear as she held him close. He kissed her and said, 'Do not be afraid, Mataji. The worst that they can do to us is to put us to death.' For a moment it was as if her young Gobind was speaking to her. She was proud that the little boys had already learnt to be so much like their father. She wiped the tears from her eyes, blessed her grandsons and let them go.

The two young boys entered the governor's presence without a sign of fear in their bearing or on their faces.

Suchanand, one of Wazir Khan's ministers, asked them, 'Have you no manners? You have come into the great Subedar's presence and you do not bow before him.'

'We have been taught, from an early age, to bow only before God and before the Guru,' Zorawar answered in a quiet but firm voice.

Wazir Khan was hoping to work out a compromise. If he could convert the boys to Islam he would not have to put them to death and he would not be guilty of violating the tenets of humanity and of Islam. If he was able to persuade them to convert to Islam he knew that he would also win the unqualified approval of the emperor.

'Your courage and your confidence have won the admiration and praise of all. There can be no doubt that you will grow up to be fine young men and that a great future awaits you, first here with me in Sirhind and later in the emperor's court. All you have to do to ensure this future is to accept Islam and become Muslims,' said Wazir Khan.

The two boys looked at each other. Then Zorawar turned back to Wazir Khan.

His voice was louder now and it was clear that he was attempting to control his temper. 'We are the grandsons of Guru Tegh Bahadur who gave up his life to protect the right of the Kashmiri pundits to practice their faith. The blood of Guru Arjan Dev, Guru Hargobind and Guru Gobind Singh runs in our veins. Like our grandfather, we will give up our lives to protect the right to practice our faith,' he said. Wazir Khan ordered that the boys be taken back to the fort. Over the next few days, he tried every trick he could think of to persuade the boys to change their religion. He offered them all kinds of rewards and inducements, but, young as they were, the boys remained implacable in their resolve.

Wazir Khan now knew that the boys would not change their minds. The qazi suggested that the boys be bricked up alive. When the wall reached their chests, Wazir Khan asked the masons to stop, and said to the boys. There is still time. Even now, if you agree to become Muslims your lives will be spared.' The boys looked at one another again and smiled. Then they looked back at Wazir Khan and shook their heads in the negative. Wazir Khan then signalled to the masons to complete their work and the boys were dead. This terrible crime was committed on 27 December 1704. Part of this wall still stands in the Gurudwara at Fatehgarh Sahib. Three days later, Mata Gujri died of a broken heart.

News of this tragedy was brought to Guru Gobind Singh while he was at Jatpura. The Guru's cup of grief was now full to the brim, but he took this tragic happening in his stride, and remained calm and strong. He was always a source of strength to his followers and inspired them to remain calm and brave and not to waver in their faith.

Chapter 20

THE FINAL YEARS

From Jatpura the Guru moved on to Dina, a village near Nabha in Patiala. As the news of the Guru's presence in Dina spread through the Punjab, his followers flocked to the village. The murder of the Guru's young sons was being talked about all over Punjab and had angered the Sikhs, and they were determined to avenge this terrible crime. They came, armed with whatever weapons they could lay their hands on, and offered their services to the Guru. The core of the new army was provided by three brothers, Shamira, Lakhmira, and Takht Mal.

When Wazir Khan heard reports of this new gathering of the Sikhs, he sent a message to Shamira to surrender the Guru to him, failing which Shamira himself would be killed. Shamira wrote back to say that he was ready to give up his life in his Guru's defence. Wazir Khan now began to prepare for battle.

The Guru heard of Wazir Khan's preparations. He had been welcomed by the people of Dina with open arms and had been given both great love and great loyalty by them. He did not wish to turn their home into a battlefield and so he moved on to Kotkapura near Bhatinda. Here too large numbers of Sikhs came to offer their services to the Guru. During this time, he was able to bring together all the Sikhs who had been scattered after the evacuation of Anandpur. In addition, many non-Sikhs were influenced by the Guru and his teachings, by his great courage and composure in the face of such intense suffering, and had become his followers. After a while, the Guru moved on from Kotkapura. It was during this time that he made peace with the descendants of Prithi Chand, the eldest brother of Guru Arjan Dev. Baba Kaul, the direct descendant of Prithi Chand, who lived in Dhilwan in Kapurthala, received Guru Gobind Singh with affection and gave him new robes. The Guru finally discarded the blue robes that he had worn to help him to escape from Gulaba's house. These tattered robes were taken up by a group of Nihangs (also called Akalis, are an armed Sikh order); and it is from them that the blue dress of the Nihangs came into being. Baba Kaul's grandson took amrit and so this branch of the descendants of the fourth Guru was brought back into the mainstream.

When the Guru reached Khidrana, the forty Sikhs who had abandoned him in Anandpur, came back to fight by his side. They had been consumed by feelings of guilt and shame ever since they had deserted the Guru and did not have the courage to offer their services to the Guru again. It was the woman warrior, Mai Bhago, who convinced them that the Guru would forgive them and led them back to the Guru.

The enemy was approaching. The Guru placed a small band of Sikhs in the grove of trees around the water tank and asked them to spread sheets and coverlets over the trees so that from a distance it seemed that the Guru's army was camping here. The Guru and his main army took up position on a hill nearly a mile away.

Wazir Khan and his army drew near and stopped a little way away from the water tank. Seeing what looked like tents, Wazir Khan was sure that the Guru himself was camped amongst the trees. He exhorted his men to give of their best in this final battle of their war against the 'infidel'.

A fierce battle followed. The Guru and his soldiers rained arrows and spears on Wazir Khan's army. The Mughal soldiers were confused because they had not expected an attack from this quarter. The small band of forty Sikhs in the forest, fought with great courage because they were determined to show the Guru that they were not cowards and to wipe away the memory of what they had done at Anandpur.

The Mughal force suffered great losses because they did not know how to cope with the Guru's attack from the hill. At the end, overwhelmed by thirst and exhaustion, they retreated from the battlefield.

There was great rejoicing amongst the Guru's soldiers, but when they came down to the tank they were greeted with dead silence. As they rode among the trees, they found that every single member of that band of brave soldiers had been killed.

The Guru found Mai Bhago, the leader of these Sikhs, severely wounded but still alive. She was carried back to the camp and her wounds were tended to: She was the sole survivor of the Khidrana Sikhs.

The Guru said a special prayer for the forty martyrs and blessed them as the Chalis Mukte or the Forty Immortals. They are remembered by all Sikhs in the *ardas* that is said at the conclusion of all Sikh religious ceremonies. Khidrana came to be known as Muktsar, or the 'pool of salvation', in memory of the *muktas* and every year a big fair is held in Muktsar to commemorate not only this battle, but also the redemption of the forty Sikhs.

The Guru spent a year travelling around Muktsar. This region is the Malwa region and the inhabitants are mostly Jats – simple, hardworking and straight-forward people, people who revel in the freedom of both of thought and action. They found the Guru's teachings to be simple and practical and that they gave freedom to people who had been bound for centuries by caste and by ceremonies and rituals. As a result many of the people from this region joined this new faith.

The Guru camped in Lakhi jungle, a forest between the towns of Bhatinda and Kotkapura, for a while, and then moved on to Talwandi Sabo, where he was greeted with great warmth by Bhai Dalla, the landlord. Dalla extended all hospitality to the Guru and made the Guru and his followers welcome to his home, and the Guru decided to stay for some time in Talwandi. Talwandi soon came to be known as Damdama Sahib, (or 'the breathing space'), and the Guru was visited by a large number of followers who brought him gifts, mainly of horses and weapons. New followers continued to join the Khalsa in ever-increasing numbers and Dalla himself was baptized.

Damdama also became the centre of great literary and cultural activity. Many of the poets and musicians, who had been with the Guru at Paonta and Anandpur, came here and joined the Guru and it seemed that the spirit of Anandpur had now come to abide in Damdama.

It was at Damdama that Mata Sundari and Mata Sahib Devan rejoined the Guru. They had been, all this time in Delhi and when their host was sure that the troubled times were over, he escorted them from Delhi to Damdama. The two ladies were overcome with grief when they heard of the loss of their four sons. But the Guru consoled them. 'Look around you,' he said, indicating the thousands of Sikhs who lived in Damdama. 'You have thousands of sons still alive. Do not mourn for what you have lost. Instead, rejoice at what still remains to you,' he added.

From Damdama, the Guru wrote a long letter to Aurangzeb who was still in the Deccan. He told the emperor the story of his flight from Anandpur and how he was attacked by the Mughal forces from behind. He accused the emperor of betrayal as the emperor had promised him safe passage if he left Anandpur. He also described, in the letter, the cruelty of Wazir Khan towards his younger sons, which was an act against the teachings of Islam. This letter was carried to Aurangzeb by Daya Singh and Dharam Singh.

Guru Gobind Singh's stay in Damdama was marked by the fortunate arrival of Bhai Mani Singh, a great scholar and a childhood friend of the Guru. The Granth compiled by Guru Arjan Dev had been copied over and over again but these copies were not always rechecked against the original Granth. As a result many mistakes and discrepancies had come into these copies and there was great need for making a new, authorized copy of the Granth, which would be free of all these mistakes. The Guru asked Bhai Mani Singh to undertake this task.

Months were spent in copying the Granth and correcting all the mistakes. The Guru also added 115 hymns composed by his father Guru Tegh Bahadur to the original text compiled by Guru Arjan Dev. He did not include any of his own compositions, however.

The Guru wrote many poems while he was in Damdama. These poems along with much of his earlier work were compiled by Bhai Mani Singh into another granth called the Dasam Granth, or Dasven Padsah ka Granth. Most of the works included in the Dasam Granth were written in Anandpur. The Dasam Granth is a compilation of eighteen works, among them Bichitar Natak, Chandi di Var, Shabad Hazare, Zafarnama, and Japji Sahib. They are written in four languages – Braj Bhasha, Hindi, Persian, and Punjabi. They contain stories from Hindu mythology, poems which are religious in nature and are used in Sikh religious ceremonies. Some works are philosophical in nature. There are also some works like the Bichitar Natak and the Zafarnama which are autobiographical and tell us about the Guru's life and personality, and about the times he lived in.

Bhai Mani Singh took nine years to complete this work, which he undertook after the Guru's death. There are many versions of the Dasam Granth in existence but the one written in Bhai Mani Singh's own handwriting is the one that is generally recognized as authentic.

The work on the new version of the Granth and the Guru's own poetic work inspired all the other scholars and writers in his group. There was great literary activity and Damdama soon came to be known as Guru ki Kashi. For a long time after the Guru's death, Damdama continued to live up to this title and there was a very strong and distinct tradition of scholarship, specially related to Sikh studies. Teachers and scholars from Damdama were regarded with special respect and copies of the Granth which had been written in Damdama, were much sought after.

Looking back now, the literary achievements in Damdama seem almost miraculous because Guru Gobind Singh's stay in Damdama was no longer than a few months. In a few short months, men who were known mainly for their skills in battle, for their courage in the face of the enemy, had set up a centre of learning and literary activity. Damdama is thus a measure of the extent to which the Guru was able to inspire his followers.

The day of the Baisakhi festival came around while the Guru was at Damdama. From Guru Amar Das' time, Baisakhi had become the most important festival for the Sikhs and Guru Gobind Singh had added a special dimension by making it the day of the birth of the Khalsa. The past year had seen resurgence in the Sikh faith, the number of devotees had increased manifold and the devotion of the Khalsa to their Guru and to their faith had grown from strength to strength. After having fought a series of fierce battles, the Sikhs at last had peace. They gave expression to all this in the fervour and joy with which they celebrated their festival. Thousands of people thronged to Damdama and the fields around the town became one big fair-ground. Since then, the celebration of Baisakhi at Damdama has become a very important occasion for the Sikhs.

Aurangzeb was still in the Deccan, in Ahmednagar. He was now ninety years old and had become frail and was so ill that he was largely confined to bed. With his age and his long illness, his mind had begun to wander.

His son, Azam, was with him in the Deccan and took care of his father. Azam was an ambitious man and hoped to be the next emperor. He knew that his brothers Muazzim and Kam Baksh nurtured a similar ambition. By keeping the news of the emperor's illness and of his impending death a secret, Azam would keep the power in his own hands. When the emperor did, finally, die, his brothers would be totally unprepared; he would declare himself emperor and strengthen his position even before the news of the emperor's death could reach his brothers. Because of this, Aurangzeb was kept under very strict guard and only his very close relatives and attendants were allowed to meet him. All other communications with the emperor had to be made through Azam.

When Daya Singh and Dharam Singh reached the emperor's court, they were asked to hand over the Guru's letter to Azam. This they refused to do. They said that their Guru's instructions were to deliver the letter to the emperor personally. The two Sikhs waited patiently and came each day to the court and requested to see the emperor and each day, this request was turned down. The days rolled into months and at last, when it seemed that they would never be admitted into Aurangzeb's presence, they sent a message to the Guru explaining their predicament. He wrote back to advise them that they should stay on in the court till such time as they were able to meet the emperor. The Guru also wrote to some very influential Sikhs in Ahmednagar asking them to use their good offices in the court to get permission for Daya Singh and Dharam Singh to meet the emperor. One of these Sikhs knew an official, Manzar Khan, from the emperor's court whom he requested to put in a word with the emperor so that the Guru's messengers would be able to deliver the letter personally. The official waited for the right moment to speak to the emperor.

The opportunity the official had been waiting for at last presented itself.

Suddenly the emperor's eyes flew open. His bony hand searched out and caught the official's wrist in a vice-like grip.

'Tell me, why doesn't anyone come to see me?' asked Aurangzeb.

'You are sick, my lord. You need all the rest that you can get. This is why Prince Azam has forbidden any visitors from coming in to you. It is out of consideration for you,' the official replied.

'Consideration for me or consideration for himself? Has he already set himself up as the emperor? Or is this merely a way of keeping my sickness from his brothers?' Aurangzeb asked.

The official realized that at this moment the emperor's mind was as lucid and clear as it had ever been. He realized that this was the oppurtunity that he had been waiting for and he seized it without a moment's hesitation and said, 'If it is the lack of visitors that troubles you, your majesty, this can be remedied immediately. You have two visitors outside who have been waiting for three months for an audience with you.'

The two Sikhs, who had been waiting for so long, were finally admitted to the emperor's presence. Manzar Khan read the Guru's letter in his deep baritone voice, 'Hail Aurangzeb, emperor of Hindustan. King of Kings, expert swordsman and rider, Aurangzeb you are handsome and intelligent. You have proved that not only are you skilled in battle but also a clever administrator. You are generous to people who follow your religion and firm in crushing your enemies. You have given away much land and wealth. Your generosity is great and in battle you are as firm as the Pole Star. You are the king of kings and ornament of the thrones of the World.'

The letter further read, 'You are the monarch of the world, but religion remains far away from you. He who respects his religion never breaks his promise. I have no faith in your promises. Anyone who respects your oath will be a ruined man. You made God your witness and gave me a promise. Yet you broke this promise. This means that you do not know God and believe not in Muhammad. If the Prophet was present in this world, I would make it my special mission to tell him of your treachery. Because you are not a man of God, your Governors and officers are not men of God. They deny Mohammad, everyday they go against the teachings of Islam. They violate the basic rules which have made Islam one of the greatest religions of the world. What Wazir Khan did to my children is common knowledge, every one knows of this. Was this in keeping with the teaching of Islam? And yet he remains unpunished. He rules as the Governor of Sirhind and is marked for special favour by you. Perhaps he did what he did at your command...'

'No, no,' the emperor said. His voice was shrill and loud and his entire frame shook with emotion. 'I swear I had no knowledge of this terrible deed. I swear I was not party to it. Believe me Gobind Singh. I know not who I am, where I shall go and what will happen to this sinner full of sins. My years have gone by profitless. God has been in my heart but my darkened eyes have recognized not His light. I have greatly sinned and know not what torment awaits me in the Hereafter. But believe me Gobind Singh, sinner as I am, that is one sin that I am not guilty of – I did not kill your sons, I did not kill your sons,' Aurangzeb added. His body shook with sobs but no tears flowed in his eyes to give him relief. Many of his listeners wept, even the Sikhs were touched by the old man's remorse.

But the emperor had not finished yet. He asked his scribe Manzar Khan to write a letter to Munim Khan, his wazir in Delhi.

'Tell him that we are very impressed by Gobind Singh's honesty and courage, by his deep and abiding faith in God, and his justice. Tell him that henceforth, all friendliness is to be shown to Gobind Singh and to his Sikhs. He must invite Gobind Singh to Delhi. Here he must convey to him our royal *firman,* inviting him to come to us here in the Deccan. Instruct Munim Khan to give him as much money as may be needed for his expenses and also to give him a royal escort so that all will know he comes as our cherished guest. Muhammad Beg, you will personally carry this letter and see that it is delivered to our Wazir. Now go,' he said waving impatiently to all those around him.

They bowed to the ailing emperor and stepped away from his chamber, the two Sikhs amongst them. They were happy that their mission had been accomplished. Mohammad Beg, the emperor's trusted macebearer, left for Delhi with the emperor's letter, and shortly afterwards Daya Singh and Dharam Singh also set out to bring the good news of the emperor's change of heart to their Guru.

However, the Guru had no idea of the two Sikhs' success at the court. At Damdama, the Guru waited for news from his two disciples. He felt that he himself must go to the Deccan. Once having taken his decision, the Guru wasted no time in carrying it out.

Dalla Singh and the other Sikhs made every effort to dissuade the Guru but, at last, they knew that they could not hold their Guru in Damdama any longer. They bowed their heads in grief and accepted the Guru's decision to leave.

The Guru knew that the journey would be difficult. He was also not sure of what awaited him once he reached Ahmednagar. So he decided to spare Mata Sundari and Mata Sahib Devan the difficulties of the journey and the uncertainty of the future. He decided that the ladies would go back to Delhi, where they would remain, till it was safe for them to join him.

Mata Sundari went about making preparations for the departure with self-confidence and authority. She carried her grief at her impending separation from the Guru with quiet dignity.

Mata Sahib Devan stood on the fringe of the crowd to catch one last glimpse of her lord as he rode away. As the Guru turned to mount his horse, he caught sight of her and hesitated. Once again she had merged herself with the crowd. She knew that she might not see him again for a long time and yet she had made no deliberate effort to come into his presence. She had remained as self-effacing as always; content merely to be under the same roof as her Guru. The Guru raised his foot to the stirrup and found that he could not go away like this; he had to acknowledge her presence, acknowledge all that she had done. He freed his foot from the stirrup and brought it down to the ground again and turned to her.

'You wait on the fringe of the crowd to see me go. Yet you make no effort to come and meet me, to say goodbye. You know that is your right,' the Guru said.

'No my Lord. That is not my right. It never was. I gave up that right in order to marry you and I have never desired it, never needed it. It was enough for me to know that you were there,' replied Sahib Devan.

'Don't you ever feel cheated; feel that your husband has been able to give you so little compared to what other husbands give their wives?' asked the Guru.

'It is enough that you should question this. In the flush of your generosity you forget how much you have given me. Till the end of time whenever a Khalsa receives *amrit* and you are named as his father, I will be remembered as his mother. You have made me immortal, you have made our relationship immortal, and you have made my motherhood immortal. Can any wife be given more; can any wife ask for more?' Saheb Devan replied.

There was nothing more to say. The Guru placed his hand

on Sahib Devan's head and blessed her. Then he turned and mounted his horse and rode out of Damdama.

The Guru was accompanied by a small band of selected Sikhs. He had forbidden all others from accompanying him. The Guru rode through Rajasthan and camped at a place called Bhangaur. It was here that he was met by Daya Singh, who was returning from Ahmednagar. Daya Singh gave the Guru details of his meeting with Aurangzeb and of the emperor's orders to the Wazir of Delhi. Shortly afterwards, came the news of the emperor's death.

Almost at once, a war of succession broke out. Prince Azam lost no time in declaring himself the emperor and began to make preparation for the battle that he knew he would have to fight with his brothers and marched towards Delhi.

Muazzim, the eldest son, was away in Afghanistan, leading a campaign. When news of his father's death reached him, he too marched back immediately towards Delhi. Both brothers knew that whoever gained control in Delhi would strengthen his claims to the throne. Bhai Nand Lal, who had at one time been Muazzim's secretary and close friend, wrote to him, advising him to seek the Guru's help in his fight against his brother. The Guru was near Delhi when he received Muazzim's appeal.

Muazzim was the eldest son of the emperor and the throne was rightfully his. When he had come to the Punjab to subdue the hill rajas, he had carefully maintained his peace with the Guru and this had given the Guru twelve valuable years in which to prepare his army. Muazzim was influenced by the teachings of the Sufi saints and was not only liberal-minded but also tolerant of other religions. The Guru decided to help Muazzim.

A detachment of Sikh soldiers, under the command of Dharam Singh, was sent to assist Muazzim. The two brothers faced each other at Jajau near Agra, on 8 June 1707 and a fierce battle raged for three days in which Azam was defeated and killed. Muazzim became the emperor and took the title of Bahadur Shah I, and sent a special messenger to the Guru to convey the news of his victory and also to thank him for his help.

The Guru set out to visit the holy cities of Mathura and Brindaban after this. While he was camping in a garden outside Agra, the emperor heard of his arrival and sent a special invitation to the Guru to visit him.

It was a very warm and cordial meeting. The emperor showed a lot of affection and respect for the Guru and thanked him for accepting his invitation and for his timely help in the battle of Jajau. Cordial relations were established and the emperor requested for another meeting. When they parted, the emperor gave the Guru many expensive presents, including a kalgi, a jewelled dagger, and a robe of honour.

The Guru felt that this was the beginning of a new chapter in the relationship between the Mughals and the Sikhs and was hopeful, that under the liberal Bahadur Shah, the Sikhs would, once again be allowed to live in peace. With this hope, the Guru stayed on in the area and met the emperor a number of times. He hoped that some positive agreement would be reached between him and the emperor before he returned to the Punjab.

But news came that Bahadur Shah's youngest brother Kam Baksh had risen in rebellion against the emperor, and the emperor left for the Deccan to suppress this rebellion. He invited the Guru to accompany him. The invitation was accepted by the Guru.

Their subsequent meetings, however, did not fulfill the promise that the earlier meetings had held out. The emperor talked vaguely of liberalism and tolerance but was not prepared to make any concrete promises and the Guru soon realized that further meetings would serve no purpose. It also became apparent that the emperor had asked the Guru to accompany him because he hoped for the Guru's support, not only against his brother, but also against the Marathas. The Guru realizing that the Sikh cause would not be served by accompanying the emperor's party any further, so he said goodbye to the emperor and broke away.

The Guru reached Nanded in Maharashtra and was charmed by the beauty of the place, especially river Godavari. It was in Nanded that the Guru met a sadhu who had renounced the world, a Bairagi by the name of Madho Das.

Madho Das came often to listen to the Guru and was greatly influenced by his teachings. One day he fell at the Guru's feet and said, 'I am your Banda.' The Guru baptized him and he entered the Khalsa Panth and was given the name of Gurmukh Singh. But he was to become famous as 'Banda Bahadur', one of the most heroic figures in Sikh history.

Once the news of the Guru's presence began to spread, Sikhs in ever-increasing numbers flocked to Nanded to get his blessings. Many Hindus and Muslims also came to listen to the teachings of the Guru. Meanwhile in Sirhind, Wazir Khan had heard reports of the help that the Guru had given to the new emperor, and of the emperor's growing affection for the Guru. He felt that at some stage, the Guru might ask the emperor to punish him for the cowardly murder of his two young sons and the emperor, in a misplaced burst of affection and gratitude might agree to do so. The only way to forestall this was to take the initiative and to murder the Guru.

He called upon the services of two loyal young Pathans, Gul Khan and Jamshed Khan. These two Pathans travelled from Sirhind and caught up with the Guru's party at Nanded. They became frequent visitors to the Guru's daily prayer-meetings and even accepted prasad from the Guru's hands. In this manner they allayed all suspicions and were soon allowed free access to the Guru's chambers.

After a few days, the two entered the Guru's room while the Guru was resting. Gul Khan stabbed the Guru twice with his dagger. The Guru reacted with the speed of lightning and, with one stroke of his sword, he beheaded the Pathan. The Sikhs outside the room heard the noise, came rushing in and killed Jamshed Khan.

The Guru's wounds were deep and there was a great deal of bleeding. But through it all, the Guru remained calm and told his followers not to panic.

Almost as soon as the attack was made, one of the Guru's visitors galloped off to Bahadur Shah who was camping nearby. Bahadur Shah immediately despatched his most experienced surgeon, Dr. Cole, to help the Guru. The surgeon examined the wounds, stitched them up and gave the Guru some medicines. When he came again to examine the Guru after a few days, the wounds had healed completely and the bandages were removed. The Guru now began to follow his normal routine. The sangat held special prayer meetings to thank God for the Guru's quick and complete recovery.

One of the Guru's devotees had presented him with a heavy bow. The Guru, who had always had a special love for weapons of all kinds, could not resist the temptation to try out his new bow. When he stretched the bow, the wounds burst open again. He bled profusely. He was given the best medical aid, but he knew that his end was near.

He asked his Sikhs to collect around him and when they had all assembled, he spoke to them, 'The one thing men dread most is death. I have always lived close to death and looked it in the face. So should each one of you, who claims to follow me. I will ride to my death as a bridegroom rides to the house of his bride. So do not grieve for me.'

He recited the Japji Sahib, the morning prayer and led the ardas. Then he went four times around the Granth Sahib, and as was the custom when a new Guru was appointed, he made an offering of five copper coins and a coconut. He told the Sikhs that they should now look upon the Granth as the spiritual representation of the Guru. The Granth would be their Guru and the teachings contained in it represented the spirit of the Gurus. Henceforth, it would no longer be the Adi Granth but the Guru Granth Sahib. He reminded them again of what he had told them at the birth of the Khalsa in Anandpur.

'Where there are five true Sikhs assembled, there will I be. Henceforth the Guru shall be the Khalsa. The spirit of the Gurus has passed into the Khalsa,' were his last words.

The Guru breathed his last in the early hours of 7 October 1708. The Sikhs put their grief behind them and conducted the funeral with great dignity. The sacred body was placed on the funeral pyre, hymns were recited, prayers said, and the pyre was lit.

For the first time the Sikhs were without a living Guru to lead them, to give them a sense of direction. This gave them a feeling of emptiness and of helplessness. Then they remembered what Guru Gobind Singh had told them before he died, and they turned with renewed faith to the Guru Granth Sahib. They read the teachings of their Gurus with great care and practised these teachings with firmness and dedication. This helped to fill up the void within them and they realized that their Guru had been right; they were as strong as they had been when he was alive.

Chapter 21

Conclusion

Guru Gobind Singh is one of the most attractive personalities in Indian history. He had captured the imagination of the people of Northern India as no other person had and this attracted people to Anandpur and Paonta in droves, both the faithful and the casual visitors. They saw the Guru and took back with them a striking picture of the Guru in their minds. They saw his handsome face, his intense eyes and his beautiful clothes. They saw him with his lean, sinewy body, walking straight and erect and proud, his kalgi seeming to sweep the heavens as he walked. They saw him riding out to battle on his beautiful blue horse, his sword flashing in the sun, ready to swoop down and strike his enemy. They saw him set out hunting, his white hawk perched on his left wrist, his horse galloping with the speed of the wind till it seemed that the Guru and his horse had merged into one and there was one life that beat in both their hearts. This was the image that the people took back with them and painted for others who had not had the good fortune to see the Guru, and this is the image that has come down over the years. Little wonder then, that even today the Guru is often referred to as *kalgidhar* – the one with the kalgi, *chittiyan bajawale* – the one with the white hawk and *neele ghode da aswar* – the rider on the blue horse.

The people of the North are a virile people who have faced the brunt of a hundred invasions; the anger of a hundred conquerors. They value physical strength, courage and valour in battle above all else and this the Guru displayed in more than ample measure. He fought against great odds and, through his personal example, led little bands of farmers against the mighty Mughal army in battle after battle. He showed great skill with the sword and with the bow and arrow, and he showed true genius as a military leader. However, there was another side of the image too. He was an image of kindness and of compassion even to his enemies. They had seen his arrows when he rode into battle, tipped with gold, to give some financial support to the dependants of the enemy soldiers, who would fall to them; they had seen him stopping his soldiers when they wanted to chase the fugitive soldiers of the defeated enemy, and they had seen him give to all who came to his doorstep.

Another image of the Guru was that of a patron of music and poetry.

For the weak, the weary, and the oppressed he was a saviour.

When we think of Guru Nanak we think first of all of a pacifist – a man who loved peace. When we think of Guru Gobind Singh we think first of all of a warrior, a man who fought many battles. No wonder then that many people think that the roles of the two Gurus contradict each other and to the layman, Guru Gobind Singh appears to have taken the Sikhs away from the path of Guru Nanak's teachings. But this appearance is deceptive. When we compare their teachings we see that Guru Gobind Singh believed in everything that Guru Nanak taught. If there seems to be a change, it is only in the extension of these teachings, which became necessary because of the change in times, and without which the panth would not have survived in the first place. Like Guru Nanak, Guru Gobind Singh believed that there was only one God, a God who was without form, who was omnipresent and omnipotent. Like Guru Nanak, Guru Gobind Singh disapproved of people renouncing the world and going up into mountains or jungles to live the life of ascetics. Guru Gobind Singh shared Guru Nanak's belief that the cure for all the miseries of life was to lead a life of prayer. Guru Gobind Singh did not even alter the form of the prayers: These were the same prayers that Guru Arjan Dev had included in the Granth. The only addition he made was to include his father's hymns in the Guru Granth Sahib. Like Guru Nanak, Guru Gobind Singh felt that the caste system was evil and worked to abolish all feelings of caste amongst his followers. Guru Gobind Singh's favourite saying was: *'Manas ki jat sabe eko pahchan bo'* i.e. 'Recognize all of mankind belonging to a single caste, that of humanity'.

Guru Gobind Singh believed like Guru Nanak, that death was the merging of the individual's soul with God and, as such, death was an event to be welcomed and not to be feared.

Guru Nanak preached that all men should be good. Guru Gobind preached that all men should not only be good but should also destroy evil. As a result, whereas Nanak said that God loved his saints and all those who lived good lives, Gobind said that God loved his saints but he also punished the doers of evil. It was the duty of every Sikh to fight against evil and tyranny. Guru Nanak said that one must always do what is right. Guru Gobind Singh went one step further. He said that not only must we always do what is right; we must also protect those who were doing right, even if it meant giving up our own lives while doing so.

The three important developments that Guru Gobind Singh brought to the Sikh faith were the creation of the Khalsa, the delegation of authority to the five faithful (Panj Pyare), and the installation of the Guru Granth Sahib as the permanent Guru of the Sikhs. By creating the Khalsa, Guru Gobind Singh made the Sikh faith pure and strong once more and gave his followers strength and courage and self-confidence so that they could stand up against all odds. It is true that by asking his followers to wear the five 'Ks' he changed their appearance. But though their looks had changed, their beliefs had not. They still believed in what Guru Nanak had taught. They had only become more assertive in their defence of these beliefs.

Guru Gobind Singh gave total authority to the five faithful; their decision was to be binding even on him. By doing this the Guru strengthened the ancient institution of the Panchayat and introduced an element of democracy into the administration of the day-to-day affairs of his followers. By declaring that henceforth the Guru Granth Sahib would be the Guru of the Sikhs, Guru Gobind removed the need of a living Guru. Thus, he was able to get rid for ever rivalries that had resulted with each change of leadership.

Two hundred years passed between the time Guru Nanak first preached his new faith (1499) and the time when Guru Gobind Singh created the Khalsa (1699). In these two hundred years Sikhism gained strength from year to year and thousands had joined the new faith. In the first hundred years of its existence, Sikhism was basically a movement of social and spiritual reform. All distinctions based on economic class or social castes were abolished amongst its followers. The Sikh Gurudwaras were open to everyone The Sikh faith worked to free the society of hypocrisy. It also worked for the upliftment of women, abolished sati, and encouraged the remarriage of widows. Religion was made simple, and hollow ceremonies and rituals were dispensed with and, as a result, the faith appealed to both Hindus and Muslims. The bridge it had provided between the two religions was symbolized by its most sacred shrine, the Harmandir Sahib, and by its holy book, the Guru Granth Sahib. The foundation stone of the Harmandir Sahib was laid by a Muslim, Mian Mir; and the building itself was raised through the labour of Hindus, Sikhs and Muslims working side by side. The Guru Granth Sahib contains not only the writings of the Gurus but also the compositions of both Hindu and Muslim saints.

In the next hundred years of its existence, Sikhism found itself being strengthened by the addition of a new dimension. It continued to be a vehicle of social reform but the martyrdom of Guru Arjan Dev gave it a new direction. Guru Hargobind gave a call to arms and made the Sikh movement a movement of resistance to tyranny and oppression unleashed by the powerful Mughal rulers.

There are many stories about Guru Gobind Singh and about his followers that have come down to us. However, some of them do not have historical evidence to support them. But they are all beautiful stories and they bring close to us some features to the Guru's personality and of his teachings. There, perhaps, could be no better way to conclude this work than by retelling some of these stories.

Amongst the thousands of Sikhs who thronged Anandpur was one called Bhai Kanhaiya. He was a very meek and humble man and there was nothing to single him out from the other Sikhs. Like so many of the other Sikhs, he would offer his services wherever they were needed and would perform chores that needed to be done without waiting to be asked to do them. His favourite task was to supply water to the langar and to the Guru Mahal. This became his special duty and people became familiar with the sight of Bhai Kanhaiya making frequent trips to the stream to carry water back in his *mashk,* his leather water-bag. This was a sight that was seen so often, that it would have been difficult for people to imagine Bhai Kanhaiya without his mashk.

He continued to perform this task even when the Guru's soldiers rode out to battle and carried water out to the detachments of the Guru's soldiers as they fought. The soldiers, tired and thirsty, welcomed Bhai Kanhaiya's visits because he brought them the welcome relief of a drink of cool water. Up and down Bhai Kanhaiya would go from the fort to the battle-field with his mashk. He could easily have been killed by a stray arrow or a stray musket shot, but he was unafraid of the danger he exposed himself to, unmindful of the risk that he was taking.

He found special happiness when he gave water to the wounded, as they lay on the battlefield, waiting to be carried back to the camp. It was the second day of the battle for Anandpur. The battle raged fiercely and Bhai Kanhaiya, as was his habit, moved among the soldiers on the battlefield bringing them a little relief with the water that he brought. He moved among the wounded murmuring prayers and offering solace when he knelt beside them.

That evening, when the fighting ended, a group of Sikhs waited upon the Guru and it was obvious that they wanted to speak to him on a matter of great importance.

The Guru asked, 'What troubles you, my friends?'

'It is Bhai Kanhaiya,' the leader of the group said.

The mention of Bhai Kanhaiya's name brought a smile to the Guru's face. He knew of the special task that this Sikh performed and of the love and comfort that he brought to the wounded.

'He brings water to the soldiers in the battlefield. He risks his life and moves from one wounded soldier to the next. Yet today he was doing something terrible. All through the day, he was busy on the battlefield, but he was bringing water, not only to our soldiers, but also to the enemy soldiers,' said one of the Sikhs.

'We all saw him Maharaj,' the Sikhs spoke in a chorus. 'He treated the enemy's soldiers with the same gentleness that he gives to our soldiers. He wiped their faces and gave them water to drink. He even spoke words of encouragement to them. I was near enough on these occasions, to hear what he said,' one of the younger members of the group added.

'And what did he say?' the Guru asked.

'He said, *'Rab sab da rakha'* – 'May God protect everyone.'

'If our own Sikhs start helping the enemy in this way, it will weaken the morale of our people,' the leader of the group said.

'Bhai Kanhaiya,' the Guru said when Kanhaiya had been ushered into his presence. 'A very serious charge has been levelled against you. You have been accused of helping the enemy soldiers during battle,' he added. Bhai Kanhaiya's head came up with a start and even in the dancing light of the torches, the look of intense shock and disbelief could be seen by everyone. The colour had drained from his face and he had lost his ability to speak. He shook his head from side to side in denial.

'Did you not bring water to those of the enemy who were wounded? Did you not lay their heads on you lap and comfort them?' the Guru asked.

Bhai Kanhaiya took two steps forward and knelt at the Guru's feet. 'It is true my Guru, I did give water to those of the enemy who were wounded. I did comfort them. But when I moved among the wounded on the battlefield, I could not tell which of them were ours and which were theirs,' he said and looked up at last into the Guru's face.

He continued, 'When I looked into the faces of those wounded soldiers, I did not see a Mughal or a Sikh. I did not see the enemy or the friend. I saw only you. Whichever way I turned, whoever I attended to, I saw only you.'

The Guru got up from his seat and drew Bhai Kanhaiya up and held him close. Then he turned to the group of Sikhs and said, 'He is my true follower, this Bhai Kanhaiya, and he has understood my mission correctly. Where there is misery make it your duty to bring relief. Where there is pain, bring comfort without discrimination.'

It is said that Bhai Kanhaiya went on to spend the rest of his days in prayer and in bringing relief and the message of hope to all those in pain. His children carried on the good work and made a study of herbal medicines and specialized in the treatment of wounds.

***

One of the most remarkable figures to come out of the Bhakti Movement was the saint, Dadu. Dadu was known for his saintliness and for various social and religious reforms that he brought about. He was also a very fine poet. His poems and his teachings had spread far and wide even during his lifetime and he had become a very famous and popular personality. He lived in a place called Naraina, not very far from Pushkar. Even after his death, people who read his teachings and his poems regarded him with great respect, and Naraina became a place of pilgrimage, and was often referred to as Dadudwara. Guru Gobind Singh had read Dadu's poems and his teachings and he too had great regard for this poet saint. On his way to Nanded, Guru Gobind Singh camped at Dadudwara. The Guru's tents were put up very close to the place where Dadu was buried. A *dargah* had come up here and there were many pilgrims who visited this shrine every day. While the Guru and his followers were riding past the dargah, the Guru remembered all the wonderful things that Dadu had said in his beautiful poems. The Guru's heart was filled with respect for the long-dead saint and as, an expression of this respect, he raised an arrow to his forehead and saluted the shrine.

When they returned to their camp, Dharam Singh, one of the original Panj Pyare, called a meeting of the Khalsa panth, of the five faithfuls. The Guru was asked to appear before the panth. The Guru himself had given them an authority which was higher than his and in deference to this authority he now appeared before them. They bowed to him and then they all took their seats. 'Today while we were riding out Guruji, you saluted the tomb of Dadu. But you yourself have said, "*Gor marhi mat bhul na mane* – worship, not even by mistake, cemeteries or places of cremation,"' Bhai Man Singh reminded the Guru, quoting from one of the Guru's own hymns.

'Yes I have said this. It is one of my teachings and an important teaching,' the Guru said.

'Then you have violated the Guru's teachings and you must be punished.' Bhai Dharam Singh pressed on.

The Guru said in all humility, 'I have violated the Guru's teachings and I will willingly undergo any punishment that the panth may decide to impose upon me.'

A fine of Rs 125 was imposed upon the Guru, which the Guru immediately paid, admitting thereby that he had been wrong to salute Dadu's tomb, no matter how holy or pious the saint had been.

The Guru having given authority to the Khalsa, was willing to submit himself to this authority, even when the Khalsa decided to punish him. The democratic set-up that the Guru had wished to introduce in the day-to-day affairs of his people was already in place and functioning efficiently during his lifetime. In spite of his towering personality and great military strength, the Guru remained a very humble man at heart; and was willing to admit his mistake in public without a moment's hesitation.

The Guru, as we have seen, was very fond of music. He was very generous to his musicians and encouraged them to give of their best. He was able to attract the best musicians both to Paonta and to Anandpur. Amongst his musicians, the most favoured were his *raagis*, who sang hymns at both the morning and the evening prayer meetings. They were, deservedly, famous all over North India and people came from far off places to listen to them.

One day, a group of the Guru's faithfuls happened to pass by the raagis' quarters. The time was about eleven in the morning. The raagis were free from their duties and usually spent this time in *riyaz* or practice. To lighten their mood a little, on this occasion, they were singing the story of the two legendary lovers of Punjab: Sohni and Mahiwal. The music was beautiful and their voices, as always, were full of emotion. The Sikhs were forced to stop and listen. As they listened to the words, they were shocked when they realized that the raagis were singing a love song. For a while they could not believe their ears, the raagis who sang such beautiful hymns, who sang of God and truth, of life and death, were singing of the profane love of a man and a woman. This was sacrilege, they thought.

That evening, after the evening prayer meeting, the band of devoted Sikhs stayed on to speak to the Guru and told him of the terrible sin that his raagis had committed.

The Guru said, 'I agree with you, this is a terrible sin that they have committed and they deserve severe punishment for it. In fact, this is so terrible a sin; I feel it should be brought to the notice of the entire sangat. The sangat should decide what punishment should be given to these great sinners. After the morning prayers tomorrow, I will put the matter to the sangat to seek their opinion as to the form of their punishment.'

The Sikhs bowed and withdrew, quite happy in the knowledge that the Guru would deal with this matter with all the seriousness that it deserved.

Sometime during the early hours of the morning the next day it began to rain and it continued raining for a long time. It was winter, and the rain intensified the cold of the morning. Each of the complainants was convinced that very few members of the sangat would attend the prayer meeting that morning and seeing the thin attendance, the Guru would not take up the matter of the raagis. Having convinced themselves thus, each one of them went back to bed and slept for a few hours more. That evening, when they went to attend the prayer meeting the Guru greeted them with a smile.

'Why my faithful Sikhs, what happened this morning? We were to discuss a very important and serious matter but you failed to turn up,' the Guru asked.

The leader of the group looked at his friends. It was clear that they wanted him to be their spokesman. 'My lord, it was raining heavily and it was very cold. We thought that very few of the sangat would come and so we went back to bed too,' he replied.

'So you got frightened by a little rain and a small blast of cold wind?' You, who swear to give your lives for me, were put off by a slight change in the weather?' the Guru asked. The leader of the group shuffled his feet uneasily and all the Sikhs stood with their heads bowed.

'What kind of faith or love is it that cannot stand up against a little bad weather? Think of this and think of that young woman Sohni's faith and love, about whom the raagis were singing. She was a young woman, just a little more than a girl. Think of the raging storm, the lashing rain and the biting wind. Think of the thunder and lightning; of the river Chenab – swollen and angry, the waves tearing at the banks, the water one vast body of raging fury. Remember that she did not know how to swim and the only support she had was an earthenware pitcher which she knew had not been baked and which would disintegrate in the water. Yet all that the girl could think of was her *mahi,* her Mahiwal, waiting for her on the other bank. Because he waited, she had to fight against all odds to try and get to him. Because he waited, she threw herself into the raging waters, knowing that she would meet her end there.' The Guru's voice had become gradually louder and now, when he paused, there was an awed silence hanging over the congregation. 'Think of this my friends,' he continued gently. 'Think of it carefully then answer my question. Were her faith and love stronger or were yours? If my raagis sing of her it is because her story deserves to be sung. Go, go all of you and if you can, you too must sing of her. Perhaps, while singing about her, you will learn from her the meaning of true love and devotion,' he added.

The Guru was not an orthodox man and was not tied down by a rigid set of values. He was extremely sensitive and had the ability to see beauty and strength even in the most unconventional situations. Above everything, he had the ability to draw upon everyday incidents to illustrate his teachings. Little wonder that he could see in Sohni's devotion to her lover, a parallel of the true devotion that a disciple should have for his Guru; for his God. He could see in Sohni's sacrifice a symbol of the ultimate form of worship.

Bibliography

1. Aarshi, P.S., *The Golden Temple,* Lancer, New Delhi, 1989.
2. Bal, Surjit Singh, *Life of Guru Nanak,* Punjabi University, Patiala, 1969.
3. Duggal, K.S., *Sikh Gurus: Their Lives and Teachings,* UBSPD, New Delhi, 1993.
4. Guru Gobind Singh Foundation, Chandigarh, *The Tenth Master: Tributes on Tricentenary,* 1967'.
5. Kohli, Surinder Singh, *Travels of Guru Nanak,'* Punjabi *University,* Patiala, 1969.
6. Singh, Dr Gopal, *History of the Sikh People,* World Sikh University Press, New Delhi, 1979.
7. Singh, Fauja, *Guru Amar Das: Life and Teachings,* Sterling Publication, New Delhi, 1979.
8. Singh, Harbans, *Guru Gobind Singh,* Sterling Publication, New Delhi, 1979.
9. Singh, Harbans, *Guru Nanak,* Punjabi University Press, Patiala, 1971.
10. Singh, Kartar, *Life of Guru Gobind Singh,* Ward Lock & Co., New York, 1967.
11. Singh, Harbans, *Guru Gobind Singh and the Mughals,* Ward Lock& Co., New York, 1967.
12. Singh, Khushwant, *A History of the Sikhs (Vol. 1),* Oxford University Press, New Delhi, 1977.
13. Singh, Puran, *A Book of the Ten Masters,* Punjabi University, Patiala, 1989.
14. Singh, Raja Daljit, *Guru Nanak,* Lahore Book Shop, Ludhiana, 1979.
15. Singh, Shanta Sarabjeet, *Nanak, the Guru,* Orient Longman, New Delhi, 1970.

16. Singh Tirlochan, *Life of Guru Har Krishan,* Delhi Sikh Gurdwara Management Committee, Delhi, 1981
17. Talib, G.S., An *Introduction to Sri Guru Granth Sahib,* Punjabi University Patiala, 1991.
18. Talib, G.S., *Guru Tegh Bahadur: Background and Supreme Sacrifice,* Punjabi University, Patiala, 1976.
19. Talib, G.S., *The Impact of Guru Gobind Singh on Indian Society,* Lahore Book Shop, Ludhiana, 1984.

ALSO AVAILABLE

Janamsakhis, as the name suggests, are stories that claim to reveal the life of the first Guru, Nanak Dev, in a chronological manner. The earliest known Janamsakhi dates back to 1658, nearly 120 years after the death of Guru Nanak in 1539. None of the Janamsakhis can claim to be the most authentic or authoritative version as, through the years, each chronicler of the Guru's life has added and altered the narrative according to the need of the times. In this volume, Dr Harish Dhillon has chosen the twenty most inspiring and interesting stories about the life and times of Guru Nanak.

A collection of mystical stories from Punjab that forces the now-ordinary and practical meaning of love to change into its illogical and irrational self it once used to be. Each story possesses both the calm and the storm of true love that consumes the body and the heart; a love that goes beyond all common sense; a love better known as *junoon* (intense passion), that finally culminates in *ibaadat* (worship) and the love of God. From Sohni-Mahiwal to Heer-Ranjha, Sassi-Punnu to Mirza-Sahiban, Harish Dhillon succinctly encapsulates the rich cultural and literary heritage Punjab is so famously synonymous with.

CONNECT WITH
HAY HOUSE
ONLINE

🌐 hayhouse.co.in **f** @hayhouseindia

📷 @hayhouseindia 𝕏 @hayhouseindia

Join the conversation about latest products, events, exclusive offers, contests, giveaways and more.

'The gateways to wisdom and knowledge are always open.'

Louise Hay

www.ingramcontent.com/pod-product-compliance
Lightning Source LLC
LaVergne TN
LVHW091626070526
838199LV00044B/954